Deleuze at the End
of the World

Deleuze at the End of the World

Latin American Perspectives

Edited by Dorothea E. Olkowski
and Julián Ferreyra

ROWMAN & LITTLEFIELD
Lanham • Boulder • New York • London

Published by Rowman & Littlefield
An imprint of The Rowman & Littlefield Publishing Group, Inc.
4501 Forbes Boulevard, Suite 200, Lanham, Maryland 20706
www.rowman.com

6 Tinworth Street, London SE11 5AL, United Kingdom

Selection and editorial matter © Dorothea E. Olkowski and Julián Ferreyra, 2020

Copyright in individual chapters is held by the respective chapter authors.

All rights reserved. No part of this book may be reproduced in any form or by any electronic or mechanical means, including information storage and retrieval systems, without written permission from the publisher, except by a reviewer who may quote passages in a review.

British Library Cataloguing in Publication Information Available

Library of Congress Cataloging-in-Publication Data Is Available

ISBN 978-1-78661-466-7 (cloth)
ISBN 978-1-5381-4974-4 (pbk)
ISBN 978-1-78661-467-4 (electronic)

Contents

Introduction   1
Dorothea E. Olkowski

SECTION I: AT THE END OF SCIENCE   17

1   Empirical Degradation and Transcendental Repetition   19
Rafael Mc Namara

2   Series, Singularity, Differential: Mathematics as a Source of Transcendental Empiricism   33
Gonzalo Santaya

3   Reading History: The Structural Logic of Difference in the Social Idea   59
Anabella Schoenle
Translated by Andrew Ascherl

4   An Embryological Approach to *Difference and Repetition*'s "Order of Reasons"   71
Sebastián Amarilla

SECTION II: AT THE END OF THE HISTORY OF PHILOSOPHY   83

5   Deleuze's Hegel: Criticism and Praise at the Edges of Thought   85
Julián Ferreyra

6   Resonances of the Voice of Being: Analogy and Univocity in Deleuze and Kant   103
Pablo N. Pachilla

7	Time and Representation: Husserlian Resonances in the Treatment of Temporal Synthesis *Verónica Kretschel* *Translated by Andrew Ascherl*	115
8	Subject and Passivity in Husserl and Deleuze: A Debate around the Contemporary Reception of Kant's Doctrine of the Productive Imagination *Andrés M. Osswald*	129

SECTION III: AT THE END OF LANGUAGE — 145

9	Double Death and Intensity in *Difference and Repetition* *Solange Heffesse*	147
10	Indirect Discourse and Ideology: Bakhtin in *A Thousand Plateaus* *Santiago Lo Vuolo* *Translated by Emilio Vergara*	161
11	Gustave Guillaume's "Obverse Causation": An Invocation to Deleuze from Linguistics *Matías Soich*	177

Index	199
Contributors	205

Introduction
Dorothea E. Olkowski

AT THE END OF THE WORLD

This is what happened. Fanny Deleuze translated a text by D. H. Lawrence into French, a text written by Lawrence as he was dying, a text called *Apocalypse*, a commentary on the biblical "Book of Revelation." Gilles Deleuze wrote the introduction for this translation, a book about the end of the world, a book about what it is to be at the end of the world, an event that Lawrence and Deleuze transform from the finality of the Judeo-Christian Apocalypse into "a book for all those who think of themselves as survivors. It is a book of Zombies."[1] Two questions arise almost immediately. First of all, why would Deleuze, renegade thinker par excellence, be inclined to take up this subject? Even given the Nietzschean influence on Lawrence's critique, how can this be relevant for Deleuze's philosophy? And second, how can a text about a book called a book about Zombies—the living dead or the living assumed to be dead—be relevant for a collection of essays from scholars who take themselves to be situated at the end of the world, this constellation of "esoteric" authors, as one of them names them? That is, is it appropriate or is it correct to engage with the apocalyptic end of the world in order to make sense of the point of view of a world so geographically distant from the Parisian intellectual hub of Deleuze and that of his more centrally located adherents that the scholars who have created this book consider their own voices to come—like Lawrence's—from the end of the world?

Lawrence was born in England but found it hostile to his anti-war views and left as soon as possible after World War I, wandering nomadically mostly between Europe, the southwest of the United States, and Central America over many years. He never visited South America but spent parts of 1922 and 1923 in Taos, New Mexico; and Chapala, Mexico, where he began one of his last novels, *The Plumed Serpent*, and he left only, it seems, because of the pending revolution. He returned to Mexico, to Oaxaca, in the fall of 1924 and probably finished the book there.[2] In Mexico, Lawrence seems to have preferred to live away from the cities, shut in by trees, writing outside leaning against a tree, barefoot in trousers and a shirt, in proximity to the activity of the villagers.[3] *Apocalypse* was written after his sojourns to Mexico in 1929–1930 in France, just prior to his death. Deleuze, as far as we know, has never visited any of these places outside of France, rarely even leaving Paris, but like Lawrence, he suffered from tuberculosis from a young age and eventually succumbed to lung disease, which led to his suicide.

No doubt, D. H. Lawrence's nomadic life was attractive to Deleuze, who was similarly drawn to T. E. Lawrence and writes of the other Lawrence that "there is a private desert that drives him to the Arabian deserts, among the Arabs, and that coincides on many points with their own perceptions and conceptions," and further that "Lawrence speaks Arabic, he dresses and lives like an Arab, even under torture he cries out in Arabic, but he does not imitate the Arabs."[4] Like D. H., T. E. Lawrence abandons, even betrays, England, and betrays the Arabs, becoming a truly dangerous man because far from being a man of action, he declares himself to be, like Deleuze, a man of Ideas, the theoretician of guerrilla warfare.[5] And like Deleuze, both Lawrences suffered bodily, tuberculosis for one and torture and rape for the other.

Focusing on D. H. Lawrence, Deleuze reveals two conceptions of the end of the world: one described as that of "modern thinkers," hungry for Power, for blood and destruction; and another, that of the aristocratic mind, the nomadic wanderer, the lover. Both can be found in the book written by Lawrence, originally intended to be an introduction to a book by Frederick Carter on the dragon of the Apocalypse. This introduction—25,000 words—eventually became Lawrence's own book, motivated not by religious fervor or even scholarly enterprise, but by a book written for very different reasons.

> Who cares about explaining the Apocalypse, either allegorically or astrologically or historically or any other way. All one cares about is the lead that the symbolic figures give us, and their dramatic movement. . . . If it leads to a release of the imagination into some sort of new world, then let us be thankful.[6]

For Lawrence "a book only lives while it has power to move us and to move us *differently*; so long as we find it *different* every time we read it," and so he concludes that given his pious childhood education, he *knows* the bible and he knows it with "an almost nauseating fixity" due to the manner in which it was constantly poured over his head.[7] But he returns to it in a state of increasing ill-health, not because he knows it but to read it differently.

What we may glean from Lawrence's account of the end of the world seems to arise, not from the biblical apocalyptic rage of its author John of Patmos, nor from Lawrence's own harsh religious upbringing, but from somewhere else, from another end of the world than the one that was forced on him as a child. As an adult near his own life's end, Lawrence recalls the imagery of Revelation as ugly, ridiculous, pompous, and unnatural. It is a text, he says for the uneducated Scotch Puritan peasants and early Christians who wished to denounce kings, rulers, and women who are actually goddesses but are defamed as whores.[8] Those readers remind him of the enemy of Jesus, the Pharisee, whose strict observance of law he thinks of as self-righteous and hypocritical, an echo of the tone of voice of the biblical Revelation, whose author "had, on the face of it, a grandiose scheme for wiping out and annihilating everybody who wasn't elect . . . and of climbing up himself right onto the throne of God."[9] This was the popular religion of his childhood, but he reflects, it was not a thoughtful religion. Its leaders dispensed not love but "a rough and rather wild, somewhat 'special' sense of power," authorized from "above."[10] The Christianity of tenderness and love overrun by that of apocalyptic self-glorification.

This division is further characterized in terms of human nature oriented by the opposition of aristocracy and democracy. Jesus, John the Apostle, and Paul are among the aristocrats Lawrence takes to be capable of the tenderness and unselfishness that comes from a unique strength—not the democratic tenderness and unselfishness of weakness and revenge coming from those who cry out for, who demand an Apocalypse—and not those whose will "wipe all worldly power, glory, and riches off the face of the earth."[11]

The author of the *Apocalypse* is also called John "but it cannot be that the same man wrote the two works, they are so alien to one another"; this because *Apocalypse* appears to be the work of a "second-rate mind" that gave energy to the idea of the Millennium, the "undying will-to-power" that "appeals to second-rate minds" and to the collective nature of humankind.[12] Because will-to-power is the law of men (even as the law of women might well be different) when this collective will-to-power is denied, its remnant, *authority*, arises in its place along with the ambitious public officials who oversee it and in so doing embrace evil and the call of mediocrity.[13] It is for this reason that Jesus was *"alone all the time."*[14] This isolation, this courage, this bravery is what Lawrence takes to be aristocratic and saintly, and he connects it to the Power of the Cosmos and the Power of the Lord of the Underworld who, like Hermes, guides the souls of the dead into an afterlife that is not the raging hellfires of the inferno.[15]

For Lawrence, the "Book of Revelation" has lost any understanding of the cosmos as a thing greater than ourselves, as "the great orb of the Chaldeans," who were known for astronomy, and the god "Helios," the Sun god.[16] Likewise, the Moon, "like a cool great Artemis," is ignored in our stupidity, and in her anger "she stares down on us and whips us with nervous whips" (a spectacular image).[17] We participants in the collective long ago, by the time of the "Book of Revelation," lost any sense of our place in the cosmos, and of the power of Sun and Moon, Saturn and Venus over us, and now, rather than being just alone, we are lonely and "lying naked like pigs on a beach."[18] Not satisfied with this stupidity, we affirm the transformation of the "amorous" Jesus from the son of man and the savior into the millennialist King of Kings, the *Kosmoskrator*—understood by religious scholars to be *both* Lord of the World *and* the Devil and his Demons—who destroys the masses of men in a bloody apocalyptic rampage.[19]

Deleuze recognizes the Nietzschean strains of Lawrence's disgust, but he focuses on a particular aspect of the Nietzschean assault on so-called slave morality as carried out by Lawrence. What draws his attention is the typology of persons, the two Johns, the one who wrote the gospel of John and the one who wrote the Apocalypse because they serve as the sign for two types of end of the world. It is the distinction between "two types of man, two regions of the soul, two completely different ensembles," that entices him to consider this.[20] The gospels of John deal with the practice of spirituality and human love but those of the other John, John of the Apocalypse, are about belief that calls cosmic terror and death, judgment and power down on mortals.[21] All of this may not be distinguished from the most urgent current concerns about the end of the world: the economic, social, ecological, biological or atomic because it has to do with a trajectory, a way of life, a preferred way of living, surviving, and judging that is the source and foundation of our current malaise. It has to do with the aristocratic way of life, meaning, the lonely life at the end of the world, the life that refuses the game of power-lord or master, the nomadic life distinguished from that of State and judicial power, which asserts itself as institutionalized, regulated, and coded in stable and stratified structures.[22]

This way of life is risky, and the risk of choosing it is that someone or "someones" will step in and take up the empty power role by claiming to serve the collective soul, but because they are lacking in humility and have never suffered bodily, never wandered nomadically, never proposed or created the Idea, they are more likely to be fearsome and cunning, cruel, and terrifying even as they falsely claim to be the real victims or the true followers of others.[23]

ANOTHER KIND OF THINKER

The first of our initial questions is answered in a shocking and harsh manner when Deleuze correlates the figure of someone who takes up the power role—disguised as a lamb but with lion's skin—with the modern thinker. What the modern thinker wants, he asserts, is power, but a secret sort of power. In order to obtain this kind of power, the modern thinker must destroy another kind of power, the kind that evinces strength, and so they proceed by insidious and seemingly reverse means. Certainly, "John of Patmos hates Caesar or the Roman Empire . . . on the other hand . . . it also wants to penetrate into every pore of power, to swarm to its centers, to multiply them throughout the universe."[24] The power of modern thinker is not an obvious sort of power; it is more devious. Deleuze calls it cosmopolitan power, world-wise, sophisticated, never in full view like that of the Emperor, but hidden in nooks and crannies, in dark corners and in the folds of the collective soul, and emanating from there to the farthest reaches of the world—to the ends of the world. From its hiding place, it is all the more able to take up its task of inventing a system of judgment, which ensures that its procurers will have the last word on every thought and every idea.[25] We begin to see what Deleuze is after.

For the ancient Greeks, the *polis*, the city-state had developed into the greatest institution of the Greek people who organized themselves in small and comparatively free communities, each with its own laws and Gods, both a community and a way of life for "men" to the extent that exile was the greatest punishment for wrongdoing.[26] By contrast, the cosmopolis—an idea Christians often associate with the disciple Paul—is mostly identified with Rome, which took itself to be an equivalent of the entire world, for the Romans managed the world as if it were one—as a cosmopolis.[27] This included extending Roman law in service to establishing an empire indifferent to the vicissitudes of its territories for the sake of its "cosmocratic tradition . . . made to stand against change."[28] Thus one who does not embrace the cosmopolis, the world as if managed by the Romans, or the Idea subject to the judgment of those who claim to know, this one is situated at the end of the world in the manner of Lawrence and in the manner of Deleuze himself. And this includes not being subject to the rule of Deleuze as much as that of anyone.

When the Emperor Constantine declared in 312 AD that Christians and pagans should be allowed freedom to worship as they pleased, and that privileges and property should be restored to them, it was celebrated by Christians as a victory for their view of the cosmos as the site of a millennialist struggle between good and evil.[29] The "Book of Revelation" was part of this victory. For Lawrence, the greatest crime committed by these thinkers was that they used their freedom to transform the Jesus of love, who saves through the power of love, into the figure of an "omnipotent conqueror flashing his great sword and destroying, destroying vast masses of men, till blood runs up to the horses bridles."[30] For Deleuze, the denial of the gift of freedom to think remains tied to the vengeance of the modern thinker, who is for him the weak one who judges and makes judgment into an autonomous faculty.

Deleuze argues that in spite of winning their freedom, the Christians, unlike the Jewish people before them, were not satisfied with living their freedom. Instead, they saw their destiny as permanently postponed; the Christians, those first modern thinkers, led by John of Patmos, transformed the waiting and the destiny into "an unprecedented and maniacal programming," the "spectacle" that is the Apocalypse, a "kind of Folies-Bergère with a celestial city and an infernal lake of sulfur."[31] The desired destruction of the masses is a mask for the destruction of the amorous figure who prefers to be alone, that is, separate from them—this destruction is not instantaneous and its replacement with Power in the guise of judgment is announced as a prediction or revelation of what is to come. Like the current technological Singularity, which is always on the way, this Power, this judgment, is always just about to arrive but never quite in front of us. Since something has to take up the time of waiting, the *Book of Revelation* becomes the primary interpretive text. It's the seven seals, seven trumpets, seven vials; it's first resurrection, millennium, second resurrection; and finally, it's last judgment, creating the feeling of self-glorification that can only come at the expense of the suffering of others, those situated at the end of the world who still speak but are not heard. Today, we offer up technology, social media, communication, and schools of thought whose speculation about the nature of reality is neither provable nor unprovable. The voice of the cosmopolitan is never quiet. But the catch is that the cosmopolitan, the one who waits for the last judgment, is waiting for the return of something they already know or understand with certainty, something, as Deleuze says, that is clearly planned or preprogrammed down to the smallest detail and not for something new, something surprising or unexpected.[32]

For Lawrence and Deleuze, filling up the time of waiting becomes the primary task of Christians before the final return and revelation. Christian visions replace Old Testament living prophesy and "programming replaces project and action, an entire theater of phantasms supplants both the action of the prophets and the passion of Christ," all of which expresses the instinct for vengeance.[33] Yet Lawrence, like Nietzsche, is fascinated by both the horrible and disgusting imagery of the Apocalypse and its author, and he is interested in the author's excessiveness and presumptuousness, which nevertheless presuppose a certain kind of charm.[34] This charm is the power of a charismatic personality who able to set out what is for themself "THE BOOK," with its secret sedimentations and pagan strata.[35] This is the case for John of Patmos but it is something else for the modern thinker. Echoing Lawrence, Deleuze declares that "THE BOOK" succeeds by capturing the "collective and popular soul" and by brandishing "vengeance and self-glorification."[36]

Lawrence again calls up his childhood when he lived among the Methodist miners who drew their power from their use of the text of the Apocalypse to bring about what Deleuze calls "the most fearsome division of a stratum so that it can be used by the Christian, mechanical, and technical world."[37] The miners preached the Apocalypse as the model for stratification and so for the machinery of an "*already industrialized organization*," of the laborer who "hammers, extends, compresses, and forges his material" in service to the end of the world, the final hour, however it may arise.[38]

THE COSMOS

Against the forging of stratification in service to the final deadly hour, Lawrence cries out that we need to situate ourselves in relation to the cosmos, because "we and the cosmos are one" and its great and vital power ripples through us exquisitely "*all the time*."[39] Yet, long ago, as long ago as the *Book of Revelation*, we consigned the cosmos to acting as the dead mechanical engineer of our fate and destiny, our human and earthly prison, from which we could be freed only by escaping the body.[40] Attuned to this, Deleuze states that "Lawrence defines the cosmos in a very simple manner; *it is the locus of great vital symbols and living connections,* the more-than-personal-life," living connections that have been lost to what he calls the Jewish alliance of the chosen people with God and the Christian soul with Christ.[41] The pagan world gave us a constant flow of creation myths, from the twelfth-century BCE goddess, Eurynome, to the Titans and the great Olympians; it gave us the harmony or balance of the elements: the chaos separated into earth, air, fire, and water, the apeiron and atoms; destruction, the effect of excess, was the principal source of injustice. Deleuze notes that in place of the cosmos we have been promised a different sort of future. A future organized, Deleuze intones, by "the military-industrial plans of an absolute worldwide State," not unlike the Christian New Jerusalem, the ultimate judicial and moral power, the city with no need of sun or moon, the holy city descended from heaven and without justice.[42]

Perhaps there exists a justice opposed to all judgment because even now, in the face of this unbearable dominant power, "existing beings confront each other and obtain redress by means of *finite* relations that merely constitute the *course* of time" and not the infinity of space and time.[43] This kind of justice begins with the system of affects and affective life, which is both dangerous and vulnerable.[44] For Deleuze, the Greek tragedies of Aeschylus do not hesitate to pit human against human. They do not wait for the judgment of God. Yes, its characters are cruel to one another. They carry out acts of unspeakable violence but "the system of cruelty expresses the finite relations of the existing body with the forces that affect it" and does not judge life in the name of "higher values" but as coming from the place where each of us finds ourselves, a *particular* place in the *cosmos*.[45] Our downfall comes each time we substitute the demand to judge and to be judged for our place in the cosmos, which is our affective life. This is the situation of Oedipus whose fate prefigures that of our modern world from which we attempt to escape into dreams, dreams of judgment and punishment but never of justice, which would be the Dionysian dreamless sleep of escaping judgment.[46]

The judgment of God seeks to elude the limit point, the limit being the barrier to infinity. Thus, it organizes the body into an organism as if it could actually accomplish this by turning into a sort of God-like being. According to Deleuze, "Lawrence ceaselessly describes bodies that are organically defective or unattractive—like Zombies or like the fat retired toreador or the skinny oily Mexican general—but are none the less traversed by this intense vitality that defies organs and undoes their organization . . . just as the moon takes hold of a woman's body."[47] This "body-without-organs" is the power to affect and to be affected and not the power to judge and to be judged, which is the power to constitute hierarchies and strata that resist dissolution and confusion.

So in the end, how can anyone who literally—geographically and affectively—inhabits the end of the world combat these powers? Lawrence asserts that Jesus preferred to be alone. Deleuze finds this isolation in Kafka, Artaud, and Nietzsche. To what end? In order to combat oneself, the most intensive combat that there can be. There is no point to combat with the Other who responds only with judgments without first confronting the forces passing through the unorganized body, whether we call them becomings, or flows, or we cite Heraclitus. "As the same thing in us is living and dead, waking and sleeping, young and old. For these things having changed around are those, and conversely those having changed around are these."[48] It is judgment that prevents the emergence of new modes of existence, new Ideas coming from the end of the world, new kinds of love and hate, agreeing and disagreeing, because the end of the world is part of the cosmos and the cosmos, our great vital symbol, consists in living connections, vibrating and expanding in every direction.[49]

THE ESSAYS

It is with this somewhat dark and heavy history in mind that the contributors to this volume write and speak and think from their place at the end of the world. They have chosen to address the mostly hidden or unexplored sources of Deleuze's work. Our goal is to insist on their value and place in the cosmos and to establish the connections that their ideas so richly put into place. However, they do not think, write, and speak merely in order to address what has already been said. It is notable that so many, if not all, of these essays address Deleuze's work from the point of view of someone or something previously unexamined in the existent literature, thereby bringing into the surface previously unexamined perspectives and ideas.

Section 1, "At the End of Science," approaches this project from the point of view of Deleuze and the natural and mathematical sciences. Rafael Mc Namara revitalizes Deleuze's conception of intensity, arguing that when in chapter five of *Difference and Repetition* Deleuze engages with some problems regarding classical thermodynamics, he does so in order to introduce the key concept of *intensity*. Almost immediately, Deleuze discovers the shadow of *good sense*, one of the greatest enemies of his philosophy insofar as it is essential to the dogmatic image of thought in the enterprise of reducing and controlling difference. Mc Namara discovers the connection between science and good sense through the notion of *entropy* and the abusive extension it was given in some of the most well-known researches on thermodynamics. The ally chosen by Deleuze in this debate is the largely unknown Léon Selme, the obscure and amateur physicist who published only one book in 1917, died two years later, and was soon forgotten. Deleuze brings him back to life to discuss the illusory character of entropy and to break the bond between thermodynamics and good sense.

Additionally, in reading Selme's book, Mc Namara finds a surprising connection between his investigations on physics and Deleuze's interpretation of eternal return. The second law of thermodynamics reveals itself as a law of nature or an empirical principle which governs the surface of things. Intensity, on the other hand, is proposed by Deleuze as a transcendental principle that governs the conservation of energy by way of the repetition of difference in a deeper dimension of space. Selme shows that, while a type of energy degrades in a given phenomenon, it always returns to nature in a transformed way and this allows Mc Namara to argue that this transformed energy can be considered a physical aspect of the doctrine of eternal return.

In a far-reaching and ambitious essay, Gonzalo Santaya explains the mathematical influences on two deeply related Deleuzian concepts: Idea and structure. In both *Difference and Repetition* and *The Logic of Sense*, the determination of these concepts follows a theme, recurrent in Deleuzian statements, namely, the resonance between heterogeneous series. Leaving aside the physical and biological sources that also take part in the conceptualization of serial communication, Santaya focuses on its mathematical aspect insofar as this underlies the necessary connection of all the notions that participate in this process. In order to achieve this, he articulates the three conditions that Deleuze poses to define structure in the eighth series of *The Logic of*

Sense, and he develops the mathematical notions involved, namely, series (both convergent and divergent), singularities, differential relations, and differential elements. Santaya then shows that this reflects the same three stages of the concept of Idea developed in *Difference and Repetition* via the differential calculus: the undetermined, the determinable, and the determination. Appealing to its mathematical sources, the inner logic that generates the determinations of real experience in the conceptual movement that characterizes Deleuze's early presentation of his transcendental empiricism, Santaya discovers a movement that goes beyond mathematics toward a new (or post-) Idealism, just as it goes toward a post-structuralism.

Anabella Schoenle's focus begins with chapter 4 of *Difference and Repetition*—"Ideas and the Synthesis of Difference"—where Deleuze takes up the concept of the social Idea. She argues that in different moments of this chapter, Deleuze develops his conception of this concept by taking up arguments from Althusser and Balibar's *Reading Capital*, and she examines the brief and only apparently marginal excerpts used by Deleuze to present his concept of a social Idea in order to provide new content and insight into the reading of Marx's *Capital* proposed by the authors in *Lire le capital*. In doing so, Schoenle mainly attends to Balibar's text "About the Fundamental Concepts of Historical Materialism" (1968). Two specific statements in regard to the problem of the social Idea are specified: (1) the interpretation made of *Capital* is structural rather than historicist; and (2) the idea that dialectic is presented as a movement of difference that is not expressed in oppositions. Developing these affirmations takes her to an understanding of Deleuze's metaphysical social Idea in its connection with a theoretical-practical perspective that allows the comprehension of what occurs in the organization of capitalist societies.

Sebastián Amarilla also takes up a crucial question in Deleuze's philosophy, one found in the fifth chapter of *Difference and Repetition*. His essay "An Embryological Approach to Difference and Repetition's 'Order of Reasons'" argues that Deleuze intends to show the way in which the virtual structure of the Idea actualizes in concrete reality. Within this framework, concepts such as "intensity" and "individuation" gain relevance as the necessary conditions for differen*c*iation to operate and promote actual empirical phenomena. Intensity dramatizes, through its expression in space–time dynamisms, via its essential process which is individuation. One of the many ambits used by Deleuze to show this movement is embryology with its central concept: the Egg (*Zygote*). The central source for Deleuze is Albert Dalcq's (1893–1973) book on embryologic dynamisms *L'œuf et son dynamisme organisateur* (1941). Amarilla's essay reconstructs some general embryological concepts present in Dalcq's work in order to clarify the "order of reasons" (differen*t*iation-individuation-dramatization-differenciation) articulated by Deleuze in *Difference and Repetition*.

Section 2, "At the End of the History of Philosophy," begins with Julián Ferreyra's foray into the numerous Deleuzian critiques of the philosophy of Hegel. He organizes these critiques according to the three books of the *Science of Logic* addressing: (1) the Doctrine of Being and the false beginning; (2) the Doctrine of Essence and negation as the engine of movement; and (3) the Doctrine of the Concept and the identity toward which all differences are conducted by the circle of return (*Rückkehr*). For Ferreyra, these criticisms are linked in an order of increasing complexity that, for him, serve to deepen the dimensions of Hegelian thought. However, the isolated consideration of these criticisms hides the nature of the problem and only organizing them into a consistent argument manifests what he argues is the truth of the Hegelian ontology. As such, Being, Essence, and Concept must be conceived in a relational way, and the boundaries of the *Science of Logic* must be surpassed toward the whole system where Hegelian logic achieves a genetic character and the Idea enlivens matter endlessly. At this point, he argues, Deleuze and Hegel seem to enjoy a sudden complicity where Hegel, according to Deleuze, would "maximally approximate the real movement of thought" and become a "thinker of genius." Nonetheless, it is also the point where Hegel will "maximally betray and distort" such real movement of thought. It is a delicate conceptual equilibrium at the razor's edge, which may turn toward one side or the other. There is not after all, Deleuze has written, "another Hegel than the forces that take him."

Following this, Pablo Pachilla takes up the problem of univocity and equivocity of being in Deleuze by contrasting the Deleuzian account with that of Kant. He argues that univocity and equivocity are present in the work of both philosophers, albeit in very different ways. Kant's point of departure is the unity of apperception, and hence, in order to relate it to the multiple given in sensibility, he must perform a transubstantiation of that unity in each of the categories. In doing so, he produces a partial equivocity of being, that is, analogy, and thus generates a merely relative unity in objectivity. There are in Kant, in this manner, two mirrored poles of unity—cogito and object—plus a variety of intermediary forms. Pachilla then argues that, on the other hand, Deleuze avoids all mediations between unity and multiplicity, predicating only one and the same sense of being of all its individuating differences. By evading all mediations between the extreme poles of unity and multiplicity, he concludes that the voice of being is directly expressed in each occasion within the process of production of the real, the nature of which is for Deleuze that of becoming or differentiation.

For Verónica Kretschel, Husserl's phenomenology initially might appear to be an example of the Deleuzian "Image of thought" developed in the third chapter of *Difference and Repetition*. In fact, she states, this is the way Husserl appears in *Logic of Sense*, as a philosopher who has raised the empirical purified to the transcendental. However, she finds that on the contrary, Deleuze does not intend to depict experience as a faculty looking for its transcendental basis, but he instead creates concepts on the basis of discovering "problems." She therefore argues that there are remarkable resemblances between the analysis that Deleuze performs on the triple temporal synthesis and the Husserlian description of time's constitution. The comparison between philosophers is made regarding three specific subjects: the authors that both take as references (Kant and Bergson), the conceptual analysis of time, and the relation between time and representation. She finds most interesting the consequences implied in the third issue because even if we can assume that Husserl's first attempt to depict temporal constitution was a representational one, we can ask if the insistence on the theme that conducts the phenomenologist to struggle with words and abandon the possibility of representing time connect him to Deleuze's understanding of time. That is, do both Husserl and Deleuze utilize certain concepts in order to construct a synthesis of time that integrates temporal instances without reducing difference?

The final essay in this section, Andrés M. Osswald's "Subject and Passivity in Husserl and Deleuze," again addresses Husserl's hidden role in Deleuze's philosophy. Conceding that even though it is very unlikely that Edmund Husserl's *Analysen ezur passiven Synthesis* (1966) has been a primary influence on Gilles Deleuze's own concept of passivity as developed in *Différence et répétition* (1968), both thinkers give passive synthesis a key role in their philosophies. The reason for this might be located in the common ground that Immanuel Kant's doctrine of "productive imagination"—particularly, in the first edition of the *Kritik der reinen Vernunft* (1781)—constitutes for Husserl and Deleuze. Given this, Osswald's paper discusses the manner in which both philosophers make use of Kant's theory of productive imagination, in order to propose an interpretation of the continuities and differences in their respective approaches to passivity. Where Husserl finds a blurring of the distinction between sensibility and understanding and, consequently, a continuity between passivity and activity, Deleuze notices a separation that divides not only the subject "I/me" (*je/moi*) but ontology itself. One the one hand, the discovery of passive synthesis leads Husserl to enlarge the field of consciousness by the recognition of its pre-reflective ground. On the other hand, the emergence of a passive foundation for activity means, for Deleuze, that subjectivity has no longer a productive, that is, transcendental, role in his ontology, indicating that the subject is just a "surface effect."

The third and final section of our volume, "At the End of Language," is inaugurated by Solange Heffesse's riveting essay, "Double Death and Intensity in Difference and Repetition." For Heffesse, Maurice Blanchot (1907–2003) and Gilles Deleuze (1925–1995) are two of the most prominent figures of contemporary French thought. As diverse as they are with regard to their styles of writing and methodological approaches toward philosophy, she argues that nonetheless, their works share vital philosophical concerns. Although Deleuze describes the atmosphere of Blanchot's works as irrespirable, he draws from it in order to construct two important notions for the development of his thought: first, the notion of *the Outside* (which is set as an image for the transcendental plane in *Foucault* and his works on Cinema); and then, Blanchot's presentation of death as *double*, found in *The Space of Literature* (1955). Heffesse focuses on the second of these to show how Blanchot's discovery of the "double death" provides Deleuze with a way to inquire about death that will not be compromised by Heideggerian approaches or categories that have been determinant for the history of philosophy concerning the question of death. She concludes with an analysis of how Deleuze integrates the alternative theorization of death inherent in the concept of *double death* into his ontology, especially in the way he characterizes the role of intensity.

Continuing the examination language's limits and ends is Santiago Lo Vuolo's essay "Indirect Discourse and Ideology: Bakhtin in *A Thousand Plateau*," which takes up a 1929 work of Voloshinov, one of Bakhtin's "disciples," *Marxism and the Philosophy of Language* as a source of Deleuze and Guattari's philosophy of language. Lo Vuolo finds that the fourth chapter of *A Thousand Plateaus* presents an elaboration of Pragmatics based on ideas found in the Russian text, and that Voloshinov's social approach to Linguistics, as well as to the experience of language, is very close to the project of Deleuze and Guattari. *Marxism and the Philosophy of Language* develops a very early critique of the postulates of abstract Linguistics, which focus on one of two possible poles of enunciation: the subjective (expression) or the objective (the grammatical system). In addition to this critical aspect, he argues that the 1929 book serves as a source of *A Thousand Plateaus* because of the study presented there about the syntax of indirect discourse. It is a study that stands out for its originality, since the social approach syntactically analyzes the transmission of another's speech with a rigor that was missing in the field of Linguistics. Deleuze and Guattari then transform the linguistic thesis of the singularity of indirect discourse into an ontological thesis on language: namely, if language does not communicate or transmit information, but instead transmits slogans, then the first determination of language is indirect discourse.

Nevertheless, Lo Vuolo's second objective is to account for Deleuze and Guattari's critique according to which, first, the relationship between ideological expression and economic content occurs in the form of a causal relationship, and second, that this relationship is possible only under the assumption of a pure formal instance (in both expression and content). The point is to bring the linguistic singularity of free indirect discourse to an ontological thesis on language itself that does not constitute an elaboration that we could take as "implicit" in Voloshinov's text, as if he had lacked the consciousness of his own idea. Rather, the contempt for the modern literary style that abuses free indirect discourse shows that there is a different transcendental device in the language philosophy of the two works.

Our book concludes with Matías Soich's "Gustave Guillaume's 'Reverse Causation': An Invocation to Deleuze from Linguistics." Soich takes up the work of the French linguist Gustave Guillaume (1883–1960), creator of a psycho-mechanical theory of language. Guillaume, like others in this volume, belongs to the constellation of "minor" authors that people the pages of *Difference and Repetition*. He makes his entrance in chapter four, where Deleuze explains the internal logic of the Idea in its double aspect, as differen*t/c*iation of the virtual/actual. For Soich, Guillaume's thought represents to Deleuze, the possibility of subtracting difference from its oppositional and negative concept in structuralism, and stands as a "technical model" that shows how the logic of the virtual/actual operates in the linguistic Idea. Regarding this second aspect, this essay presents the Guillaumean view of the operational field in linguistics, consisting of three fields: "obverse causation" (*causation obverse*), "constructed caused" (*causé construit*), and "reverse causation" (*causation déverse*). Guillaume identifies the latter with discourse, that is, the actual uses of language, second with the language (*langue*) as a construction that in a first moment (*tempus primum*) is produced in pure thought and then (*tempus secundum*) is covered with corresponding and more or less resembling physical signs. Soich focuses on the first field, that is, on the central concept of the obverse causation. He argues that according to Guillaume, this names a purely mental and virtual field, whose power of differentiation accounts for the production of all possible linguistic structures, their deploying in the existing languages and the variety of their discursive uses. Based on the Guillaumean text, he examines the concept of obverse causation by detailing three of its traits: its genetic power, its invisibility with relation to empirical linguistic research, and its lack of resemblance with its effects. Throughout this description, Soich calls attention to the affinities of Guillaumean obverse causation with the Deleuzian virtual, thus making explicit the connection between this linguistic theory and the Deleuzian theory of the Idea.

This volume of essays is the first of its kind, the first to gather together the words and ideas of these accomplished scholars for a largely Anglophone audience. It is our hope that it will only be the beginning of cooperation and the exchange of ideas between these authors, these minoritarian points of view, and the majoritarian academic world. As Deleuze and Guattari have made clear, each perspective exists in relation to the other and only survives and is promulgated insofar as they remain in conversation with one another. So, we celebrate these essays as the source for creative ideas, new ideas, which is to say, the creation of concepts that is philosophy.

NOTES

1. Gilles Deleuze, "Nietzsche and Saint Paul, Lawrence and John of Patmos," in *Essays Critical and Clinical*, trans. Daniel W. Smith and Michael A. Greco (Minneapolis: University of Minnesota Press), 1997, 37.
2. https://lakechapalaartists.com/.
3. https://lakechapalaartists.com/.
4. Gilles Deleuze, "The Shame and the Glory, T. E. Lawrence," in *Essays Critical and Clinical*, 117.
5. Deleuze, "The Shame and the Glory," 118, 121.
6. D. H. Lawrence, "Introduction," *The Dragon of the Apocalypse*, cited in D. H. Lawrence, *Apocalypse and the Writings on Revelation, The Definitive Cambridge Edition* (Cambridge: Cambridge University Press, 2002), 50. Also on https://read.amazon.com/.Location 472.
7. D. H. Lawrence, *Apocalypse* (New York: Viking Press, 1982), 1; Kindle edition location 1161.
8. Lawrence, *Apocalypse*, 5. https://read.amazon.com/.Location 1203.
9. Lawrence, *Apocalypse*, 6. https://read.amazon.com/.Location 1215, 1226.
10. Lawrence, *Apocalypse*, 7. https://read.amazon.com/. Location 1249.
11. Lawrence, *Apocalypse*, 9. https://read.amazon.com/.Location 1266.
12. Lawrence, *Apocalypse*, 11. https://read.amazon.com/. Location 1288, 1304.
13. Lawrence, *Apocalypse*, 13. https://read.amazon.com/.Location 1325.
14. Lawrence, *Apocalypse*, 14. https://read.amazon.com/.Location 1347 (emphasis added).
15. Lawrence, *Apocalypse*, 20. https://read.amazon.com/. Location 1438.
16. Lawrence, *Apocalypse*, 22. https://read.amazon.com/. Location 1460.
17. Lawrence, *Apocalypse*, 23. https://read.amazon.com/.Location 1480.
18. Lawrence, *Apocalypse*, 25. https://read.amazon.com/.Location 1501.
19. Lawrence, *Apocalypse*, 28. https://read.amazon.com/.Location 1562; Deleuze, "Nietzsche and Saint Paul," 36; see also http://classic.studylight.org/lex/grk/view.cgi for Kosmoskrator.
20. Deleuze, "Nietzsche and Saint Paul," 36.
21. Deleuze, "Nietzsche and Saint Paul," 36.
22. Gilles Deleuze and Félix Guattari, *Anti-Oedipus*, trans. Robert Hurley, Mark Seem, and Helen R. Lane (Minneapolis: University of Minnesota Press, 1987), 40; 352–53.
23. Deleuze, "Nietzsche and Saint Paul," 38.
24. Deleuze, "Nietzsche and Saint Paul," 38.
25. Deleuze, "Nietzsche and Saint Paul," 38.
26. Francis Wolff, *Polis* (Princeton, NJ: Princeton University Press), 801–2. http://assets.press.princeton.edu/chapters/s4_10097.pdf.
27. Catherine Edwards and Greg Woolf, "Cosmopolis: Rome as a World City," in *Rome, The Cosmopolis*, ed. Catherine Edwards and Greg Woolf (Cambridge: Cambridge University Press, 2003), 3.
28. Edwards and Woolf, "Cosmopolis: Rome as a World City," 5, 6, 7.
29. Dr. Sophie Lunn-Rockliffe, "Christianity and the Roman Empire," BBC.http://www.bbc.co.uk/history/ancient/romans/christianityromanempire_article_01.shtml. Accessed September 2019.

30. Deleuze, "Nietzsche and Saint Paul," 40. Lawrence, *Apocalypse*, chap. 6, 81.
31. Deleuze, "Nietzsche and Saint Paul," 40.
32. Deleuze, "Nietzsche and Saint Paul," 41.
33. Deleuze, "Nietzsche and Saint Paul," 41. Deleuze points to Jewish, that is, Old Testament, sources for the Christian dogma but credits them with operating in life whereas the Christian visionaries operate in the realm of death; the afterlife is all that matters.
34. Deleuze, "Nietzsche and Saint Paul," 43.
35. Deleuze, "Nietzsche and Saint Paul," 43.
36. Deleuze, "Nietzsche and Saint Paul," 43.
37. Deleuze, "Nietzsche and Saint Paul," 43–44.
38. Deleuze, "Nietzsche and Saint Paul," 44.
39. Lawrence, *Apocalypse*, 24.
40. Lawrence, *Apocalypse*, 24.
41. Deleuze, "Nietzsche and Saint Paul," 45.
42. Deleuze, "Nietzsche and Saint Paul," 46.
43. Gilles Deleuze, "To Have Done with Judgment," *Essays Critical and Clinical* (Minneapolis: University of Minnesota Press, 1997), 127.
44. Deleuze, "To Have Done with Judgment," 129.
45. Deleuze, "To Have Done with Judgment," 128, 129.
46. Deleuze, "To Have Done with Judgment," 130.
47. Deleuze, "To Have Done with Judgment," 131.
48. Deleuze, "To Have Done with Judgment," 133. https://www.iep.utm.edu/heraclit/#H3. Hermann Diels and Walther Kranz. *Die Fragmente der Vorsokratiker*. Zurich: Weidmann, 1985, DK22B88.
49. Deleuze, "To Have Done with Judgment," 134.

BIBLIOGRAPHY

Deleuze, Gilles and Félix Guattari. *Anti-Oedipus*. Translated by Robert Hurley, Mark Seem, and Helen R. Lane. Minneapolis: University of Minnesota Press, 1987.
Deleuze, Gilles. *Essays Clinical and Critical*. Translated by Daniel W. Smith and Michael A. Greco. Minneapolis: University of Minnesota Press, 1997.
Edwards, Catherine and Greg Woolf. "Cosmopolis: Rome as a World City," in *Rome the Cosmopolis*, edited by Catherine Edwards and Greg Woolf. Cambridge: Cambridge University Press, 2003.
Lawrence, D. H. *Apocalypse and the Writings on Revelation, The Definitive Cambridge Edition*. Cambridge: Cambridge University Press, 2002, 50. Also https://read.amazon.com/.
Lunn-Rockliffe, Dr. Sophie. "Christianity and the Roman Empire." BBC. http://www.bbc.co.uk/history/ancient/romans/christianityromanempire_article_01.shtml.
Wolff, Francis. *Polis*. Princeton, NJ: Princeton University Press, 801–2. http://assets.press.prince ton.edu/chapters/s4_10097.pdf.

Section I

AT THE END OF SCIENCE

Chapter 1

Empirical Degradation and Transcendental Repetition

Rafael Mc Namara

Good sense is the ideology of middle classes who recognise themselves in equality as an abstract product. It dreams less of acting than of constituting a natural milieu, the element of an action which passes from more to less differenciated [. . .]. It therefore dreams less of acting than foreseeing, and of allowing free reign of action which goes from the unpredictable to the predictable (from the production of differences to their reduction). Neither contemplative nor active, it is prescient. In short, it goes from the side of things to the fire: from differences produced to differences reduced. It is thermodynamic.
—Gilles Deleuze[1]

The belief in the increase of entropy [. . .] has not had, as it appears, a serious base. And when scientists who admire Clausius repeat his famous and full of abusive dogmatism sentence: "universe's entropy tends to a maximum; the world has, as an end, an absolute rest, the death of all," it doesn't matter how booming it might be, all we have to see there is a false extrapolation.
—Léon Selme[2]

INTENSITY

The main goal of chapter 5 of *Difference and Repetition* is to develop a new concept of *intensity*. This concept should render the genetic conditions of the sensible thinkable. In order to achieve this, Deleuze starts with a study of the science of intensities *par excellence*: thermodynamics. In evaluating the efficiency of thermal machines, the main concern of this science is to study the production of work through differences in intensity; this is why it is relevant to Deleuze's approach. It has even been said that given its problematic rather than theorematic character, thermodynamics could be considered a minor science in Deleuze and Guattari's sense of the concept.[3] A science is minor when, far from the "matter-form" schema over which royal sciences are built, it uses a "material-forces" schema to "determine singularities in the matter, instead of constituting a general form."[4]

Although that description may be a satisfactory interpretation of certain aspects of thermodynamics, this discipline soon started using, at least in its classical investigations, general or even dogmatic postulates. With respect to a philosophy of intensity, one ought to distinguish two aspects of its dialogue with this science. First, thermodynamics stresses the genetic role of difference: in order to produce work, a difference in intensity is needed. The most basic one is the difference between hot and cold. The canonic theory on this regard was developed by Nicolas Léonard Sadi Carnot and continued by Ludwig Boltzmann and others. The second aspect is indebted to but at the same time somewhat contrary to the first one. Once phenomena are triggered by intensive differences, the movement following those differences is usually one of equalization. In other words, difference provokes the phenomenon, but it is also canceled in the work it produces. Intensities seem to always follow the same path: from difference to leveling.

The leveling process can be understood as a passage from molecular order to disorder. The state of order is one of disequilibrium. It gives birth to an articulation of differences (called "dissymmetry"). Disorder, on the other hand, must be understood as a state of equilibrium derived from a balancing of intensities. For instance, imagine a container with two compartments separated by a gate. Let us now suppose that one compartment contains hot water while the other contains cold water. In this case, the molecules of water are *ordered* in two dissymmetric halves, that is, the system is in a state of thermal *disequilibrium* and *can* produce work. If we open the gate that separated the two halves of the container, the molecules will mix. This results in a leveling of the whole at an average temperature. The difference in intensity will have been nullified, producing a thermal *equilibrium* which is also a *disordered* state of the molecules (they are mixed up).

To measure this kind of phenomenon, physics uses a special magnitude called "entropy," which is the extensive factor of caloric energy. This magnitude gives an account of the fact that, in an isolated system (such as those imagined by nineteenth and early twentieth century thermodynamics), order is not spontaneous. Left to its own molecular tendencies, any closed system will look for equilibrium, that is, disorder. Let's take another example: if one drops some grains of salt in a glass of water, the ensemble will tend to spontaneously mix the molecules of both materials until the water turns salty. The system will remain in the state of equilibrium in which all molecules are mixed up (disordered), unless one applies a new intensive difference. In this case, once we mix molecules of salt and water, the only way to separate them is to apply heat until the liquid evaporates.

What these simple experiments show is that in any given system, order tends to decrease, and entropy is the measure of that decrease. In light of this, heat acquires a special status in relation to other types of energy. In thermodynamics, physicists talk about noble energies and degraded energies, but in fact, the only degraded energy is heat. This is because, in comparison with noble energies, which produce work in high proportions, heat is less productive. Thus, classic thermodynamics expresses certain facts which only correspond to this form of energy. Notoriously, caloric energy is the only energy that shows an increase of its extension (entropy) as the correlate of an intensive variation. On the other hand, noble energies (such as electric or hydraulic energy) are said to preserve their correspondent extension in energetic movements.

The universal tendency toward leveling intensities is also expressed by the concept of *irreversibility*, which defines what the physicists have called "the arrow of time." Given the natural tendency of matter to move to states of equilibrium, the movement from order to disorder is perhaps the only phenomenon that makes perceptible the passage from the past to the future. This is based on the fact that for all work, whether generated by electric, gravitational, hydraulic, or any other energy, caloric energy emerges as a nonprofitable residue (for instance, in the grazing and rubbing between the parts of any machine). This means that although noble energies can be transformed almost with integrity in some kinds of work, it frequently happens that some part of that activity produces heat, which results in lost energy.

Speculation around such facts led physicists to postulate the state of equilibrium as the final destiny of the universe. This claim is the conclusion of the second aspect of thermodynamics. Considered from a cosmological point of view, if all differences tend to stabilize at an average temperature, and the capacity to produce order through work is finite, one can conclude that the universe as a whole is leading to a thermal death, that is, a state of maximum entropy.

The first aspect of thermodynamics, the production of work through intensive differences, is essential to Deleuze's approach because it supports his search for the differential conditions of phenomena. The second aspect, which postulates the equalizing of intensities as a general law and as the final destination of the universe, belongs, on the contrary, to the paradigm of *good sense*. By reducing differences to equality and the improbable to the probable, good sense is one of the enemies of the philosophy of difference. In chapter 5 of *Difference and Repetition*, Deleuze defines good sense as "partial truth in so far as this is joined to the feeling of the absolute."[5] That chapter separates the second law of thermodynamics as a partial or empirical truth from the conclusion that makes it the general destiny of matter as such, a conclusion that is no more than a fallacious generalization. In order to eliminate this belief and block the marriage between good sense and the science it expresses, Deleuze takes into account a work that, after producing a heated debate when published in 1917, fell into oblivion: *Principe de Carnot contre formule empirique de Clausius*, by Léon Selme. According to Deleuze, this author "made a profound discovery. In opposing Carnot and Clausius, he wanted to show that the increase of entropy was illusory."[6] In what follows, we will give an account of this strange source.

THE GRAND ILLUSION

The theory of the increase of entropy, while widely accepted, had an opponent who was as strong as he was unknown in the figure of Léon Selme. Little is known about Selme, except that he was a foreman in a factory, that he was completely self-taught in advanced physics and mathematics, and that he died two years after publishing his only book. These facts were taken from the footnotes of articles that discuss his ideas. They manifest the astonishment of the scientific community of that time with the emergence of this unknown man who questioned that which the most prestigious physicists considered to be true. Adding more to the mystery, there are even doubts regarding Selme's first name, since he only signs all his publications with an enigmatic "L" before his surname. In a book that is another source of Deleuze's engagement with thermodynamics, Rougier calls him "Louis," while Félix Michaud refers to him as "Léon."[7] Without a way to confirm with certainty which one is correct, we might as well follow Michaud and Deleuze in using "Léon" as Selme's first name.

One of the author's main argumentative strategies for bringing the illusory character of the increase of entropy to light is to reject the qualitative difference between noble and degraded energies. In Selme's own words, one has to "arrive at the supposed 'class struggle' of energies" in order to demonstrate that "there's no such thing as a cast of supposedly noble energies that would have a kind of birth right opposed to heat, which would be a wasted energy. All energies degrade, and in the same way, all energies have their nobility."[8]

To overcome this difference between energies, Selme proposes a generalization of Carnot's principle. This principle establishes that the magnitude corresponding to the efficiency of any real thermal system is lower than the ideal; that is, it is less than one, due to the inevitable loss of heat. In other words, it is impossible to turn heat into work without losing energy. Selme's hypothesis is that this is the case for every kind of energy.

As the title of Selme's book indicates, his investigation also revolves around another famous name in the history of thermodynamics: Rudolf Clausius. This physicist postulated the existence of a strange magnitude which tended to grow in the real processes of transmission of heat. This magnitude, which is precisely *entropy*, seemed to be bonded to the dissipation of molecules. In the ideal model created by Carnot, entropy remains constant during the route of caloric energy. Let us not forget that Carnot's cycle was an idealized thermal machine in which vapor, when heated, would put a piston in motion and then would cool without wasting any energy. But this machine doesn't exist in reality. In real processes, entropy always tends to grow. Another way of taking account of this magnitude consists in considering it as the measure of efficiency within a machine. From this point of view, the quantity of work is inversely proportional to the quantity of entropy. This means that, as entropy grows, the capacity to do work diminishes. At the crossroads of those two researchers, Selme has no doubt: while Carnot's principle is true, Clausius' theory is completely deceitful. For any kind of energy, be it hydraulic, electric, and so on, the extensive magnitude remains the same in closed systems. According to Clausius and his followers, the only exception is heat. In generalizing Carnot's principle, Selme rejects that exception. He thinks instead that in every energetic exchange there is nonprofitable energy that degrades itself. What happens, according to his theory, is that this degraded energy is actually transformed into other types of energy, while the extension remains constant.

Selme gives a classic example to explain Clausius' reasoning: take a closed mass at a temperature $T1$ and another at temperature $T2$.[9] Suppose that $T1$ is higher than $T2$. When the two bodies are in contact, a quantity of heat goes from the hotter body to the cooler one until both reach an average temperature. This translation of heat can be understood as a movement of entropy from the first body to the second. When heat moves from the hot body to the cold one, the first body's entropy diminishes while that of the second one grows. This variation of entropy is calculated as a quotient between the magnitude of heat (Q) and the temperature (T); it is then expressed as $-\frac{dQ}{T1}$ for the first object, and as $+\frac{dQ}{T2}$ for the second. The negative sign expresses a decrease of entropy, while the positive indicates an increase. The letter d means that we are dealing with a differential that expresses a pure variation. Since $T1$ is higher than $T2$, the decrease of entropy for the first body is lower than the increase of the same magnitude for the second. This means that $\frac{dQ}{T2}$ is always higher than $\frac{dQ}{T1}$. Once it reaches an average temperature, the entropy of the whole system consisting of the two bodies increases as $\frac{dQ}{T2} - \frac{dQ}{T1}$ is always positive. From this result, Clausius concludes that entropy increases in every translation of heat.

Selme's strategy consists in applying the same reasoning to other types of energies. In an article discussing Selme's book, Louis Rougier offers the following example.[10] Consider the potential energy of a mass of water at a certain altitude. The extensive magnitude corresponding to that energy, volume (V), can be calculated as a quotient between the magnitude of the hydraulic energy of the potentially falling water (E) and height (H) (that is to say: $V = \frac{E}{H}$). The relation between volume (V) and the quotient $\frac{E}{H}$ is analogous to the relation between entropy and the quotient $\frac{Q}{T}$ (heat and temperature) in the previous example. Now imagine two containers with water at different levels, $H1$ and $H2$. If we insert a tube between the recipients in such a way that the water will move from one container to the other, the difference in height will be equal. The leveling of the water contained in the two containers results in a quantity of volume that goes from the higher level ($H1$) to the lower level ($H2$). This means that while the first one decreases, the second increases to the point where they meet at an intermediate level that can be called mH (medium height). The variation in volume of the first recipient is expressed by the formula $-\frac{dE}{H1}$; the second one is $+\frac{dE}{H2}$. Since $H1$ is bigger than $H2$ before the leveling at mH, $\frac{dE}{H1}$ is lower than $\frac{dE}{H2}$. In perfect analogy with the previous example, the variation of volume for each segment of time is always positive.[11] If this calculation is correct, it means that the total volume of liquid would have undergone an increase during the equalizing of both levels of water.

This second result is, of course, completely absurd. In a case like the latter—where something takes place—the total volume of water remains the same. The only phenomenon registered consists in the translation of a certain quantity of volume from one container to the other. Selme asks himself: why should it be different in the case of heat? The problem is that, contrary to what happens with other extensive magnitudes, entropy is not perceptible. This derives, according to Selme, from a series of mistakes that arise when we compare heat with other types of energies. For example, it is believed that an absolute zero is possible for temperature, while no physicist would admit this for any other type of energy. On the other hand, the extension corresponding to temperature, entropy, is said to tend toward a maximum, while the extensive magnitudes of the rest of the energies, like mass or volume, are said to remain constant. Lastly, the rate of transformation in work for heat energy is considered to be always less than one (by Carnot's principle), while for noble energies that rate equals one.[12]

According to Selme, when one verifies an increase of entropy in a thermal system, the system can only be considered closed in an imaginary way.[13] The same happens when we see an increase of volume in a hydraulic system: it means that liquid was poured from the outside.

> When an isolated object is warmed, we see an elevation to a higher temperature; the hypothesis that makes appear, from nothingness, the exact wished quantity of entropy so that the object reaches that increase in temperature has nothing to do with science. If anything, it shows an imagination so fertile in fantasies as poor in true relations.[14]

To avoid this mistake, Selme uses multiple analogies between heat and other energies. For instance, when a body's electric charge is elevated to a higher power, the only thing that changes is the distribution of electric charges in a greater ensemble that includes that body. Another example: when we elevate the falling power of a mass of water, we change the relative positions of the parts of an ensemble including that mass of water and the Earth. Selme gives multiple examples of that sort until he arrives, not without irony, at the following conclusion:

> When someone affirms that the elevation in temperature of a body is not a change in the distribution of electrons or ions, but a revelation of a miraculous emergence of entropy, are we not authorized to ask for the proofs on which such an arbitrary claim is based? The best thing about this doctrine is that, conversely, when an isolated body is cooled, there is no disappearance of entropy. No, that would be too simple. Instead they say that there's still emergence of entropy. According to this, the leveling of temperature is not a decrease of efficient thermal quantity, but the result of a creation of entropy![15]

ANALOGIES

The Deleuzian reader might have found something curious in the preceding arguments: they are completely based in analogical reasoning. This method is explicitly rejected by the philosopher in the first chapter of *Difference and Repetition*, where he points to it as one of the ways in which classical philosophy blocked the emergence of a radical thought about the difference. But physicists didn't need Deleuze for them to realize this aspect of Selme's theory. In fact, a great part of the debate around his book revolved around this argumentative strategy.

Louis Rougier, for instance, not only approves these arguments but also gives more examples of his own in the same vein. Contrary to this stance, Félix Michaud rejects the generalization of this way of thinking in an article responding to Rougier's. Michaud begins by considering the difference between reversible and irreversible processes in physics. The analogy between energies can be applied to the reversible processes, and according to Michaud, "if we look carefully, Carnot's principle does not give caloric energy a particular treatment."[16] This means that with regard to reversible processes, this principle does not imply a hierarchy of noble and degraded energies. If we now consider irreversible processes, heat does have a singular place. On the plane of irreversibility, the reigning structure is not analogy but antilogy, meaning that is impossible to compare irreversible processes analogically.[17] "Carnot's principle explains analogy, and the principle of degradation of energy is an expression of antilogy. These two principles are irreducible to one another."[18] In irreversible processes, heat is the only energy that produces entropy.

Selme does not accept this distinction, and far from rejecting the principle of degradation, he extends it to all energies with Carnot's principle. From this point of view, noble energies are not only partly transformed in heat during certain processes, but there are other phenomena that show that sometimes those energies turn into other types of energies such as sound waves. In some cases, heat can even turn into electricity. For example, in the Kelvin, Seebeck, and Peltier effects, which, as we showed elsewhere, Selme uses as examples in some of his arguments.[19] This is, in fact, one of the aspects of Selme's book attacked by Michaud, who mentions and compares specifically the liberation of heat in the Joule effect and the thermoelectric Kelvin and Peltier effects in order to demonstrate Selme's mistake.[20] The analogy made by Selme between those effects is, according to Michaud, completely false, due to the fact that, while the Kelvin and Peltier effects are reversible, the Joule effect is not. The latter belongs undoubtedly to the irreversible type of phenomena and is not produced by a difference in temperature or potential as in the Kelvin and Peltier effects. Instead, the Joule effect is a simple transformation of electric energy in heat. In this way, Michaud states, it is not a phenomenon of translation of entropy, but a creation of it.[21]

The result of this debate was not favorable for Selme's ideas, which soon fell into oblivion. Today, no physicist would accept his refutation of the increase of entropy through analogies with other types of energies. But that's not the point of Deleuze's appropriation. The virtue of Selme's theory is that, although it's been refuted in some of its points, it is still interesting and forces us to think about the nature of intensities. As Miguel de Beistegui writes, "The empirical principle of degradation, while unquestionable, does not account for complex phenomena such as the creation and evolution of life."[22] These phenomena imply the emergence of new differences in intensity in spite of their empirical leveling. As we will see in the following text, Selme still has some things to say on this matter. With these problems in mind, we will be able to insert his thought into the core of Deleuze's philosophy.

FROM EMPIRICAL DEGRADATION TO TRANSCENDENTAL REPETITION

In some decisive passages, Deleuze's thought is organized through triads of synthesis which systematize distinct ontological processes. The synthesis of time and the unconscious, developed in chapter 2 of *Difference and Repetition*, is among the most well known. But in the same book, there is a third triad, less famous but equally important: the pure synthesis of space. It arises in chapter 5, and although this chapter does not revolve around synthesis in the same way as chapter 2 does in relation to the synthesis of time and the unconscious, there is a clear parallel between both formulations:

> We should not be surprised that the pure spatial syntheses here repeat the temporal syntheses previously specified: the explication of extensity rests upon the first synthesis, that of habit or the present; but the implication of depth rests upon the second synthesis, that of Memory and the past. Furthermore, in depth the proximity and simmering of the third synthesis make themselves felt, announcing the universal "ungrounding."[23]

Although a complete account of this subject is beyond the scope of this essay, the main goal of bringing up the spatial synthesis is to situate Deleuze's reference to Selme with the highest possible precision.[24]

Selme is very briefly mentioned in a footnote in chapter 2, where Deleuze discusses the nature of intensive systems, but chapter 5 is where his thought really has a key role.[25] His ideas are, in fact, a bridge between the first and the second synthesis of space, and are not, therefore, just another reference to the field of thermodynamics. They have a different role to play. Deleuze mentions Selme immediately after the paragraph devoted to the relation between thermodynamics and good sense (first synthesis), and his theory opens the door to the development of the concepts of *depth* and *spatium* (second and third synthesis, respectively).[26] Selme is the only physicist mentioned in the third paragraph of chapter 5, while all the remaining sources from the field of thermodynamics (Rougier, Rosny, and Boltzmann) are mentioned in the first two paragraphs, where the first synthesis of space, although not explicitly mentioned, is constructed.[27] The problem of the illusion linked to entropy is essential to tackle and solve both the problem of good sense and that of intensity. Let us review what consequences this has for Deleuze's philosophy of difference.

After advancing from the first synthesis of space to the second and third, and once he develops the three characteristics of intensity (the unequal, affirmation, and implication), Deleuze reformulates (and partially corrects) Selme's thesis about the illusory character of entropy while making a distinction between two orders of implication. There is a first implication, which gives an account of intensity's envelopment and conservation in itself, and a second one, which shows that intensity cancels itself in explication; that is, it is nullified and partly lost in the extensities and qualities it creates. "The illusion is precisely the confusion of these two instances."[28]

Toward the end of his book, Selme seems to have a similar intuition. In order to grasp it, we should turn to his criticism of the heat death of the universe. According to what has been said in this chapter about his theory it could seem that, far from refuting the thesis of the universal heat death, Selme's arguments tend to reenforce it. If all energies degrade, and not only heat, we would reach the death of the universe even faster. Let us see what Selme has to say about this subject.

The physicists of his time, he says, considered the universe to be a closed system on which nothing external acts. They maintained the laws of the dissipation of energies and the increase of entropy to be true principles. In this way, the universe is condemned, sooner or later, to the state of equilibrium or heat death. Selme says that the problem with this reasoning is that it considers the world to be isolated from the cosmic medium in which it is submerged. But this medium must be considered to be an endless source of energy, of intensive differences with unlimited capacity to generate work and order. In this line of thought, and although it could appear as an enunciation fantastically in excess, Selme thinks that the Maxwell hypothesis is much more interesting. Maxwell's "little anti-destruction demons" work in favor of a continuous regeneration of energy.[29] For instance, if we consider a gas whose molecules move at different speeds, these "demons" would keep the faster ones separated from the slower. In this way, they would prevent the leveling of differences in intensity generating work that could be measured in joules. In any case, it is not necessary to postulate such demons: "They are replaced by gravitational forces that play a similar role in separating the molecules at different speeds."[30] This contributes to the generation of new intensive differences. When we negate this, according to Selme, we only expand the very special conditions of our earthly medium to the universe as a whole. This is a false extrapolation. We ought to say instead that "what is lost for ourselves is not lost for nature. What we leave behind *returns* to it. [. . .] New forms of potential energy are thus prepared."[31]

Selme's thesis on this point is far-reaching. In order to put more light on it he offers the following example:

> A waterfall erodes the layers of a mountain and uncovers, here and there, some blocks of granite. The fall of the torrents remove the sand around those blocks slowly but surely, and one day arrives the moment when these blocks become elevated masses that threaten to collapse. Degradation gave birth to potential energy.[32]

There are at least two processes at work in the description of this phenomenon. They can be distinguished using Deleuze's distinction between the two orders of implication we saw above. On the one hand, we have an empirical degradation; on the other hand, that same degradation produces a virtuality. This virtuality is not illusory in the least. The threat of collapse is absolutely real, but not actualized. Although these processes are two sides of the same phenomenon, one must distinguish them from an ontological point of view. The water falling can be considered lost energy. But from that apparent loss emerges a new force of nature in the shape of threatening blocks of granite. The dissipating energy is not simply lost. It travels across a space with the capacity of transforming it in potential energy which, if we had the proper technology, could be used. That is to say that the degradation of energies goes always with a "regeneration of usable energy."[33]

In the preceding lines, we can therefore find not only the germ of the Deleuzian concept of intensity and the two orders of implication, but also their relation to eternal return. Indeed, the constant transformation of degraded energy into potential energy allows us to state that there is a true transcendental repetition as a correlate of empirical degradation. At the same time that the intensive differences follow a degrading fall, they are conserved in themselves and return to the world as potential energy. It does not seem that it is forcing Selme's text by saying that here we can find a physical version of the doctrine of eternal return as read by Deleuze.

From all this, we can conclude that, apart from certain problems, or even mistakes, found in Selme's book by his counterparts, some aspects of his thought deserve to be rescued from darkness. Even Michaud, his most incisive critic, said that his ideas had "the merit of calling to attention the necessity of a revision of the classical discourse of thermodynamics," which still had a lot of unsolved problems.[34] At the moment of *Difference and Repetition*'s publication, Selme was, perhaps, the best scientific source for the critique of thermodynamic good sense. This obscure character, a complete outsider in the academic world, is a strange singularity in the history of science. He refused to accept the good sense thesis that "the universe will cool itself to death." Using Deleuzian concepts, we can say that the principle of degradation of energy (or second law of thermodynamics) rules the process of the *explication* of intensities in the genesis of extension. But that law is no more than an empirical principle that has, as a correlate, a transcendental principle of *implication* and intensive repetition. It would be a terrible mistake for science and for philosophy to confuse both aspects. As we saw in this chapter, Selme's study of energetics allows us not only to prevent such confusion but also to give a physical account of the doctrine of eternal return as the transcendental repetition of difference.

NOTES

1. Gilles Deleuze, *Difference and Repetition*, trans. Paul Patton (New York: Columbia University Press, 1994), 225.
2. Léon Selme, *Carnot's Principle versus Clausius Empirique Formula* (Paris: Dunot et Pinad, 1917), 105.
3. See Manuel DeLanda, *Intensive Science and Virtual Philosophy* (London/New York: Continuum, 2002), 179–80.
4. Gilles Deleuze and Félix Guattari, *A Thousand Plateaus: Capitalism and Schizophrenia* (Minneapolis: Minnesota University Press, 1987), 369.
5. Deleuze, *Difference and Repetition*, 224.
6. Deleuze, *Difference and Repetition*, 228.
7. Louis Rougier, *En marge de Curie, de Carnot, et d'Einstein* (Paris: E. Chiron, 1922), 96; Félix Michaud, "La dégradation de l'énergie et le principe de Carnot," *Revue de métaphysique et de morale* (Paris: Librairie Armand Colin, 1919), 209.
8. Léon Selme, "Dynamique généralisée et dégradation de l'énergie," *Revue de métaphysique et de morale* (Paris: Librairie Armand Colin, 1917), 430; Selme, *Principe de Carnot contre formule empirique de Clausius*, 8.
9. See Selme, *Principe de Carnot contre formule empirique de Clausius*, 101.
10. See Louis Rougier, "Encore la dégradation de l'énergie: l'entropies' accroitelle?," *Revue de métaphysique et de morale* (Paris, Librairie Armand Colin, 1918), 192–93.
11. The sum of $-\frac{dE}{H1}$ and $+\frac{dE}{H2}$ (or $\frac{dE}{H2} - \frac{dE}{H1}$) is positive.
12. See Selme, *Principe de Carnot contre formule empirique de Clausius*, 113.
13. See Selme, *Principe de Carnot contre formule empirique de Clausius*, 105.
14. Léon Selme, "L'entropie, extension conservative," *Revue de métaphysique et de morale* (Paris: Librairie Armand Colin, 1919), 93.
15. Selme, "L'entropie, extension conservative," 93.
16. Michaud, "La dégradation de l'energie et le príncipe de Carnot," 199.
17. Michaud creates the term "antilogisme" to oppose to "analogisme." The latter means, in French, "analogical reasoning." By contrast, we interpret that "antilogisme" means the opposite, that is, a kind of asymmetric logical structure where one cannot compare relations as we did in the previous paragraph. In this case, contradictions arise.
18. Michaud, "La dégradation de l'energie et le príncipe de Carnot," 199–200.
19. See Rafael Mc Namara, "Léon Selme y el problema de la entropía," in *Deleuze y las fuentes de su filosofía II*, ed. Verónica Kretschel and Andrés Osswald (RAGIF, Buenos Aires), 68.
20. The Kelvin or Thompson effect shows that an electricity conductor with a difference in temperature in its extremes absorbs or exhales heat, depending on the material in which is manufactured (copper, cobalt, steel, etc.). On the other hand, Peltier effect (which is the opposite of the Seebeck effect) consists in the creation of a difference in temperature through a difference in electric potential.
21. See Michaud, "La dégradation de l'energie et le príncipe de Carnot," 204–5.
22. Miguel de Beistegui, *Truth and Génesis: Philosophy as Differential Ontology* (Bloomington: Indiana University Press, 2004), 300–301.

23. Deleuze, *Difference and Repetition*, 230.
24. This account was made in my PhD thesis. See Rafael Mc Namara, *Deleuze y la ontología del espacio*, PhD diss. (Facultad de Filosofía y Letras, Universidad de Buenos Aires: 2019). For a short version of some key concepts developed in that thesis, see Rafael Mc Namara, "Apuntes para una ontología del espacio," in *Lo que fuerza a pensar. Deleuze: ontología práctica I*, ed. Solange Heffesse, Pablo Pachilla, and Anabella Schoenle (Buenos Aires, RAGIF: 2019), 109–20.
25. See Deleuze, *Difference and Repetition*, 318, note 25.
26. In his study of *Difference and Repetition*, Henry Somers-Hall gives a brief account to the synthesis of space convergent to ours. See Deleuze's *Difference and Repetition* (Edinburgh: Edinburgh University Press, 2013), 171.
27. The English version of *Difference and repetion* does not include, in its index, the complete division of paragraphs and their pages. See Gilles Deleuze, *Différence et répétition* (Paris: PUF, 1968), 408.
28. Deleuze, *Difference and Repetition*, 240.
29. Selme, *Principe de Carnot contre formule empirique de Clausius*, 135.
30. Selme, *Principe de Carnot contre formule empirique de Clausius*, 136.
31. Selme, *Principe de Carnot contre formule empirique de Clausius*, 134 (emphasis added).
32. Selme, *Principe de Carnot contre formule empirique de Clausius*, 134.
33. Selme, *Principe de Carnot contre formule empirique de Clausius*, 135.
34. Michaud, "La dégradation de l'energie et le príncipe de Carnot," 205.

BIBLIOGRAPHY

Beistegui, Miguel de. *Truth and Génesis: Philosophy as Differential Ontology*. Bloomington: Indiana University Press, 2004.

DeLanda, Manuel. *Intensive Science and Virtual Philosophy*. London/New York: Continuum, 2002.

Deleuze, Gilles and Félix Guattari. *A Thousand Plateaus: Capitalism and Schizophrenia*. Translated by Brian Massumi. Minneapolis: Minnesota University Press, 1987.

Deleuze, Gilles. *Difference and Repetition*. Translated by Paul Patton. New York: Columbia University Press, 1994.

Deleuze, Gilles. *Différence et répétition*. Paris: PUF, 1968.

Mc Namara, Rafael. "Apuntes para una ontología del espacio." In *Lo que fuerza a pensar. Deleuze: ontología práctica I*, edited by Solange Heffesse, Pablo Pachilla, and Anabella Schoenle, 109–20. Buenos Aires: RAGIF, 2019.

Mc Namara, Rafael. "Deleuze y la ontología del espacio." PhD diss., Facultad de Filosofía y Letras. Universidad de Buenos Aires, 2019.

Mc Namara, Rafael. "Léon Selme y el problema de la entropía." In *Deleuze y las fuentes de su filosofía II*, eds. Verónica Kretschel and Andrés Osswald, 62–70. Buenos Aires: RAGIF, 2015.

Michaud, Félix. "La dégradation de l'énergie et le principe de Carnot." *Revue de métaphysique et de morale*, 199–210. Paris: Librairie Armand Colin, 1919.

Rougier, Louis. "Encore la dégradation de l'énergie: l'entropies'accroitelle?" *Revue de métaphysique et de morale*, 189–97. Paris: Librairie Armand Colin, 1918.

Rougier, Louis. *En marge de Curie, de Carnot, et d'Einstein*. Paris: E. Chiron, 1922.

Selme, Léon. "Dynamique généralisée et dégradation de l'énergie." *Revue de métaphysique et de morale*, 429–53. Paris: Librairie Armand Colin, 1917.

Selme, Léon. "L'entropie, extensión conservative." *Revue de métaphysique et de morale*, 90–118. Paris: Librairie Armand Colin, 1919.

Selme, Léon. *Carnot's Principle versus Clausius Empirique Formula*. Paris: Dunot et Pinad, 1917.

Somers-Hall, Henry. *Deleuze's Difference and Repetition*. Edinburgh: Edinburgh University Press, 2013.

Chapter 2

Series, Singularity, Differential: Mathematics as a Source of Transcendental Empiricism

Gonzalo Santaya

INTRODUCTION

Everything can be serialized. There are series everywhere. It is no exaggeration to say that the world is made of series—and ourselves as well. In consequence, the word "series" should not refer solely to an audiovisual phenomenon, as it actually does for most people in the era of entertainment. The engines of our vehicles are serialized, and so are our smartphones, using serial numbers which differentiate them within the series of similar objects that come out of the same assembly line: the *principium individuationis* in times of massive serial production. In a similar way, each bill or banknote has a serial number, index of the indispensable control of the government over money issuance. Historians research series of historical events; psychologists, of psychological events; geologists, of geological events. In their analysis, each one outlines a quite different temporal series. Life involves an interaction of multiple series of different levels, from protein connections to cell development, and from organic growth to species evolution. Artists are accustomed to producing series: series of engravings, drawings, paintings, and sculptures. Each one of our days is made of a series of daily or regular events, although, from time to time, a singular event comes to disrupt and modify that series, and a new daily life has sprung. A speech is made of a series of statements; a statement, of a series of words; words, of a series of letters; and letters—as structuralism has shown—are nothing considered isolated from the series of terms that form a certain alphabet.

According to the dictionary, the word "series" refers mainly to "a number of events, objects, or people of a similar or related kind coming one after another."[1] But let's not be too hasty at this point. In the first place, "events, objects or people" sounds quite vague, pre-philosophical, either not technical enough or assuming too much already. We will simply say that a series is composed of *terms*. Second, "number," while implying plurality, seems to point to a condition of closure, yet we know there are open series—the series of our days, for instance. Third, the "similarity" between the terms must not make us forget about their *differences*—which are just as necessary to obtain a series. And finally, the condition of "coming one after another" presupposes a temporal succession, an empirical direction in the chain of relations which we are not yet allowed to presuppose here. Taking all this into account, we should say that a "series" is all that which is composed of terms mutually related by patterns of differences and repetitions—as it is by virtue of these two things that the relations between the terms can be established.

In addition, series are not necessarily preexisting and fixed tracks where terms go by in a smooth and flawless course. They often interact with one another, twisting their course, reaching points of rupture, and modifying themselves and others. In fact, it is almost impossible to isolate any kind of interaction whenever we are thinking of a series. Historians know that a series of historical events can lead back to a series of psychological or geological events, and so on. In turn, the interaction between series can give birth to a new series, or to a phenomenon that cannot be reduced to a simple juxtaposition of the previous interacting series. Social and economic series are so intimately intertwined that it is impossible to affirm their independence, and in their complex bonds we can discern, thanks to Marx, the surfacing of the multiple series (legal, political, ideological, and so on) that organize society's lives. It is as if the physical series of ripples that constitute a wave of a certain kind (sound, light, superficial, and so on), when communicating with another, would generate an *interference* where the peaks of the resulting wave were not reducible to the mere sum of the previous ones. Something like that seems to happen between the vibrating chords in a guitar. Life, it is supposed, started because of the intersection of electrical, chemical, weather, and atmospheric series. The transcendental philosopher—Kant, to begin with—speaks of the world as the series of the conditioned, where each and every one of the terms (phenomena) which compose it are connected via categories of relation. It is not exaggerated—but it is rather incomplete—to say that the world is made of series.

Gilles Deleuze speaks of series often, in a wide range of texts throughout his work, to refer to systems of the most diverse nature; he seems to try and make us feel "ultimately, all the divergent series constitutive of the cosmos."[2] This is especially notorious in his great philosophical oeuvres of the late 1960s, *Difference and Repetition* and *The Logic of Sense*, but also in some secondary writings of this period, like "The Method of Dramatization" and "How Do We Recognize Structuralism?" We can find in those texts a recurrent description, used to explain such fundamental concepts as "system" or "simulacrum," or "structure." This description takes as its basis the notion of a *communication between heterogeneous series*.[3] By virtue of its recurrence, I would like to draw a parallel between what we could call Deleuzian "Idealism" and his "structuralism." Indeed, we can go from his concept of structure to his theory of the Idea, showing how both of them originate with a common source, which is the differential calculus. If Deleuze's philosophical objective is to stand for a plane of radical immanence, in which difference operates as the fundamental ontological principle (i.e., a principle of *sufficient reason*), the aforementioned description seeks to conceptualize its functioning, and it does so by turning to mathematical terminology.

In this description, which aims to explain the ontological genesis of a "thing in general," the concept of *series* has the central role. Let's see an example. In the eighth series of *The Logic of Sense*—a series-organized book—we find the minimum conditions that a *structure in general* has to fulfill to be considered as such: (1) at least two heterogeneous series are required to communicate with each other somehow (in the classical formulation of structuralism, following de Saussure, this duality of series corresponds to the duality of the *sign*: signifier and signified); (2) the terms of both these series are nothing considered independently of the series itself, that is, outside of the relations that they hold with each other, and these relations determine *singularities* that define the space corresponding to the structure; and (3) there is a paradoxical object toward which the series—even if divergent—*converge*, an element that works as the "differentiator" of the series: absent from its own place, without self-resemblance, without identity, it moves through both series but does not belong to either of them, or belongs to both at once as its function is to communicate and ramify the series, assuring the distribution of terms and, by doing this, *producing sense*.[4]

This description will sound undoubtedly familiar to Deleuze's readers who have already gone over the aforementioned texts. It introduces a group of interrelated concepts, which goes to the core of Deleuze's transcendental empiricism, and that we will try to clarify in the following pages—the convergence and divergence of *series*, the *singularities* that emerge from them and bond them, and the *differentiator* that, within the series, relates differences with differences through difference itself. We will analyze the three stages in their mathematical background, trying to keep it simple for nonexpert readers but without neglecting the rigor of the exposition. We aim to show the resonances between the concepts of Idea and structure (both deeply related with the Deleuzian concept of *problem*), and to clarify the nexus between *structure and existence* (or problem and *solution*) within Deleuze's philosophy of difference. Even though Deleuze does not speak of mathematics as a language immediately attached to the very truth of Being—as Badiou will later suggest—he does hold it in high esteem whenever he is creating philosophical concepts.[5] Mathematics is, in fact, a privileged source for Deleuze's conceptual construction throughout his whole work, and particularly in *Difference and Repetition* and *The Logic of Sense*. In those books, many notions of mathematical analysis are redeployed in the context of the ontological movement of immanent self-determination of a problem. By virtue of this process, virtual problems generate by themselves the *conditions* under which they can receive an actual individual solution, or a *series* of solutions—and yet, problems "insist and persist in these solutions."[6] In spite of the roughness and abstraction implied by high mathematics, nothing better illustrates this ontological movement lying beneath every actual configuration of real experience than the singular points that articulate a series of regular points—all of them produced by differential relations. Moreover, it is *because* of its high abstraction that mathematics is a suitable language to extract the tools to map the ontological movement of the problematic transcendental field. This does not mean, however, that mathematics are *themselves* the virtual, or the ontological source of existence. Yet they are an immense inspiration for Deleuze, which allow him to define the three stages of his concept of structure (and also of Idea). Each of these stages is inspired, as we will see in the following, by a certain aspect of the calculus of series carried out by mathematical analysis; we need to disassemble these stages carefully in order to reconstruct the whole movement *at the end*. We will try to make the mathematical roughness worthwhile, by showing how it determines the way in which Deleuze thinks the actualization of a virtual, the incarnation of a structure, or the solution to a problem.

SERIES AND SINGULARITIES

The first condition set by the aforementioned description of a structure is serial organization. We have seen many examples in our introduction, but in mathematics, series are sums whose terms—the addends—form an infinite succession. In consequence, to solve a series does not mean to add infinitely many times, but to search for a *limit value*—that is, a number—toward which the series tends as more and more terms are added. This operation is then a progressive approximation.[7] For example, the series

$$\frac{1}{2}+\frac{1}{4}+\frac{1}{8}+\frac{1}{16}+\ldots+\frac{1}{2^n}+\ldots \approx 1$$

tends toward or approaches, as the "$\approx$" sign indicates, the *limit* 1. This means that the more terms we add, always following the pattern $\frac{1}{2^n}$, the closer we get to 1, without ever actually reaching it, but also never exceeding it. In

Series, Singularity, Differential   37

other words, the more terms we add, the smaller the remainder becomes (the remainder is the difference between the limit value and that of the terms actually added). When $n \to \infty$ the sum would coincide with 1. This property of a mathematical series is called *convergence*: the series of the example converges to the limit value 1. Even if nobody ever actually added the infinite terms of the series, mathematicians have come up with procedures to evaluate the convergence of a series in a finite number of operations. When a series is convergent we will say it is solvable, meaning by this, not that it is "equal to" a number, as happens in a regular sum, but that it "tends toward or converges to" a number.

However, a series may not tend toward or converge to a determinate value. There are unsolvable series that do not converge because they tend to infinity or because they result in quite different values as we add the terms. For instance, the series

$$1+1+1+1+\ldots$$

does not tend to a finite number, but to infinity, whereas the series

$$1-1+1-1+1-\ldots$$

tends alternatively to 0 and 1, depending on where we stop adding. In those cases, we say that the series is *divergent*, as it does not go toward a determinate limit value.

When Deleuze speaks of series in mathematical terms, he refers to a particular kind of series called "power series," which are characterized by the presence of a quantity that repeats itself in each next term raised to a higher power than in the former.[8] The terms of this kind of series, and also the limit value toward which they converge, are not numbers but more complex mathematical entities called *functions*. A function is a relation between variable quantities: it is a mathematical operation that contains a variable quantity (generally named x), that is, an unassigned amount that can receive different numerical values, so the operation itself will result in different numerical values (generally y, also referred to as $f(x)$). Power series are used in analysis to approach the value of a function around a determinate value of its variable. Given any function $f(x)$, we choose a fixed point x_0 around which we wish to evaluate its behavior (it is usual to consider $x_0 = 0$ for comfort reasons), from which the function is developed as $f(x_0 - x)$, where x_0 is constant and x variable. A power series is a tool to express a function of a certain complexity by a series whose terms are simpler functions than the former. Let's see it in some examples.

The function $f(x) = \sin x$ is a trigonometric function—that is, a function that relates angles or arc lengths to right triangles. They have many applications, for example, in physics, to describe the sound or light waves. Yet they are hard functions to calculate accurately without a calculating machine (mostly because they imply the irrational number π). A way to simplify this is given by a power series expansion. The power series corresponding to $f(x) = \sin x$ approached around $x_0 = 0$ is a convergent series of the form

$$\sin x \approx x - \frac{x^3}{3!} + \frac{x^5}{5!} - \frac{x^7}{7!} + \frac{x^9}{9!} - \ldots$$

Whenever we assign to x a value in the right member of this expression, the sum will result in an approximation to the value of $\sin x$ for that value, and the more terms we add the closer we get to the exact result of $\sin x$. The main advantage of this kind of series is that they let us express as polynomials—that is, as sums—functions that in any other case would be very difficult to solve.

Nevertheless, by considering functions that can be expressed by a *single* power series, like $\sin x$, we have not reached the first condition of the structure laid out by Deleuze: we needed *at least two* different series. To satisfy that condition we ought to consider a rational function, that is, a function defined by a quotient or a fractional structure (a *ratio*). For instance:

$$f(x) = \frac{1}{1+x}$$

When $x = -1$, the denominator of the quotient becomes 0, and the function becomes unsolvable at that point (because division by 0 is not defined). This mathematical phenomenon is referred to by saying $f(x)$ has a *singularity* in $x = -1$. There are different kinds of mathematical singularities, but all of them indicate a determinate value that *stands out* from the other values corresponding to a function. It can be a maximum or a minimum value, an inflection point, or an indefinite value—which is the case of the rational function of the example. This did not happen in the function considered previously ($\sin x$), as there is no value that, assigned to x, does not result in a definite value (this property of a function is called "continuity"). Whereas in a rational function, like the aforementioned, the existence of a singularity in its domain is expressed by a rupture or discontinuity of the function (we can see this graphically in figure 2.2). This implies—and this will be a crucial point of Deleuze's argument—that *the function cannot be expressed in a single power series*.

When $x = -1$ the series, like the function, diverges: it tends to infinity. In those cases, where a determinate value makes the series diverge, the series corresponding to the function diversify. The power series around $x_0 = 0$, that is, at the right side of the singularity, is

$$\frac{1}{1+x} \approx -1 + x - x^2 + x^3 - x^4 + x^5 - \ldots$$

While for values smaller than $x_0 = -1$, that is, at the left side of the singularity, for instance, in $x_0 = -2$, the series becomes

$$\frac{1}{1+x} \approx -1 - (x+2) - (x+2)^2 - (x+2)^3 - (x+2)^4 - \ldots$$

Thus, the whole function must be expressed in two heterogeneous series. At −1 the function presents a singularity that breaks the simplicity of the serial expression. At the singularity, one series dies while another one is born.

In the case that we have just analyzed, the function has only one singularity, but other functions can have more than one. Also, we have analyzed cases of functions of a single variable, but other functions with more variables are possible. The single-variable function is the simplest case; it is geometrically represented by a curve, which can be topologically referred to as a one-dimensional manifold. A function of two variables expresses a surface, or a two-dimensional manifold, and a higher number of variables leads us to the complex field of hypersurfaces. The more variables a function has, the more singularities it may count in its domain, and the more singularities there are, the more heterogeneous series will be required to express the function. Each series expresses the behavior of the function *between* two singularities, so these can be said to "cut" a continuous or regular tendency into a new one which is born at each one of them. At the same time, singularities differentiate and articulate heterogeneous series, giving form to complex spatial figures.

Geometry often has ways to illustrate the abstract laws of algebra or analysis, somehow making "visible" those intellectual operations. In this sense, it is clarifying to see how power series expansions work in the context of the graphical representation of functions. The graphical representation of a function locates each point of the curve corresponding to the function in a system of Cartesian axes—with as many axes as variables in the function. In these graphics, we can visualize a way of solving the problem posed by a mathematical function, and in this problem-solving process, both series and singularities play a crucial role: the first ones by allowing a progressively accurate approximation of the curve; the second ones by locating the structural points that define its global spatial configuration. Let's see how this appears in the functions we have just analyzed to draw out some initial conclusions about Deleuze's use of mathematics.

Similar to what happened with its numerical values, the curve corresponding to a function can be progressively approached starting from a given point by adding the successive terms of its power series. Figures 2.1 and 2.2 show

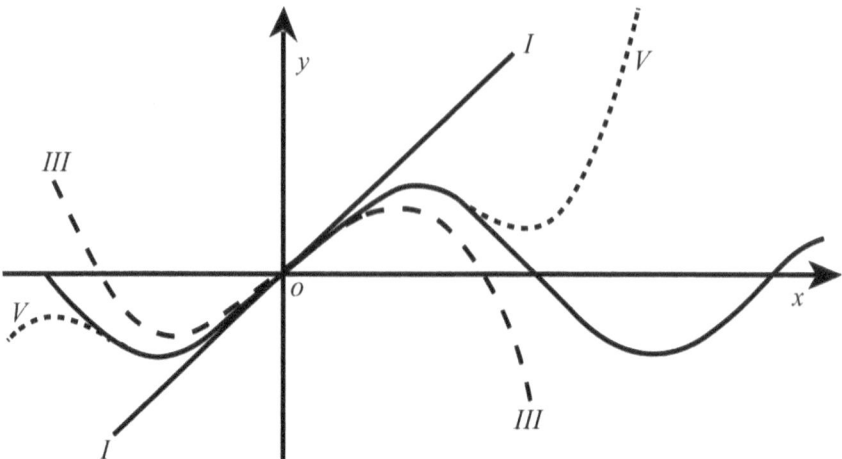

Figure 2.1 The Power Series Expansion of sin *x*.

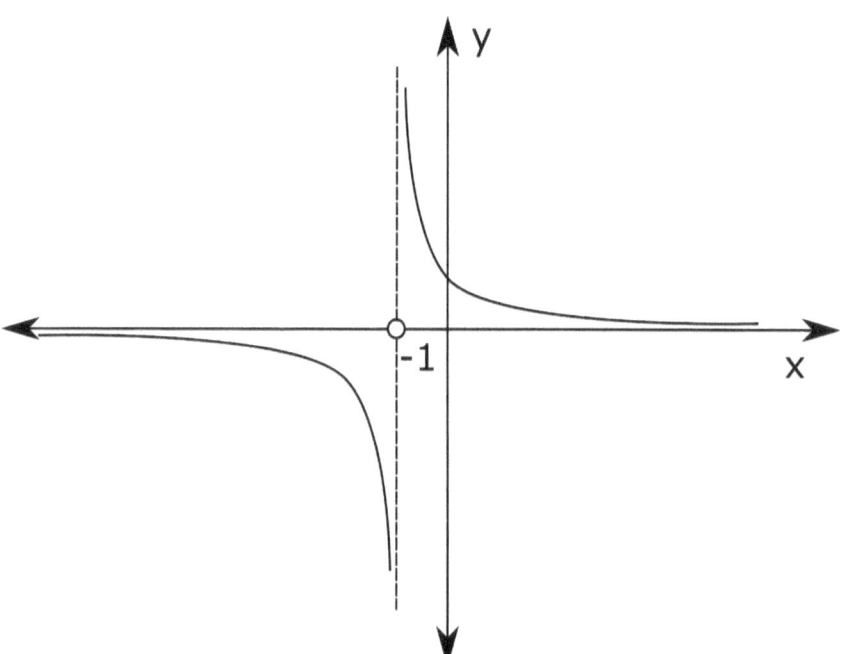

Figure 2.2 The Asymptote Articulating Two Symmetrical Curves.

the graphs corresponding to the examples we have seen so far. Figure 2.1 corresponds to the power series expansion of sin x. That function determines an oscillating and continuous curve that repeats itself all along the horizontal axis, and which is represented as a continuous curved line in the graph. On the other hand, we have a straight line (I) and two curves represented by dotted lines (III and V). These lines are determined by the progressive approximation of the function by its power series. The straight line (I) is the representation of the first term of the power series expansion of sin x alone (which was just x), a line that cuts the continuous curve in the coordinate center. The dotted line (III) is the graph corresponding to the function defined as the sum of the first three terms of that same series (i.e., $x - \frac{x^3}{3!} + \frac{x^5}{5!}$), resulting in a curve that gets closer to sin x in more points around the Cartesian coordinates center, and then ramifies in an infinitely ascendant curve at right and an infinitely descendant curve at left. The other dotted line (V) corresponds to the function defined as the sum of the first five terms (i.e., $x - \frac{x^3}{3!} + \frac{x^5}{5!} - \frac{x^7}{7!} + \frac{x^9}{9!}$), which approximates sin x in a wider range. This shows graphically what we said before: the more terms of the series we consider, the closer we get to the original function. Adding successive terms of the series and building the corresponding graph results in a series of curves more and more coincident with the original function's curve. Those curves, called osculating curves, coincide with the original curve in what is called a radius of convergence bigger and bigger, outside of which the values get more and more distant.[9]

Figure 2.2 represents our second example, the function $\frac{1}{1+x}$. We see a dotted straight line parallel to the y-axis that represents the *cut* on the curve defined by the singularity. The value $x = -1$ defines an asymptote toward which the two curves, corresponding to the two series that develop the function, approximate indefinitely. Through the singularity, we pass from one curve to the other as if jumping to the other side of the mirror. The power series analyzed at the right side of the asymptote defines a series of osculating curves progressively coincident with the right branch of the curve. The same thing occurs with the power series corresponding to values minor to -1 and the left branch of the curve. Nonetheless, it is not necessary to calculate the infinite dots that form the trajectory of these curves to describe this behavior: we know that the function does not result in any assignable number in $x = -1$, and by calculating a finite amount of terms at one side and the other we reach a certain degree of knowledge about the global behavior of the curves.

The mathematical notion of singularity and the series associated with it show how a given space that is generated according to the conditions set by a problem provides a solution to that problem. Once we have reached the knowledge of the existence and distribution of singularities that reside in the domain of a function, we have what Deleuze calls a *complete determination* of it.[10] This does not mean that the curve is *entirely* determined, which implies actually drawing the curve or calculating the values of the function for a whole part of its domain. Complete determination refers to the minimum conditions that a problem—in this case, a mathematical function—requires to be solved—calculated or drawn. Deleuze uses this to characterize the structuring role of singularities in the determination of the spatial configuration that solves a problem. On the one hand, singularities belong to the space they structure, but on the other hand, they *go beyond* that space, as they are not mere solutions but those points that make solutions effectively real. The different regular tendencies of the values of the function, as well as the regular or continuous dots of the curve, are completely determined *within* the problem inasmuch as its singular points are found. The curve or the values of the function, that is, the *solution* to the problem, are those regularities that lay *between* the singularities.

This *double* aspect of mathematical determination corresponds to the Deleuzian metaphysical distinction between the virtual and the actual, or between the plane of differen*t*iation and that of differen*c*iation. One part of the problem-solving process refers to the virtual complete determination of singular points, the other aspect projects that complete determination into the construction of the actual curve that corresponds to the function.

> Mathematicians ask: What is this other part represented by the so-called primitive function? [. . .] Whereas differentiation determines the virtual content of the Idea as problem, differenciation expresses the actualisation of this virtual and the constitution of solutions (by local integrations). Differenciation is like the second part of difference, and in order to designate the integrity or the integrality of the object we require the complex notion of different/ciation. The *t* and the *c* here are the distinctive feature or the phonological relation of difference in person. Every object is double without it being the case that the two halves resemble one another, one being a virtual image and the other an actual image. They are unequal odd halves.[11]

These "unequal halves" coexist in the Deleuzian inversion of classical logics. The continuous parts of a curve or the regular tendency of the values of a function are an actual image, they imply the *actualization of a problematic field* raised by the function, and the singular points are those *virtual* images that determine that actualization in a process that is immanent to the problem. In philosophical terms, the distinction between the singular and the regular—the virtual and the actual—implies distancing from the classic logical distinction between particular and general. It replaces a logic of subsumption between subject and predicate for a logic of inner self-differentiation operated by ideal or virtual events—that is, singularities—in an individuation process. Deleuze attributes this discovery to Leibniz, which put simply, affirms that the "singular" is that which escapes from and determines regularity. "It's that mathematics already represents a turning point in relation to logic. The mathematical use of the concept 'singularity' orients singularity in relation to the ordinary or the regular, and no longer in relation to the universal."[12] This "new" logic has important implications for the theory of determination. We do not determine an individual from outside, once we have applied the significance given by an abstract or transcendent universal to it, subsuming the singular under it (i.e., universals are not general categories that apply to different individuals by some criteria of resemblance). The singular carries a principle of immanent self-determination, insofar as it determines its surrounding regularities by positing a difference from within its own space. Every individual will thus be defined as a dynamical spatio-temporal configuration that depends on a certain number of singular points. The universal is not the generality subsuming the individual but the set of singularities by virtue of which *this* individual comes to be (this implies a radical inversion in the viewpoint of classical logic). This is the case in the curve of the function, considered as a mathematical individual: it is not defined by its external resemblance to other curves or functions, but by its intrinsic singularities that inform the space of the curve from within.

> Thus, in the neighborhood of a singularity, something changes: the curve grows, or it decreases. These points of growth or decrease, I will call them singularities. The ordinary one is the *series*, that which is between two singularities, going from the neighborhood of one singularity to another's neighborhood, of ordinary or regular character.[13]

What is a series then? We have reached a new characterization of it: it is a regular tendency that extends between two singularities. And what is a singularity? It is a virtual point, a "blind spot," determined but not representable, in which a series changes or from which a new series is projected. The singular-regular pair is mutually dependent, and moreover, it is not strictly speaking a "pair," as it implies a multiplicity. Multiple regular points are articulated around singular points, forming the space of a given individual. Different sets of singularities determine different kinds of individuals. A square has four singular points, among which four infinite series of ordinary dots converge to form the figure (to set the distribution of those singular points means to determine completely the construction of the square). But other kinds of singular points can be shown at different levels, like in the series of the squares. For instance, the square whose side is $= 1$, in front of which

Pythagoreanism saw the monstrous irruption of irrationals (its diagonal = $\sqrt{2}$, an incalculable value at the time). For each object, an indefinite chain of regular–singular–regular– . . . links can be projected. "The serial form is thus essentially multi-serial. This is indeed the case in mathematics, where a series constructed in the vicinity of a point is significant only in relation to another series, constructed around another point, and converging with, or diverging from, the first."[14] Yet singularities are not the last word in Deleuze's theory of determination.

SINGULARITIES AND RELATIONS BETWEEN THE TERMS

We have just exposed the first condition laid out by Deleuze to characterize a structure in general (the communication between heterogeneous series), but as we did so, we were forced to introduce elements from the second condition. We saw this when, while speaking about serial communication, we had to speak about the *singularities* that determine this communication. This shows the deeply imbricating nature of the elements that form a structure. But the second condition expressed specially the necessary mutual dependence of the terms that compose the communicating heterogeneous series—singularities being a product of the relations that those terms hold between each other. The inquiry now leads us to the relations between terms, and to those between terms and singularities. In order to examine this, let us recall the first example of a power series given in the previous section:

$$\sin x \approx x - \frac{x^3}{3!} + \frac{x^5}{5!} - \frac{x^7}{7!} + \frac{x^9}{9!} - \ldots$$

At first glance, we see the terms of the series linked by the simplest arithmetic relations: addition and subtraction. Those relations do not seem to reflect the necessary mutual dependence we were talking about. Addition and subtraction seem to only juxtapose terms that keep their fixed individuality and relative independence out of the relation itself. We can see how 12 can express the synthetic activity of adding 7+5, but there is absolutely nothing *in* 12, 5, or 7 that make those terms dependent on the relation "+." Each number keeps its own identity outside the relation, they *are something* considered outside their relation. Addition thus depends on its terms, and not the opposite. In the case of a power series, we can also consider each of the terms separately. In isolating each term from the rest, we will see that it can be considered as an *individual* function. We can, for instance, extract the second term of the series and we will obtain the function $y = -\frac{x^3}{3!}$ or extract the fifth term and obtain the function $y = \frac{x^9}{9!}$, and so on. As independent functions, each of them defines its own variation regime, that is, its own set of values and its own geometrical representation on the Cartesian axis. In consequence, we must see if there is a deeper set of inner necessary relations that grounds the exterior relations of addition and subtraction. If this is the case, mathematics would also show us the functioning of that *inner* logic that generates both the singularities *and* the series of regular terms, whose importance for the theory of determination we saw in the previous section.

The feeling that this is the case grows stronger if we remember that, within the series, each term contributes to the progressive approximation of the value of the original function. The relation of addition testifies to a mutual dependence of the terms inasmuch as they contribute to form the original or *primitive* function toward which the whole series converges. Beneath the apparent independence of the juxtaposed terms of the series that the expression of a sum suggests, the power series seems to hide a principle of *reciprocal determination*, by virtue of which each term contributes to completely determine a function. The *complete determination* by which Deleuze referred to the distribution of singular or structuring points is thus supported by a *reciprocal determination* between the elements that develop the problem.

In mathematical analysis, this is based on an interesting property of the approximation of functions by power series expansions: each next term of the series is obtained by *differentiation* of the former, or in other words, each next term includes a derivative of the function included in the former. A derivative, in analysis, is a function obtained from a primitive function by differentiation. This derivative constitutes a privileged resource to obtain the singular points of the primitive function, especially in the expression that includes all of its derivatives in the power series. For instance, when a value assigned to x turns the first term of the series into zero, there will be a maximum or a minimum of the curve on that value; when the second term of the series becomes zero, we will have there an inflection point; when the first term tends to infinity, there we will have a pole (i.e., the case of singularity we examined in figure 2.2), and so on.

The terms of the series can reveal a singularity at a given point, and we can thereby analyze the behavior and the effective construction of the graph of the function by extending the regular points between the singular ones, as we saw in the previous section. The power series is not made up of an arbitrary juxtaposition of functions, but constructed by rigorous operations of function differentiation. The search for singular points is thus dependent on those operations, as well as the progressive coincidence of the osculating curves with that of the primitive function. Each new osculating curve, as each new term of the series, has a different qualitative nature, and all of them together form a totality that is more than a mere aggregate of parts. In consequence, there must be a principle of reciprocal determination functioning below, on the one hand, the heterogeneous terms that form the series, and on the other hand, the heterogeneous series extended through the different singularities that broke the continuity of a series and communicated it with another.

All of this finds its profound metaphysical meaning in Deleuze's theory of Ideas. While complete determination, as seen in the last section, had to do with the composition of a figure or the solution of a problem, reciprocal determination has to do with the exploration of the elements of the problem, exploration that leads eventually to its complete determination. The reciprocal determination between the terms of a power series, that is, the reciprocal determination between the primitive and derivative functions, leads to a concept of synthesis based exclusively on difference, developed with mathematical tools.

> The effectively synthetic function of Ideas is presented and developed by means of a reciprocal synthesis [. . .] When the primitive function expresses the curve, $\frac{dy}{dx} = -\left(\frac{x}{y}\right)$ [i.e., the derivative] expresses the trigonometric tangent of the angle made by the tangent of the curve and the axis of the abscissae [. . .] This is only a first aspect, however, for in so far as it expresses another quality, the differential relation remains tied to the individual values or to the quantitative variations corresponding to that quality (for example, tangent). It is therefore differentiable in turn, and testifies only to the power of Ideas to give rise to Ideas of Ideas. [. . .] This is what defines the universal synthesis of the Idea (Idea of the Idea, etc.): the reciprocal dependence of the degrees of the relation, and ultimately the reciprocal dependence of the relations themselves.[15]

This passage is crucial in order to avoid a common inaccuracy that I believe can be found in some commentators on Deleuze and mathematics and which is supported even by some of Deleuze's own expressions: a differential relation is always linked to the individual solution to a problem, and does not exist *in itself*.[16] In defining this purely differential synthesis we see that, unlike the relation of addition or subtraction, *the differential relation, $\frac{dy}{dx}$, is such that its terms are dependent on the relation, and cannot be considered as individual values outside of it, but at the same time it is necessarily connected to a set of individual values that it determines*. We should then ask ourselves: what is the metaphysical nature of this relation?

Or what are those differential elements that the reciprocal determination requires to take place? Indeed, a series is not a structure; the structure, or the Idea, *lays beneath* the series as a set of differential relations between differential elements reciprocally determined, which generates the individual terms of the series and their mutual dependence. We should advance in this direction, which will also take us further in the description of the conditions for a structure in general.

DIFFERENTIAL RELATIONS AND THE "DIFFERENTIATOR"

Once again, then, the development of one of the Deleuzian conditions for defining a structure gave rise to elements corresponding to the next one: the reciprocal determination between the terms of a series implied a reference to the differential relation $\frac{dy}{dx}$. The third Deleuzian condition for the structure referred to a paradoxical element that circulates through the communicating series without resting in a fixed place, but instead producing and distributing the terms and singularities—this is mostly inspired by Lacanian psychoanalysis, where the paradoxical element is identified with the *phallus* as the circulating undetermined object that connects the terms of the significant chain. In the context of the mathematical operations here exposed, this refers undoubtedly to the element that allows obtaining the successive derivatives that compose the mutually dependent terms of the power series. This operation was, as we saw, differentiation; and the element which makes that operation possible is the differential element, *dx*, insofar as it appears within a differential relation, $\frac{dy}{dx}$. As a matter of fact, only in this relation do we find the second condition fully satisfied: in the differential relation, no independence whatsoever can subsist, as each term is something *only* in its relation to the other. The reciprocal determination finds its core in the differential relation: the mutually dependent terms of the series are generated by the synthesis of reciprocal determinations between the differential elements. These form the *true* universal, as they have no individuality or significance whatsoever:

> *dx* and *dy* are completely undifferenciated [*indifferencies*], in the particular and in the general, but completely differentiated [*differenties*] in and by the universal. The relation $\frac{dy}{dx}$ is not like a fraction which is established between particular quanta in intuition, but neither is it a general relation between variable

algebraic magnitudes or quantities. Each term exists absolutely only in its relation to the other: it is no longer necessary, or even possible, to indicate an independent variable.[17]

The main feature of the differential element, following the metaphysical interpretation of Deleuze, is its *indetermination*. We find here again a radical inversion of the categories of predicative logic. "General" and "particular" are not relevant categories to determine the differential element, which in turn constitutes the true or *concrete* universal. A pure power of genesis corresponds to this undetermined element, as it is the source of the process of emission of singularities that gives raise to complete determination, and thus to determine concrete existence.

Mathematically speaking, dx is an unassignable quantity, insofar as no actual value can be attached to it, but always a smaller one than any that is given. Applied as an increment to the variable x of a function $f(x)$, the differential element will produce a concomitant variation in the values of the function (y); the differential relation results in the relation between that increment and this variation, and it is equal to the derivative of $f(x)$:

$$f(x+dx) = y + dy \rightarrow \frac{dy}{dx} = f'(x)$$

where $f'(x)$ means the derivative of $f(x)$. Differential elements bring to analysis the possibility of generating, in some cases, an indefinite succession of functions from a given primitive function. They do this by introducing a zone of indiscernibility *in* the function, under the form of undetermined increments to its variables. Just as differentiation makes the power series construction possible, the differential element makes differentiation possible. This is why Deleuze grants this mathematical tool nothing less than the title of "the symbol of difference" [*Differenzphilosophie*].[18]

The status of differential elements is indeed problematic. They are neither fixed, actually existing quantities, nor useful fictions, nor mere variables. They are instead that which grounds quantity, as they lead the genetic process of the terms of the series.[19] Whenever we consider dx under the categories of quantity, we reduce it to an element of the same nature as that of the order of magnitudes it grounds (constant or variable quantities). One of the greatest questions for eighteenth-century mathematicians was: "What is dx?"[20] The attempts to define this paradoxical element within the regime of preexisting magnitudes left aside its sub-representative or extra-propositional nature.[21] Irreducible to other magnitude types, the differential element held an eminently *problematic* status. Within Deleuzian metaphysics, this means that it is simultaneously a producer of solutions and yet inexistent in the order of solutions it produces. Differential relations testify to the presence of irreducible *inner* relations beneath the apparently external relations between the apparently independent terms which are grounded on them. dx thereby functions as the "differentiator" that circulates through the terms of the power series by means of the successive differentiations, and grounds the communication between series by generating and distributing the singularities corresponding to the differential relations. It does all of this without identifying itself with its products, and in fact without identifying itself at all, as there is no possible value assignable to x such that $dx = x$.

It could be objected that Deleuze, who often appeals to the differential calculus, did not make this explicit identification of dx with the paradoxical instance he calls the "differentiator." He usually reserves to dx a *symbolic* function, to designate the terms or the places of the structure insofar as they are inseparable of their relations. He does so in "How do we recognize structuralism?" where the differential elements and relations appear as the very nature of the symbolic order, but do not reappear when speaking of the empty square [*la case vide*] or the differentiator.[22] He does so even in the eighth series of *The Logic of Sense*, when he refers to the differential calculus only in the context of the second condition for the structure we have seen.[23] However, we should bear in mind that the different "names" Deleuze gives to the paradoxical element are borrowed from literature (as in Carrol's *Snark*), from the history of philosophy (Stoic's *blituri*), or from psychoanalysis (Lacan's *phallus*), and not from mathematics. Yet there is no reason, as far as I can see, not to consider the differential as the strictly mathematical "differentiator" in the case of the problems referred to power series expansions. In fact, if differential elements are the essence of the symbolic, the paradoxical element that circulates through the structure is *eminently* symbolic.[24] We could say that the mathematical symbol of infinitesimal difference, d, circulates through the whole power series without appearing in any of the actual terms it generates. As we have seen, all of the inner bonds between the terms and singularities of the series are tied by force of the differential relations that articulate the whole. (Other types of serial communication should be evaluated under other paradoxical elements, as they may take many forms according to the order or nature of the structure.)

When considering this strong inner bond that ties together the different stages of a structure, we should not forget the movement that constitutes its *existence*. Even if *virtual*, a structure always has a real and concrete existence, insofar as its differential relations and ideal singularities are necessarily incarnated in *actual terms* or phenomena. In the case of a power series, their actual existence is given by the individual functions that constitute their terms. A function is a mathematical individual which constitutes a problematic field that powers immanently its own individualization process (expressed in the calculation of its values or the drawing of its curve). Following Deleuze's characterization of individuation as a process determined by his concept of *intensity*, we should see every individual as composed of other heterogeneous individuals, as intensities envelop other intensities, changing in nature as they divide.[25] Thus the mathematical operation induced by a power series is like an unfolding or a *development* (in Deleuze's technical sense) of a given mathematical individual in the series of its enveloped intensive "parts." Those parts, however, are in turn heterogeneous individuals as well, as intensities are not divisible without a change in their nature. It is in this sense that Deleuze affirms: "The reciprocal synthesis $\frac{dy}{dx}$ is continued in the asymmetrical synthesis which connects y to x. The intensive factor is a partial derivative or the differential of a composite function."[26] The differential elements reciprocally determined in their structural or virtual relation determine real experience insofar as they determine the series of intensive thresholds that incarnate the affects of actual existence, for any given form of sensibility—in this sense, we must consider a singularity to be a mathematical event that affects a given set of values corresponding to a function.[27] Considered outside of this *existential* relation, once again, differential elements are nothing.

CONCLUDING REMARKS

"In short," writes Deleuze, "*dx* is the Idea—the Platonic, Leibnizian or Kantian Idea—the problem and its being."[28] Indeed, in the philosophical concepts we have drawn out from the preceding analysis of mathematical series, we have gone through the three stages of Deleuze's concept of Idea, but "in reverse." By these stages, I mean: the undetermined, the determinable, and the determination, that is, the three logical values that correspond with the three moments of Deleuze's reformulation of the ontological principle of sufficient reason: determinability, reciprocal determination, and complete determination. Each of these moments is mapped by Deleuze from the different moments of the differential element, the differential relation, and the constitution of power series. If the description of the structure carried us from the divergent series to the problematic or paradoxical element, the description of the Idea goes from *dx*—the undetermined, problematic element—to the complete determination of the ideal series and its emission of singularities.[29] Should we conclude that Idea and structure are one and the same thing?

"Structure" may indeed be one of the many *names* that the Idea receives in *Difference and Repetition*.[30] (Other names for it could be: problems, transcendent objects of thought, the expressed, or the "*n*th" power of thought.) Yet to simply identify all these as mere synonyms or as instances of a general concept would imply erasing their nuances and the different changes of perspective they impose—something quite controversial when it comes to Deleuze's philosophical peculiarity. It would be strange to say the structure is equal to the Idea, when the Idea cannot be said to be strictly equal to itself, being a principle of pure difference. Instead, it is as if the concept of Idea and the concept of structure were *territories* that the philosophical discourse constitutes as it deals with different problems. Engaging, on the one hand, with the philosophical tradition (Plato, Leibniz, Kant), and, on the other hand, with his intellectual contemporaries (Althusser, Lacan, Lévi-Strauss, Foucault, Barthes) may have been the occasion for Deleuze to turn to one concept rather than the other, and to define it following his own criteria (neither his concept of Idea coincides with that of the tradition, nor does his concept of structure follow that of the "classical" structuralists). As noted in the preface to *Difference and Repetition*: "Concepts, with their zones of presence, should intervene to resolve local situations. They themselves change along with the problems."[31] What matters is the common movement that lays beneath the concepts and their local contexts, the immanent genetic activity that they suppose and that pushes constantly beyond themselves as it corresponds to an unceasing production and reorganization of differences.

In this sense, Deleuze's philosophy is a living thing: his description of what it means to think recalls the very activity that reading him demands in the reader's spirit. Reading him is problematic, problematizing; he awakes the necessity of producing sense when our will to systematize (or to identify) crashes against its own powerlessness. That very impotence may have haunted the attempts to give to dx a univocal meaning in the mathematical language preceding it and powered all the creation of concepts of mathematical analysis. Ideas are those differential elements, which entail the disintegrating *and* genetic movement that manifests the highest weakness of thought, but also "that point at which 'powerlessness' is transmuted into power," at which nonsense forces itself to produce sense, or the undetermined pushes itself toward determination.[32] A genetic structuralism is thus constituted, or a transcendental empiricism.

Indeed, insofar as this movement seeks to explain the genesis of both thought and being, Deleuzian Ideas hold a transcendental mark. Kant spoke of the world as the series of the conditioned: every phenomenon presents itself in the context of a causal chain, being both cause and effect, linked to the whole system of experience. Yet it is rather incomplete to see the world as a mere chain of a phenomenal series: this would sink us in a fragmentary or disperse network of empirical terms, each referring to one another, up and down to infinity. That is why Kant showed our need for an Idea, a rational organizing principle which would function encompassing and totalizing the series of the conditioned as a whole:

> Reason seeks in this synthesis of conditions, which proceeds serially [. . .] the completeness in the series of premises that together presuppose no further premise. Now this *unconditioned* is always contained *in the absolute totality of the series* if one represents it in imagination. Yet this absolutely complete synthesis is once again only an idea.[33]

This Idea, the Idea of the world, allows the human understanding to achieve a maximum of systematic unity when applying to multiple exterior phenomena. Kantian Ideas present the philosophical advantage of being impossible to consider as objects of knowledge, but only as regulative horizons of the series of objects of experience. Deleuze rescues this notion of the Idea in its problematic status, heuristic function, and vivifying nature, but he attributes to it an inner genetic power, liberated from all kind of dependence to a transcendent or preexisting order of representational concepts or intuitions (the Kantian categories and his pure forms of space and time).[34]

The world is made of divergences between heterogeneous series, of structures lying beneath the varied connections between the terms of those series, of singularities which break and pass through a series to jump into another. Ideas are those differential elements that carry thought to its "nth" power, where a new series is born. Mathematical notions configure thus an immanent ontology of difference, which becomes a genetic principle of real experience. The differential relation and its correlative distribution of singularities are translated into the ontological description of the cosmos as the set of all divergent series: *chaosmos*. This does not imply, however, that the world is mathematically structured, or absolutely reducible to mathematics. The divergent series of the cosmos do not reduce to dx, but rather the opposite: dx, the differential element invented by Leibniz, represents *a* divergence, a rupture point, *between* the series of the cosmos: "The differential calculus belongs entirely to mathematics, even at the very moment when it finds its sense in the revelation of a dialectic which points beyond mathematics."[35] The world is not written in mathematical language, but mathematics encodes, in its own way and in its specific notions, the dialectical or ideal movement that produces reality, a movement which is diversely encoded in diverse degrees. Mathematics, as the science of quantity, forms a limited domain, a partial configuration of the ontological movement. It can, however, be granted an enormously important propaedeutic function: that of revealing to us the differential dialectics that points beyond the existing scientific domains into the production of novelty. Other domains, other configurations find their differentiator, their relations, and their singularities elsewhere, each configuration being partial, variable, and multiple. The transcendental process repeats itself in different structures under different forms, configuring the differential pulse of the divergent series. Series diverge by virtue of that permanently moving ground and communicate producing new series. It corresponds to each repetition in the task of thought, in each case and each domain, to explore the differentiator that connects the series and jumps into a new serialization.

NOTES

1. This definition corresponds to the "series" entry of the *Oxford Dictionary*, as can be found on https://www.lexico.com/en/definition/series, accessed August 20, 2019.

2. Gilles Deleuze, *Difference and Repetition*, trans. Paul Patton (New York: Columbia University Press, 1994), 121. The expression is used by Deleuze to refer to James Joyce's and Raymond Roussel's literature.

3. We can find this description associated with the notion of "system," from physical to literary ones in Deleuze, *Difference and Repetition*, 117–21; then, referred to the notion of "structure," in Gilles Deleuze, *The Logic of Sense*, trans. Mark Lester with Charles Stivale (New York: Columbia University Press, 1990), 50–51; also, referring to the process of individuation of a "thing in general," in Gilles Deleuze, "The Method of Dramatization," in *Desert Islands and Other Texts*, trans. Michael Taormina (New York: Semiotext(e), 2004), 96–97; and referred again to the "structure" concept in "How Do We Recognize Structuralism?," in *Desert Islands and Other Texts*, 182–84. In all cases, we can find differences and nuances between these different presentations, as it appears in different contexts and is used to set forth different concepts. We do not intend to say that this is all strictly the same, that Idea and structure and system are mere synonyms in Deleuze's philosophy (see our Concluding Remarks). However, we want to focus on the common movement that lays beneath these descriptions, with the aim of exploring and showing that movement as a fundamental stage of Deleuze's transcendental empiricism.

4. See Gilles Deleuze, *The Logic of Sense*, 50–51.

5. See Alain Badiou, *Being and Event*, trans. Oliver Felthan (New York: Continuum, 2005), 13.

6. Deleuze, *Difference and Repetition*, 163.

7. The mathematical developments that follow are based on the work of the professors of mathematics of the National Technological University of Argentina (UTN): Jorge Ferrante and Sandra Barrutia, *Solución de ecuaciones diferenciales mediante series de potencias* (Buenos Aires: edUTecNe, 2014), 21–53. We also follow the presentation of Felix Klein, *Elementary Mathematics from an Advanced Standpoint. Arithmetic, Algebra, Analysis*, trans. E. R. Hedrick and C. A. Noble (New York: Dover Publications, 1945), 223–36.

8. Deleuze refers to this specifically in chapter IV of *Difference and Repetition*, while developing the concept of the "element of pure potentiality," which corresponds to his theory of differential Ideas, and in virtue of which the Idea holds a power of

indefinite self-differentiation e.g., (Idea of the Idea). See Deleuze, *Difference and Repetition*, 174–75. We are obliged to refer here to Simon Duffy as one of the pioneers in the field of Deleuze and mathematics. Duffy has shown the importance of power series, from Taylor's algorithm to Weierstrass and Poincaré's improvements, when approaching Deleuze's use of differential relations. See Simon Duffy, "The Mathematics of Deleuze's Differential Logic and Metaphysics," in *Virtual Mathematics. The Logic of Difference*, ed. Simon Duffy (Manchester: Clinamen Press, 2006), 128–32.

9. *Osculari* comes from Latin and means "to kiss." This word certainly illustrates the progressively intimate contact between the curves, merging more and more in the original curve. For more graphical examples of this procedure (including the case sin x), see Felix Klein, *Elementary Mathematics from an Advanced Standpoint. Arithmetic, Algebra, Analysis*, 225–26; and for the notion of radius of convergence, see Klein, *Elementary Mathematics from an Advanced Standpoint*, 228. Klein develops this subject taking into consideration the complex plane and the Riemannian surface of the analyzed functions, drawing a far more exact scene of what Deleuze has in mind when dealing with these mathematical concepts. We have limited the introduction of technical mathematical notions to ease the exposition the most we could. A longer and more philosophical development of all this can be found in Jules Vuillemin's book, known and praised by Deleuze: Jules Vuillemin, *La philosophie de l'algèbre* (Paris: PUF, 1962), 303–65.

10. See Deleuze, *Difference and Repetition*, 175–76.

11. Deleuze, *Difference and Repetition*, 209–10.

12. Gilles Deleuze, *Sur Leibniz. Cours Vincennes-St. Dennis. Cours du 04/29/1980*, trans. Charles J. Stivale, accessed August 27, 2019. https://www.webdeleuze.com/textes/55. In this quotation, "universal" should be understood as an abstract generality, and not as the "true universal" that corresponds to Deleuzian Idea, and that we will see appear in the third condition of the structure.

13. Gilles Deleuze, *Sur Leibniz. Cours Vincennes-St. Dennis. Cours du 04/29/1980*; the emphasis on "series" is ours. For a deeper insight into the whole impact that the theory of singularities associated with Leibnizian thought has on Deleuze's philosophy, see chapter 2 of *The Fold*: Gilles Deleuze, *The Fold: Leibniz and the Baroque*, trans. Tom Conley (Minneapolis: University of Minnesota Press, 1993), 14–26. The theory of singularities goes beyond a new characterization of the general and the particular, to a new conception of the subject-object relation, based on the notion of event.

14. Deleuze, *The Logic of Sense*, 37.

15. Deleuze, *Difference and Repetition*, 172–73.

16. It can be easily understood that the differential elements determinate *each other* reciprocally in the differential relation, therefore becoming *something* they were not *before* the relation, as if something that was undetermined before entering a relation, becomes determined in itself by virtue of the relation. See, for instance, Duffy, "The Mathematics of Deleuze's Differential Logic and Metaphysics," 125:

> The undetermined differentials, or infinitesimals, dy or dx, are only determinable insofar as each is involved in a differential relation to one another, dy/dx. What counts

is that it is within the differential relation itself that the differential possesses rigor and coherence; that the undetermined are determinable, by a process of reciprocal determination.

I believe it is crucial, in explanations like this, to stress that "determinable" does not mean that the undetermined becomes *in itself* determined. This is impossible if we follow Deleuze's remark on the differential element as the "undetermined *as such*" (Deleuze, *Difference and Repetition*, 171; my emphasis). The virtual "determination" consists exclusively in the singularity, while only the differential relation is "determinable," insofar as it emits its corresponding singularity, but the differential element itself remains undetermined, as the objective problematic horizon that continues to surround the conditions under which a problem becomes solvable. In this sense, reciprocal determination never involves uniquely the differential relation as such, but the chain of derivatives (solutions) that constitute the power series: reciprocal determination supposes not only the differential relation (and its elements) but the network of derivatives mutually connected by them. The importance of stressing this lays in avoiding to see the differential relation as *preexisting* its products, as it if belonged to an absolutely separated dimension of reality, generating the functions from outside. Excellent Deleuze scholars like Simon Duffy, Aden Evens, or Daniela Voss have thus expressed a priority of the differential relation with respect to the primitive function (see Simon Duffy, *Deleuze and the History of Mathematics: In Defense of the New* (London/New York: Bloomsbury Academic Publishing, 2013), 33–4; Aden Evens, "Math Anxiety," *Angelaki: Journal of the Theoretical Humanities* 5, no. 3 (2000): 111; and Daniela Voss, *Conditions of Thought: Deleuze and Transcendental Ideas* (Croydon: Edinburgh University Press, 2013), 123). I think this priority of the differential relation has to be explicitly and uniquely referred to the generative virtual process of emission of singularities, but not to the primitive function itself. The reciprocal determination has to be understood in relation to an asymmetrical or intensive synthesis defined by the relation of the variables, that is, the function (see Deleuze, *Difference and Repetition*, 244), and where no ontological priority can be easily assigned. To affirm a priority of the virtual plane over the intensive one is something that has been largely put to discussion in recent scholarship; see, for instance, the whole eleventh volume of *Deleuze Studies*, devoted to this problem: *Deleuze Studies* 11, no. 2 (May 2017). By stressing the reciprocal bond between reciprocal determination and asymmetrical synthesis, I want to emphasize instead the complex and intertwined nature of the "levels" of Deleuzian ontology, which resist, in my view, to an absolute priority or "good sense" in the ontological process. I have gone over this interpretation of the reciprocal determination in Gonzalo Santaya, *El cálculo transcendental. Gilles Deleuze y el cálculo diferencial: ontología e historia* (Buenos Aires: RAGIF Ediciones, 2017), 175–93.

17. Deleuze, *Difference and Repetition*, 172.
18. Deleuze, *Difference and Repetition*, 170.
19. Deleuze follows here Hoëne Wronski's conception of dx as a rational Idea—in a Kantian sense—that presides the process of generation of quantities. Starting from a given function as the problem to solve, the differential element, via the Idea of infinity, grounds the process of generation of finite quantities that actualize the solution

to that problem. See Deleuze, *Difference and Repetition*, 175: "In this sense, the differential is indeed pure power, just as the differential relation is a pure element of potentiality."

20. I have studied in some detail this historical problem in Gonzalo Santaya, *El cálculo transcendental*, 47–102. When referring to this problem, Deleuze quotes Carl Benjamin Boyer's book, *The History of the Calculus and Its Conceptual Development* (New York: Dover Publications, 1959).

21. See Deleuze, *Difference and Repetition*, 178.

22. See Deleuze, *Desert Islands and Other Texts*, 176, where Deleuze, speaking about the differential relation as the purely symbolic form of structural relations, affirms:

> The mathematical origin of structuralism must be sought rather in the domain of differential calculus, specifically in the interpretation which Weierstrass and Russell gave to it, a *static and ordinal* interpretation, which definitively liberates calculus from all reference to the infinitely small, and integrates it into a pure logic of relations. (Emphasis original)

23. But then, while speaking of the differentiator and the empty square, he does not explicitly identify those instances with the differential element (see Deleuze, *Desert Islands and Other Texts*, 178–82, and 184–88). See Deleuze, *The Logic of Sense*, 50–51, where the differential calculus appears only as a part of the second condition for a structure in general, and not in the first nor in the third. Note 2 of that series (Deleuze, *The Logic of Sense*, 339) mentions again Weierstrass and his foundation of a mathematical structuralism, and refers to the book of Boyer we have cited in note 20.

24. See Deleuze, *Desert Islands and Other Texts*, 176 and 184. The name "Object = x," given to the paradoxical element, should not make us think about the mathematical variable x, whose relations Deleuze characterizes as imaginary and not as symbolic in a structural way (176), and that is attached to the viewpoint of abstract generality in *Difference and Repetition*, 171.

25. Because of space limitations, I cannot go into details over the concept of intensity here. It is important to remark, however, its *serial* nature. Chapter V of *Difference and Repetition* begins characterizing intensity as a system described by the very notion of serial communication that we saw at the beginning of this article. See Deleuze, *Difference and Repetition*, 222: "In so far as a system is constituted or bounded by at least two heterogeneous series, two disparate orders capable of entering into communication." The different terms of those intensive series are described, as the chapter progresses, as a manifold of individuals communicated by relations of envelopment and development, by which intensities organize themselves. In their development, they tend to *explicate*, that is, to constitute the extensive fixed magnitudes and qualities that populate the empirical plane. Deleuze borrows here his conceptual tools to biology and embryology rather than mathematics (see Deleuze, *Difference and Repetition*, 244–54). Actual intensive series are then in constant communication with virtual ideal series, producing empirical existence. The resonant communication between both series constitutes the infinite world of difference in itself.

26. Deleuze, *Difference and Repetition*, 244.

27. In this sense, Deleuze recalls Lewis Carrol's characterization of a parallelogram "longing" for its angles or a curve which suffers from "sections and ablations," insisting in the priority of ideal events over every form of metaphor or anthropomorphizing of mathematics (see Deleuze, *The Logic of Sense*, 55).
28. Deleuze, *Difference and Repetition*, 171.
29. For a complete description of this, see Deleuze, *Difference and Repetition*, 171–76.
30. See Deleuze, *Difference and Repetition*, 183, where Deleuze *defines* the Idea as a structure by following the Riemannian concept of multiplicity, which is in turn interpreted via the three conditions of being composed of (1) differential elements (2) mutually related and (3) necessarily incarnated in actual *terms*.
31. Deleuze, *Difference and Repetition*, xx.
32. Deleuze, *Difference and Repetition*, 200.
33. Immanuel Kant, *Critique of Pure Reason*, trans. Paul Guyer and Allen W. Wood (New York: Cambridge University Press, 2000), 464 [A416-B443–444].
34. See Deleuze, *Difference and Repetition*, 168–70. In this point, Deleuze follows the post-Kantian critiques to Kant regarding the mutual exteriority of the parts of his system. Kantian Ideas incarnate in three different and exterior moments (the self, the world, and God) the three intrinsically interrelated moments of *the* Deleuzian Idea: undetermined, determinable, and determination. However, Deleuze rejects the "dogmatic" post-Kantian notion of a superior or absolute Unity, for erasing the true nature of Difference. Daniel Smith has shown the importance of Kantian Ideas within the Deleuzian philosophy as a whole, and the importance of the post-Kantian tradition in it: see Daniel Smith, "Dialectics: Deleuze, Kant, and the Theory of Immanent Ideas," in *Essays on Deleuze* (Croydon: Edinburgh University Press, 2012), 106–21.
35. Deleuze, *Difference and Repetition*, 179.

BIBLIOGRAPHY

Badiou, Alain. *Being and Event*. Translated by Oliver Felthan. New York: Continuum, 2005.

Boyer, Carl Benjamin. *The History of the Calculus and Its Conceptual Development*. New York: Dover Publications, 1959.

Deleuze, Gilles. *Desert Islands and Other Texts*. Translated by Michael Taormina. New York: Semiotext(e), 2004.

Deleuze, Gilles. *Difference and Repetition*. Translated by Paul Patton. New York: Columbia University Press, 1994.

Deleuze, Gilles. *Sur Leibniz. Cours Vincennes-St. Dennis. Cours du 04/29/1980*. Translated by Charles J. Stivale. Accessed August 27, 2019. https://www.webdeleuze.com/textes/55.

Deleuze, Gilles. *The Fold: Leibniz and the Baroque*. Translated by Tom Conley. Minneapolis: University of Minnesota Press, 1993.

Deleuze, Gilles. *The Logic of Sense*. Translated by Mark Lester and Charles Stivale. New York: Columbia University Press, 1990.

Duffy, Simon. "The Mathematics of Deleuze's Differential Logic and Metaphysics." In *Virtual Mathematics: The Logic of Difference*, edited by Simon Duffy, 118–44. Manchester: Clinamen Press, 2006.

Duffy, Simon. *Deleuze and the History of Mathematics: In Defense of the New*. London/New York: Bloomsbury Academic Publishing, 2013.

Evens, Aden. "Math Anxiety." *Angelaki: Journal of the Theoretical Humanities* 5, no. 3 (2000): 105–15.

Ferrante, Jorge and Sandra Barrutia. *Solución de ecuaciones diferenciales mediante series de potencias*. Buenos Aires: edUTecNe, 2014.

Kant, Immanuel. *Critique of Pure Reason*. Translated and edited by Paul Guyer and Allen W. Wood. New York: Cambridge University Press, 2000.

Klein, Felix. *Elementary Mathematics from an Advanced Standpoint: Arithmetic, Algebra, Analysis*. Translated by E. R. Hedrick and C. A. Noble. New York: Dover Publications, 1945.

Santaya, Gonzalo. *El cálculo transcendental. Gilles Deleuze y el cálculo diferencial: ontología e historia*. Buenos Aires: RAGIF Ediciones, 2017.

Smith, Daniel. "Dialectics. Deleuze, Kant, and the Theory of Immanent Ideas." In *Essays on Deleuze*, 106–21. Croydon: Edinburgh University Press, 2012.

Voss, Daniela. *Conditions of Thought: Deleuze and Transcendental Ideas*. Croydon: Edinburgh University Press, 2013.

Vuillemin, Jules. *La philosophie de l'algèbre*. Paris: PUF, 1962.

Chapter 3

Reading History: The Structural Logic of Difference in the Social Idea

Anabella Schoenle

Translated by Andrew Ascherl

What we can imagine always exists, on another scale, in another time, clear and distant, like a dream.

Ricardo Piglia
El último lector

INTRODUCTION

How do philosophers think about society? Are intellectuals concerned about social problems? In particular, how concerned are certain political militants with society? Why should intellectuals and militants be Marxists? Who are we, each one of us, in the society where we are inserted in? In the context of his argument about the ideal synthesis of difference in chapter IV of *Difference and Repetition* (1968), Gilles Deleuze develops the notion of the *social Idea* as a problematic concept, responding in particular to some of the arguments in *Lire le Capital* [*Reading Capital*] (1965[1970/2016]), the original edition of which consists of papers written by five different authors—Louis Althusser, Étienne Balibar, Roger Establet, Pierre Macherey, and Jacques Rancière—in Althusser's annual seminar. These Marxist militant-intellectuals offered readings of Marx's *Capital* that were meant to support the Leftist movements of the time. In 1967, Althusser decided to publish a pocket edition of the book and rejected proposals to republish the original text in two volumes, opting instead for an abridged version. In 1969, a translation of this shorter version appeared in Argentina with the title *Para leer el Capital*, which included only the texts by Althusser and Balibar.[1]

Deleuze cites *Reading Capital* and in a theoretical gesture analyzes the elaboration of a practical theory in order to think, in his own work on metaphysics, a problem that articulates the central issues of everyday life in a singularly profound way, that is, phenomena which cause us anxiety because of their urgency: daily suffering, ubiquitous lack and excess, violent illnesses, and the cycle of life and death.

We will cover the brief fragments in which Deleuze discusses the social Idea—which is resignified in the arguments proposed by the authors of *Reading Capital*—focusing primarily on Étienne Balibar's contribution, "*Sur les concepts fondamentaux du matérialisme historique*" ["The Basic Concepts of Historical Materialism"], which Deleuze specifically cites. One of the objectives is to develop two specific affirmations that relate to the problem implied by Deleuze's elaboration of the social Idea *on the basis of* and/or *with* these Marxist readings. These affirmations are: (1) that Balibar's interpretation of *Capital* is structural rather than historicist; and (2) that the dialectic is a movement of difference that is not expressed in opposing terms (a view that forms part of Deleuze's critical reading of Hegelianism).[2] The development of these affirmations will guide us toward understanding the connection between, on the one hand, the metaphysical social Idea proposed by Deleuze and, on the other hand, Balibar's theoretical–practical perspective, which makes it possible to read what takes place in the organization of capitalist societies in relation to what Deleuze conceives of as the faculty of sociability.

FIRST AFFIRMATION: BALIBAR'S INTERPRETATION OF *CAPITAL* IS STRUCTURAL RATHER THAN HISTORICIST

Is it possible to read history? Can we read Marx as deterministic? How can a structural reading open itself up to history without becoming a historicist reading? Deleuze arrives at the notion of the social Idea in chapter IV of *Difference and Repetition* while looking for examples of how to think the Idea as a multiplicity in which structure and genesis are noncontradictory. In this regard, he mentions three kinds of Ideas—physical, biological, and social. Reflecting on the social Idea, Deleuze asks, "are there social Ideas, in a Marxist sense?" and later affirms that "the social Idea is the element of quantitability, qualitability, and potentiality of societies."[3] There doesn't seem to be a Marxist vocabulary for Deleuze's definition of the Idea, although there is something here that places us within the horizon of Marxist thought: social revolution. How many people have given up their power in the current social order? Is it the same power that allows us to discern how much we can do and how much we will be able to do it? How much can we do as a society? Just a few pages before he begins defining the social Idea, we find an earlier mention of the elements that constitute Deleuze's understanding of the Idea:

> Just as determinability pointed towards reciprocal determination, so the latter points towards complete determination. All three form the figure of sufficient reason in the threefold element of quantitability, qualitability, and potentiality.[4]

For Deleuze, all Ideas are related to movements of determination. The social Idea in particular is related to the quantitative, the qualitative, and the potential of societies, and these three elements, related to the movements of determination of an idea, compose the figure of sufficient reason. That is to say, when we think the social Idea we are dealing with a virtual idea that allows us to consider social problems in relation to the qualities, quantities, and potentialities that configure its determinations. Thus, there are social Ideas, and they have a specific Marxist meaning. But what is this meaning? Deleuze explains:

> [The social Idea] expresses a system of multiple ideal connections, or differential relations between differential elements: these include relations of production and property relations which are established not between concrete individuals but between atomic bearers of labour-power or representatives of property.[5]

In principle, society consists not simply of men but also of work to be done. The point in question is how social relations were established such that some men are reduced to their labor power and others are representatives of private property.

Therefore, in order to understand the social Idea as Deleuze considers it here, it is necessary to elaborate on—in relation to Balibar's contribution to *Reading Capital*—the way in which Marxism's structural rather than historicist interpretation allows us to think the problem of the social. We can find some pertinent reflections in the section of Balibar's text titled "History and Histories: On the Forms of Historical Individuality," which problematizes both the methodologies that read history as *a* history and the way in which the question of *history* (singular) or *histories* (plural) is connected to the problematization of concepts related to the reading of history. These concepts include the subject of history, time and temporality, the object of history, moments of history, or history as succession. Balibar's paper also addresses the concept of labor under two converging perspectives: one which holds that the mode of production is the determination of labor, and another that views man as a worker reduced to labor power. Structure (in this case, production) appears as a fundamental element for reading history, but how are we to understand the concept of structure here? How is genesis articulated *with* and *in* structure to produce solutions? How are we able to say that rejecting a historicist reading does not reject what is historical in the process but rather takes into consideration a different, nonlinear, nondeterministic form of comprehending changes in temporality? Deleuze focuses his reflections on the limitations of Marxism's historicist interpretation and emphasizes the structuralist reading developed in the papers published in *Reading Capital*. In this regard, he argues that the structural aspect of Marxism should be understood as structural and dialectical in a movement configured in difference. Therefore, genesis and structure are not mutually exclusive.

> Ideas are multiplicities: every idea is a multiplicity or a variety [. . .] multiplicity must not designate a combination of the many and the one, but rather an organisation belonging to the many as such, which has no need whatsoever of unity in order to form a system. The one and the many are concepts of the understanding which make up the overly loose mesh of a distorted dialectic which proceeds by opposition.[6]

A combination of the many is not the same thing as the organization of the many *as such*. On this point, Deleuze follows Althusser's advice at the beginning of *Reading Capital* in a section titled "To the Reader": "the terminology we employed was too close in many respects to the 'structuralist' terminology."[7] This structuralism, which proposes a formalist reduction to a combinatory, is supplanted by one that considers the variation of the elements of a given structure. Therefore, "Marxism is not a 'structuralism' " in a formalist sense but rather insofar as it acquires structure by being thought as a space in which different practices and times are articulated.[8] To this end, Balibar discusses the *differential forms of historical individuality*, a concept that allows us to think of a different mode of history based on the Marxist proposal to redefine the concept of man in a structure as a form of individuality that enters into a dependent relationship with the forms of production.

> Each relatively autonomous practice [that of the productive forces and that of the worker] thus engenders forms of historical individuality which are peculiar to it. [. . .] For each practice and for each transformation of that practice, they [men] are the different forms of individuality which can be defined on the basis of its combination structure.[9]

Thus, Balibar adopts a conception of transformation that allows us to understand that the elements of the combinatory give shape to a history that departs from the linearity of historicist readings in which men embody different forms of individuality. The idea here is to think a structure of temporal development, since every process that occurs in social reality develops according to its own temporality and alongside the temporalities of other processes. This allows us to explain the relation between history and dynamics, and idea of structure as something characterized by movement. Examining the relation between structure and dynamics, Balibar discusses Marx's analysis:

> If men were the common supports of determinate functions in the structure of each social practice, they would "in a manner express and concentrate" the entire social structure into themselves, i.e., they would be the centres from which it would be possible to know the articulation of these practices in the structure of the whole. At the same time, each of these practices would be effectively centred on the men-subjects of ideology, i.e., on consciousnesses. Thus the "social relations," instead of expressing the structure of these practices, of which individuals are merely the effects, would be generated from the multiplicity of these centres, i.e., they would have the structure of a practical intersubjectivity.
>
> As we have seen, Marx's whole analysis excludes this possibility. It forces us to think, not the multiplicity of centres, but the radical absence of a centre. The specific practices which are articulated in the social structure are defined by the relations of their combination before they themselves determine the forms of historical individuality which are strictly relative to them.[10]

Is every subject both part and the whole of a structure? If we think the answer is yes, it may be because we believe that every subject relates to structure as both a determinate and a determining instance. Thus, the subject not only expresses structure but also helps sustain it; in extreme cases, even more than helping to support structure, it also engenders it. Can we therefore say that any one of us—as subjects of a structure—"doing" something different could change the structure that articulates every social fact? In principle, no, because it would only impact a singularity and not a structure: a particular situation, a determinate moment, by and for specific people and with a singular objective. However, does this mean that "someone doing something else" has no differential meaning? Would this space in which someone does something else not be different at all if that someone did what everyone does/what one does/what one should do/what one is accustomed to doing? Does doing the same thing have the same effect as doing something different? From another perspective: what would happen if there were no subject-center of structure and only practices? Instead of focusing on the subject and its actions, we would think relations, articulations, nonformal combinations. There would then be something to do in relation to structure since relations configure individualities, not the other way around. That is to say, we cannot ask the oppressor or the oppressed to cease playing their roles. Nor can we make these individualities stop existing. What we can do is think of how to produce in another way so that other individualities can be configured on the basis of new relations.

Deleuze discusses these conceptions, interprets Balibar's Marxist analysis in nonformal structural terms, and thinks the social Idea as variation. This reading distances itself from historicism in that linear time forces us to think transformations in succession and with a transitivity that only recognizes sudden disruptions as moments of change.

> *The concept of history in general, unspecified, is simply the designation of a constitutive problem* of the "theory of history" (of historical materialism): it designates that theory as a whole as the site of the problem of the articulation of the different historical times and the variants of this articulation. This articulation no longer has anything to do with the simple model of the insertion of one time into another; it accepts coincidences not as obviousnesses, but as problems: for instance, the transition from one mode of production to another may seem to be the moment of a collision, or collusion, between the times of the economic structure, of the political class struggle, of ideology, etc. The question is to discover how each of these times, e.g., the time of the "tendency" of the mode of production, becomes a historical time.[11]

The Deleuzian social Idea can affirm social problems in differentiation without relying on the genesis of a historical subject to be able to think the genesis of movements that involve the formation of new individualities. This is not the history of disruption expressed in the possibility of thinking a break in the historical mode of social development in order to produce a change. Given that Deleuze's proposal involves the history of movement, we can begin to think "the economic":

> "The economic" is never given properly speaking, but rather designates a differential virtuality to be interpreted, always covered over by its forms of actualisation; a theme or "problematic" always covered over by its cases of solution. In short, the economic is the social dialectic itself—in other words, the totality of the problems posed to a given society, or the synthetic and problematising field of that society.[12]

Therefore, the economic is considered to be a structural space in which the disposition of elements that offer solutions through *combinatories* and variability is at stake. In Deleuze's words, "the economic conditions of a problem determine or give rise to the manner in which it finds a solution within the framework of the real relations of the society."[13] That is to say, the interpretation of *Capital* he is analyzing is structural rather than historicist, and the structure in question is the economy as a dynamic/dynamicizing element, a structure whose process of structuration occurs in time and is related to the possibilities for solutions opened up by it.

The *social Idea in a Marxist sense* therefore satisfies structural and genetic conditions proper to the Idea, since the economic is the dynamic structure (the organization of the multiple) in which modes of production are articulated (with variations) that, being dynamic, are expressed in solutions (a structure can have various structurations), which exceed the elements of the structure themselves (economic structure brings about problems in biologically, physically, and socially structured spaces).[14]

SECOND AFFIRMATION: THE DIALECTIC IS A MOVEMENT OF DIFFERENCE THAT IS NOT EXPRESSED IN OPPOSING TERMS

Deleuze presents the dialectic as a noncontradictory movement without oppositions, which is to say, as an affirmative movement of difference in which a combinatory of differential elements is developed. The relation between differen*t*iation and differen*c*iation emerges here to explain that Deleuze's idea of the dialectic disregards negation, which allows us to understand the dialectic in terms of differen*c*iation rather than opposition. This is because one mode of differing is not opposed to another but instead is expressed in another space and/or in another way. There is both virtual space and actual space. Deleuze writes: "Problems are always dialectical: the dialectic has no other sense, nor do problems have any other sense. What is mathematical (or physical, biological, psychical, or sociological) are the solutions."[15] Therefore, the social Idea is the solution, namely, the problem of the economic. That is to say, poverty as the impossibility of feeding, clothing, educating, and/or finding work for oneself is not a social problem but rather a social solution of the economic problem, and this problem is expressed in the distribution of its elements in the structure. It is another way of defining the problem of distribution within the economy. "The problematic or dialectical Idea is a system of connections between differential elements, a system of differential relations between genetic elements."[16]

From this, we can connect Deleuze's reflections to Balibar's explanation of the link between history and dynamics that problematizes the historical conception of linear time and expresses the way in which difference forms part of the logic of structure. Structure and difference appear as parts of the movement that makes possible the combinatories that shape what Balibar calls the *differential forms of historical individuality*, which we mentioned at the beginning of the present text. This relationship is connected to two Deleuzian concepts: (1) the social Idea, which expresses a system of multiple ideal relations, or differen*c*ial relations between differential elements; and (2) the variety of relations that is embodied in the differentiated concrete works that characterize a particular society.

Deleuze interprets the structure of the economic as the set of regulations in society that addresses social problems. This does not mean that "the economic" can resolve these problems, since all problems are, as Deleuze argues, embedded in a *dramatization*.[17] That is to say, the concept-problematic is configured in the mode of a drama in which the problem unfolds on one level. If the structure of the economic is a level on which certain problematic concepts develop, then the social problem can be performed there as a drama (it has a way to develop itself) which could generate another schema of movements on another level.[18] Therefore, we think that the problematic field proposes fields of resolution, and the fact that the structure of the economic is where social problems manifest suggests that there is a level of the structure on which solutions to these problems can be found. That is, the problem is ramified toward spaces of solution found in the possibility of a relation to another level of the structure.

It is necessary to be clear that the structural aspect here is dynamic, and this aspect—if we think of the social Idea as that which addresses the problems of living in a society—is the structural economic aspect. That is to say, in the economy as structure one *virtually* (in the sense of real rather than actual) finds the affirmations that embody social reality.

What then is the relationship between the social Idea and social reality? First, like everything that is virtual, the social Idea is real, and in this sense, social reality can be equivalent to the social Idea.[19] However, we should remember the everyday sense of reality—that which unceasingly happens all the time and which must urgently be modified or improved in order to live in one way or another. We believe that we are referring here to another reality because it is urgent, but it is actually the same embodied reality. Rather, the question is, why do we believe this embodied reality is a solution if it is so disappointing?

In principle, we can identify the central idea as that of connecting problems and solutions which appear as dialectical affirmation—that is, all movement that articulates problems and solutions is to be taken as affirmation. There is an embodied reality that is connected to (virtual or real) Ideas, and the fact that what happens happens the way it does not mean that there are no other possible forms of embodiment. However, in order for these to exist, they must be articulated with other Ideas. To think this from the punctual perspective of the social Idea, we must address the problem that appears here as the dynamicizing aspect, the dynamicizing structure: the economy. When we think that the virtual is real, we place emphasis on the fact that in the virtual there is nothing to actualize because supposing otherwise would mean that the virtual has no reality. Therefore, we ask again: is there a virtual idea—of another possible society, for example—waiting to be actualized?

This question mistakenly expresses a relation between the virtual and the actual, as the characteristic immanence of these concepts obliges us not to separate them from one another. The virtual Idea is as real as the actual idea. However, where is potentiality if every Idea is real? In order to think this, we must ask: are there affirmations that can be made even if they are not factual? Yes and no. What is factual is affirmation of affirmation of affirmation, and the factual can only be such by entailing what has been affirmed or in the mode of affirmation—all of these redundancies are legitimate. Negation has no place here because movement and transformation are permanently given in the encounter of different configurations.

With this in mind, we can suggest that it is in the mode of affirmation that we can address the problems and solutions related to understanding the dynamics of structures and authorize new configurations within them. The problem of "the economic," therefore, is not a problem because it generates economic problems but rather because it is expressed in nonvital social realities—because it kills. Killing here is an affirmation that entails a closure because it obstructs the continuous movement of affirmations. It is the end of the movement, the end of the dialectic understood as such. The way in which economic structure is unified is problematic. However, does this mean that all problems are economic and that social problems do not exist? Absolutely not. As Deleuze writes:

> Social problems can be grasped only by means of a "rectification" which occurs when the faculty of sociability is raised to its transcendent exercise and breaks the unity of fetishistic common sense. The transcendent object of the faculty of sociability is revolution. In this sense, revolution is the social power of difference, the paradox of society, the particular wrath of the social Idea. Revolution never proceeds by way of the negative. [. . .] Practical struggle never proceeds by way of the negative but by way of difference and its power of affirmation.[20]

The faculty of sociability makes it possible to think social problems and establish their potentialities in difference because the Idea is embodied multiplicity, and there is no transference between the Idea and praxis. The Idea is one of the modes in which life develops, and therefore, it is the problematic mode of life as solution. In this sense, the faculty of sociability appears here as a promise of virtuality and thus of reality. According to Deleuze, the element of social transformation emerges from social multiplicity and the transcendent objects it generates.

CONCLUSION

In order to avoid the potential absence of closure to the present text and in turn, to offer an affirmation that allows space for the expression of closure, we will express our agreement with certain points and suggest what ought to come next. We agree that: (1) structure expresses *its own organization of the multiple* that enables continuation and transformation; (2) subjects in history and in structure proceed by making multiplicity possible in both history and structure; (3) in the development of society, there are different times that relate to one another; and (4) one can think in order to produce, given that there is a permanent movement of affirmation that makes this possible. Furthermore, we understand that it is important to relate the concept of the *social power of difference* Deleuze mentions in the passage cited previously regarding the possibility of social transformation to Balibar's reflections on the *forms of individuality* in order to rethink both the subject and history. This next step can only be posed as a question: how can we, *in this time and on this scale*, think about inventing another mode of living? It is important not to forget here that *what we can imagine always exists*.

NOTES

1. [The original English translation of *Lire le Capital* (*Reading Capital*, trans. Ben Brewster, London: NLB, 1970) also only included the texts by Althusser and Balibar. A complete English translation of the book, including the papers by Establet, Macherey, and Rancière, was finally published in 2015.—Tr.]

2. Julián Ferreyra, "Hegel lector de Deleuze: una perspectiva crítica sobre la ontología afirmativa a partir de las objeciones a Spinoza en *La ciencia de la lógica*," *Kriterion* 127 (2013): 89–107.

3. Gilles Deleuze, *Difference and Repetition*, trans. Paul Patton (New York: Columbia University Press, 1994), 186.

4. Deleuze, *Difference and Repetition*, 176.

5. Deleuze, *Difference and Repetition*, 186.

6. Deleuze, *Difference and Repetition*, 182.

7. Louis Althusser, Étienne Balibar, Roger Establet, Jacques Rancière, and Pierre Macherey, *Reading Capital: The Complete Edition*, trans. Ben Brewster and David Fernbach (New York: Verso, 2015), 13.

8. Louis Althusser and Étienne Balibar, *Para leer el capital*, trans. M. Harnecker (Buenos Aires: Siglo XXI, 2012), 4. This phrase (and the paragraph in which it appears) is present in the Spanish translation but not in the English translation or the original French text. This curious discrepancy is one of the notable signs of the South American perspective on the sources of Deleuze's thought.

9. Althusser and Balibar, *Reading Capital*, 306.

10. Althusser and Balibar, *Reading Capital*, 307.

11. Althusser and Balibar, *Reading Capital*, 345 (italics in original).

12. Deleuze, *Difference and Repetition*, 186.

13. Deleuze, *Difference and Repetition*, 186.

14. Deleuze, *Difference and Repetition*, 184.

15. Deleuze, *Difference and Repetition*, 179.

16. Deleuze, *Difference and Repetition*, 181.

17. "Given a concept, we can always discover its drama, and *the concept would never be divided or specified* in the world of representation *without the dramatic*

dynamisms that thus determine it in a material system beneath all possible determination," Gilles Deleuze, *Desert Islands and Other Texts*, trans. Michael Taormina (Los Angeles: Semiotext(e), 2004), 98.

18. Gilles Deleuze and Félix Guattari, *What Is Philosophy?*, trans. Hugh Tomlinson and Graham Burchell (New York: Columbia University Press, 1994).

19. Deleuze, *Difference and Repetition*, 208.

20. Deleuze, *Difference and Repetition*, 208.

BIBLIOGRAPHY

Althusser, Louis, Étienne Balibar, Roger Establet, Jacques Rancière, and Pierre Macherey. *Reading Capital: The Complete Edition*. Translated by Ben Brewster and David Fernbach. New York: Verso, 2015.

Deleuze, Gilles and Félix Guattari. *What Is Philosophy?*. Translated by Hugh Tomlinson and Graham Burchell. New York: Columbia University Press, 1994.

Deleuze, Gilles. *Desert Islands and Other Texts*. Translated by Michael Taormina. Los Angeles: Semiotext(e), 2004.

Deleuze, Gilles. *Difference and Repetition*. Translated by Paul Patton. New York: Columbia University Press, 1994.

Ferreyra, Julián. "Hegel lector de Deleuze: una perspectiva crítica sobre la ontología afirmativa a partir de las objeciones a Spinoza en *La ciencia de la lógica*." *Kriterion* 127 (2013): 89–107.

Chapter 4

An Embryological Approach to *Difference and Repetition*'s "Order of Reasons"

Sebastián Amarilla

INTRODUCTION

The entire world is an egg. The egg is a theater. The egg provides us with a model of the order of reasons. These are some of the appearances of this mysterious concept, scattered here and there, in *Difference and Repetition*.

"The entire world is an egg," we said an instant before: in what sense? What does "world" mean in this context? What does egg signify? Here, we might consider that "world" refers to any phenomena, everything that takes place, every system in general that can be isolated, or that is able to be considered separately, that is, any physical, biological, psychic, social, astronomic, molecular, protean, geological, or conceptual system (just to mention some possibilities); in other words: *anything*.[1]

And what about the egg? Maybe when we read the word "egg," the first thing that comes to mind is that ovoid thing that hens lay and the poultry industry package in convenient half-dozen packs for us to buy and eat. But in this context it is necessary to disambiguate this term: "egg" refers, in general, to the embryological ambit. And the embryological expresses, according to Deleuze, that instance that encloses the processes related to the gestation, formation, germination, or emergence of *anything*—objects, individuals, ideas, qualities, places, events, and so on. More specifically, it refers to those primordial movements that correspond to initial phases of things; those phases that have more potential and determine the features or characteristics from which things will be identified once developed. Although the fact that a thing reaches its "adulthood" means that it acquires, at least in appearance, more or less stable features that give it certain identity, its becoming isn't closed: it continues to be undermined by forces and intensities that go through it and transform it. However, for one thing, these transformations will never again belong to the embryological domain: what the egg lives can only be lived by it once and irreversibly.

If we focus in the domain of living beings of the animal realm that reproduce themselves sexually, "egg" refers, in particular, to the *zygote*, that is to say, the incipient individual product of the union between both female and male gametes.

In the fifth chapter of *Difference and Repetition*, "Asymmetrical Synthesis of the Sensible," Deleuze aims to characterize the way in which the structural virtual multiplicity of the Idea actualize in "concrete and empiric" reality. Within the frame of this process, the concepts of *difference of intensity* and *individuation* become especially relevant, as necessary conditions for differenciation to operate and therefore promote the actual and empirical phenomena. It is through intensity that the multiplicity of the Idea is dramatized in spatiotemporal dynamisms and differenciates in species and parts.[2]

According to Deleuze, the egg can help us understand this ontogenetic process, providing us with a model for the order of reasons:

> The world is an egg. Moreover, the egg, in effect, provides us with a model for the order of reasons: (organic and species related) differentiation-individuation-dramatisation-differenciation. We think that difference of intensity, as this is implicated in the egg, expresses first the differential relation or a virtual matter to be organized. This intensive field of individuation determines the relations that it expresses to be incarnates in spatio-temporal dynamisms (dramatization), in species which correspond to these relations (specific differenciation), and in organic parts which correspond to the distinctive points in these relations (organic differenciation). Individuation always governs actualization: the organic points are induced only on the basis of the gradients of their intensive environment; the types determined in their species only by virtue of the individuating intensity. Throughout, intensity is primary in relation to organic extension and to species qualities. Notions such as "morphogenetic potential," "field-gradient-threshold" put forward by Dalcq, which essentially concern the relations of intensity as such, account for this complex ensemble.[3]

We will aim to clarify this brief but conceptually dense passage using embryology in general and in particular the work of Albert Dalcq as intercessors.

EMBRYOLOGY

Albert Dalcq (1893–1973) was an eminent representative of a generation of embryologists that came up from the junction of two very different lines of investigation of that which we can call "life," at the dawn of the molecular revolution in biology: on the one hand, that which focuses on global properties of organisms; on the other hand, that which emphasizes on the study and characterization of basic molecular constituents of cells.[4] Near the year 1930, Dalcq—who belonged to the first tradition—started with a biochemical approach to his experimental practices.

How can Dalcq's work contribute to comprehend the order of reasons? In the chapter of Dalcq's volume quoted by Deleuze, the author starts distinguishing three main regions present in any vertebrate: the head, the trunk, and the tail, and then he asks how it is possible to explain that the head forms on one end and the tail on the other: is it a qualitative difference, or there is a more profound quantitative difference?[5]

Dalcq rejects a popular position from that time, which stated that each organ is formed by a progressive cell assimilation to its structure, as if it were, for example, a miniature liver which keeps growing little by little. This type of extensive growth by cellular assimilation is inherent to terminal phases of the kinematics of the gastrula, and it is only a complementary and secondary aspect of the organizing dynamism of the egg. It cannot reveal what is truly important: the genesis of the parts of the embryo.

At this point, we need to present some basic embryologic notions, at least schematically. We shall distinguish three major phases in embryonic development: cleavage, gastrulation, and organogenesis:[6]

1. The product of the union between the female gamete (ovum) and the male gamete (sperm) is called *zygote* or fertilized egg. In the first phase, called cleavage, this primordial cell undergoes a fast mitotic division (following a geometric progression with ratio 2 with no significant growth; however, the division speed is higher in a zone (the animal pole, where cells are more numerous and smaller) than in the diametrically opposed (the vegetal pole, where cells are less numerous and bigger). Except for this, there is not much difference between cells, meaning that, at this point, they have the potential to become any organ (see figure 4.1).

   The new cells derived from cleavage are called blastomeres. After certain quantity of divisions (that varies from species to species, but at least four are needed, that is to say, sixteen cells), a dense ball of cells is formed, called morula. When a number of seven cleavages are reached, blastomeric cells reorganize, placing in the periphery of this ball to form a fluid-filled hollow sphere, whose cavity is called blastocoel. This stage has been named blastula (see figure 4.2).

2. In the next phase, the gastrulation, a critical reorganization of blastula's cells, is produced. Once a certain threshold is reached in a zone of the periphery of our young blastula, a revolutionary cell group invaginates, folding inside the blastocoel. This dramatic bio-topological ballet produces the appearance of three cell layers: an external layer (ectoderm), a middle layer (mesoderm), and an interior layer (endoderm). Additionally,

Animal Pole

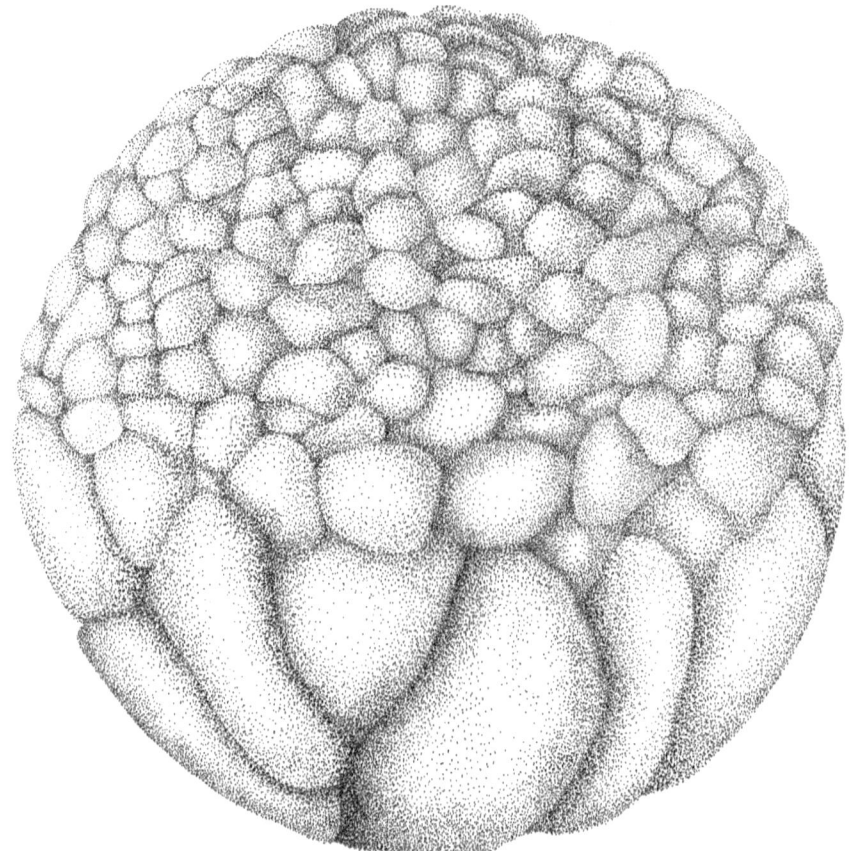

Vegetal Pole

Figure 4.1 Vegetal and Animal Poles of the Morula.

a new cavity is delimitated (archenteron), which communicates with the outside through an opening called a blastopore. Depending on the species, this primitive hole will become either the anus (deuterostomes) or the mouth (protostomes) (see figure 4.3).

3. Consequently, in the organogenesis, each cellular layer of the gastrula that still is undifferenciated but has a territory—we will come back to this point in a moment—becomes, respectively, the epidermis, the nervous tissues, and the sensitive organs; the digestive and breathing tubes, digestive glands, and bladder; and the dermis, heart lining, circulatory system, kidneys, gonads, the skeletal, and muscular systems.

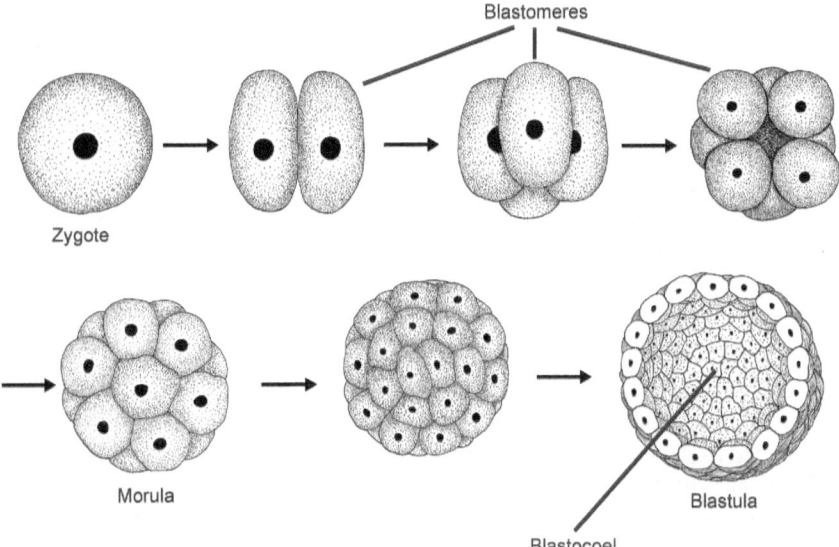

Figure 4.2 From Zygote to Blastula.

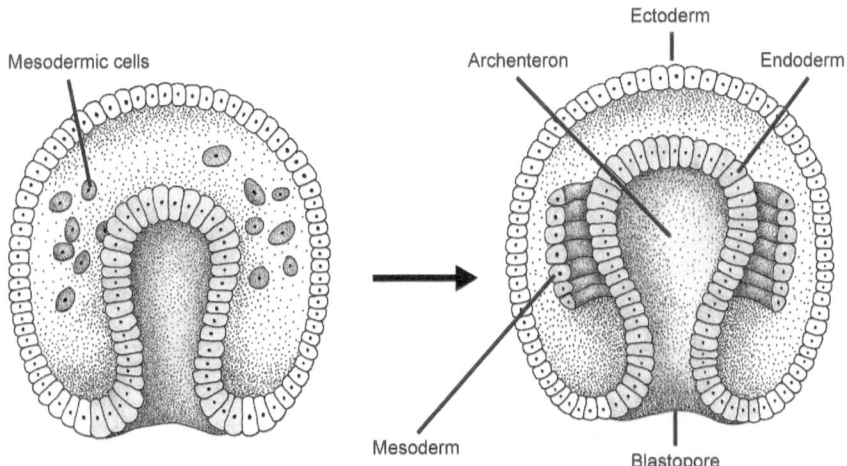

Figure 4.3 Gastrulation.

To comprehend Dalcq's ontogenetic proposal, the concept of "morphogenetic potential" becomes especially relevant. Following Dalcq, it is necessary to understand this concept in order to realize the "capital process that happens in the gastrulation: the disjunction of continual cellular patterns, segmented in groups of elements that are the primordial organs."[7] These territories are carriers of a morphogenetic potential. Embryologists of that time called this demarcation either "segmentation" or "differentiation," but Dalcq rejects the latter term to rename the early movements that take place in the young embryo, pointing out that it evokes the appearance of cytoplasmic structures, granules, fibrils, and so on, that is to say, certain types of cellular structures which account for a specific function. In other words, differenciation corresponds to a histological level, a late process of the embryo: as far as we are concerned, it is not a question of any *visible* difference out of the territorial demarcation of primitive cell groups.

Quoting Deleuze:

> Embryology shows that the division of an egg into parts is secondary in relation to more significant morphogenetic movements: the augmentation of free surfaces, stretching of cellular layers, regional displacement of groups. A whole kinematics of the egg appears, which implies a dynamic. Moreover, this dynamic express something ideal. Transport is Dionysian, divine and delirious, before it is local axes of development, the differential speeds and rhythms which are the primary factor in the actualization of a structure and create a space and a time peculiar to that which is actualized.[8]

EMBRYONTOLOGY

The early movements that take place in the egg involve spatiotemporal dynamisms that express the differential relations and singularities that determine them. And reciprocally, those dynamisms, those primary movements are, in their turn, supposed by the double differenciation in species and parts that characterize the adult individual, that is to say, the actual qualities and extensities. "It is the dynamic processes which determine the actualization of Ideas."[9]

A whole drama takes place in the egg and evokes a citation mentioned previously:

> The world is an egg, but the egg itself is a theatre: a staged theatre in which the roles dominate the actors, the spaces dominate the roles and the Ideas dominate the spaces. Furthermore, by virtue of the complexity of Ideas and their relations with other Ideas, the spatial dramatization is played on several levels: in the constitution of an internal space, but also in the manner in which that space extends into the external extensity, occupying a region of it.[10]

Spatiotemporal dynamisms are real *dramas*, and that which is dramatized are Ideas. And if we consider the complexity of the Idea and the relations it engages with other Ideas, we realize that everything we focus our attention on implies an abyssal depth. As regards to living beings of the animal realm that reproduce sexually, as described previously, and superficially, we show a series of dynamisms that found space and time in the egg and determine their internal environment. But this internal environment is, at the same time, constituted by a number of other series of movements and interactions: a whole protean theater, with its own dramas, spaces, roles, and larval actors. All of this is even more complex if we consider the external environment of an individual with its own demographic and ecological dynamisms, which constitute the way it interacts with other living beings and with its setting. These connections, relations, and integrations can occur in multiple ways: "Everywhere a staging at several levels."[11] The analytical perspective we assume determines a limitation to the series, which otherwise will reveal what they are: infinite

Space-time dynamisms are therefore the agents that stage a double synthesis which corresponds to the two distinctive aspects of anything: on the one hand, a qualification or specification, and on the other hand, a partition or organization in extension. This synthesis, this process is that we understand by differenciation, and it constitutes one of the two "halves" of anything, the actual "half." We lack a whole other "half," which without being actual is very real.

In this respect, we have not stopped to invoke the Idea. We have said that that which is dramatized by dynamisms are Ideas. And if dynamisms command the double empiric synthesis of qualities and extensities in the Idea, then we should find two characters that correspond without resemblance to those two aspects. Our hypothesis is that, within this context, genetic information, as it is present in cell nucleus, expresses the ideal level.[12]

On the one hand, ideal genetic information is populated by differential relations (dy/dx) between differential elements (dy and dx) which only find their *raison d'être* when they are linked in a relation. dy and dx are not anything on their own; they are completely undetermined outside of any relation corresponding to a principle of determinability. But they are mutually determinable, one in relation to the other, corresponding to a principle of reciprocal determinability. A reciprocal synthesis of differential relations between undetermined elements is required. Moreover, distributions of singular and ordinary points correspond to those differential relations: a singular point is the origin of a series that prolongs itself through ordinary points toward the neighborhood of another singular point, whether converging or diverging, in favor of a principle of complete determination. This dialectic of the ideal synthesis is what is named by the word differen*t*iation.

Thus, the Idea is formed as a multiplicity of differential relations and bright singular points that already constitute the completely differen*t*iated state of the Idea that is the other half of anything: the virtual half. Therefore, variable differential relations correspond to *qualities*, while ideal singular points correspond to *parts*; a whole ideal variety. It is the Idea that poses the problems and questions; and the egg and its dynamisms are themselves cases of solutions to problems, answering the questions posed by the genetic material, the layouts of multiple space-time coordinates.

But there is a question of crucial relevance which must be asked of any dynamism that presumes to operate with specifications and partitions. That question is *who?*

"*Who?*" always determines a field supposed by dynamisms and in which they are produced. The question "*who?*" asks always for the individual and sets an intense field of individuation, in which differences or intensities (differences of intensity) are distributed in depth. Despite the fact that intensities are presented to us already qualified and developed in extension, we must conceive intense fields of individuation as the previous condition to any specification and partition. They are true plexuses of pure intensities enveloped in depth.

As Dalcq says, referring to the cell territorialization we showed earlier:

> A term is necessary to characterize this process, this is the individuation. This neologism will designate the acquisition, by the organs, of its individuality. Also, it will embrace everything that confirms that individuality: the complication of the cord and, mostly, of the brain, the appearance of sensory organs, the heart and the blood vessels, the excretory organs, the gradual diversification of the enteric tract, etc.[13]

Individuation exerts its influence through individuation fields, which impress in each primordial group of cells a territorial character that determines the progressive structural development of the organism. It modulates the kinetic dynamisms which provoke the appearance of the organs and embrace the conditions that regulate the stabilization of the morphogenetic potential. It is possible, following Dalcq, to think the individuation fields as present in the more premature states of the egg, even when the actual differentiation of each organ has not been performed.

Individuation fields are presented as fields of mutual inductive influence, in which different territories conform to systems of reciprocal determination, which are responsible for the amplification of the structures of the organism. We can consider the morphogenetic potential of a given territory as a proliferation capacity or growth power; as if it were causing an inductive influence on other territories. The acquisition of a differentiated cytological character depends on it, that is to say, an adequacy to certain biological needs required for the specific functions of each tissue, a further sign of effective individuality.

As a cellular group reaches this point, it also acquires a specific metabolism. Thus, biochemical specificity comes up in each organ or tissue, giving rise to the appearance of, for example, neurofibrils, myofibrils, glycogen, myosin, collagen, and so on. These already differenciated tissues and elements are responsible for carrying out all the functions that an organism is capable of. Thereupon, we can state that egg's blastomeres possess, from the very beginning, all functions: they combine assimilation, excretion, breathing, and excitability. What Dalcq points out is that differenciation will focus on one of these functions and placate the others.

Quoting Deleuze:

> Individuation does not presuppose any differentiation; it gives rise to it. Qualities and extensities, forms and matters, species and parts are not primary; they are imprisoned in individuals as though in a crystal ball, in the moving depth of individuating differences or differences of intensity.[14]

In an adult organism, differences in morphogenetic potential stabilize, resulting in the balance between different organs and tissues each with their own proportions and functions. In other words, the cells of a well-formed kidney cannot become heart cells. However, it may happen that this balance is perverted, triggering pathological modification of cells. One of the most known effects of this cellular deterritorialization is cancer.

When plumbing the intensive *spatium* of the egg, we find a whole depth, the theater of any metamorphosis. The egg is itself an individuation field which at the same time envelopes and is comprised within another multiple individuation fields: field of individuation of the liver, field of individuation of the right arm, field of individuation of a red cell, field of individuation of a protein, field of individuation of this group of pampas hares, field of individuation of pampas steppes biome. Relations of relations in an intensive depth announce the universal ungrounding.

It has been frequently asked if intensity is ideal or actual, but the question is not well posed this way. Intensity is the expression of difference. It is the potency of difference. In the very same way that lighting has a dark precursor before striking, which communicates the different intensive series in order to make it happen, at the level of the egg we find all kinds of gradients and thresholds or morphogenetic potential, which induce by proximity the appearance of the qualified parts of the body. Cell migrations that take place in the embryo are extensive, but beneath these extensive movements underlay passages and becomings from another nature: intensive passages and becomings through intensity lines. For example, if, like a biological alchemist, we grab some cell group from a zone of the embryo and relocate it in another, at specific moments of the embryo development, we shall induce very interesting transformations in the adult individual (see figure 4.4).

Every individual is an intensive system of the signal-sign type, where "signal" designates at least two heterogeneous series that are capable of

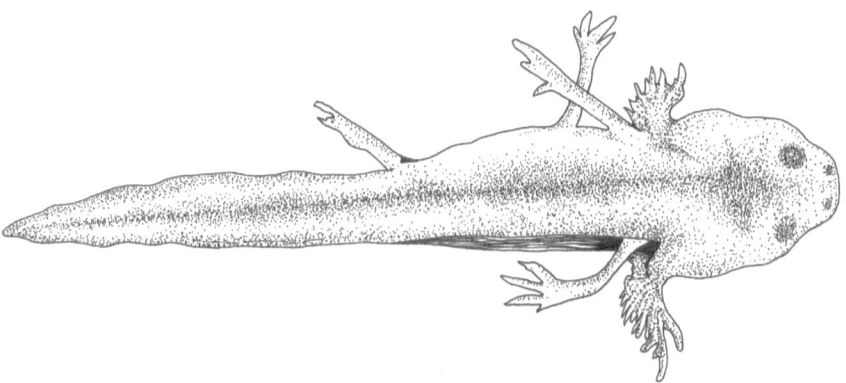

Figure 4.4 Monstrous Transformation in Adult Amphibian Product of Early Embryo Manipulation.

entering into communication, bounding the system, and giving it an internal resonance, and where the sign is the phenomenon that flashes between those two series, brought about the communication, which lasts all the time it takes to extinguish the constitutive difference of that particular system.

If the egg provides us with a model of the order of reasons, it is because we find in it differential relations or a virtual matter that, in some way, inhabits the differen*t*iated genetic material. This virtual matter is expressed by differences of intensity which create intensive fields of individuation that stage or dramatize spatiotemporal dynamisms and, at the same time, determine actualization in species and organic parts, which correspond to differential relations and distinctive points in these relations (specific and organic differen*c*iation).

The development of the egg is the movement of a waterfall, which goes from the highest to the lowest level. At the top, the zygote, potential differences are maximal and as the organism explains itself, the intensity of the waterfall decreases until it reaches its adult form. However, to consider that intensities tend to an unfailing and final nullity means to fall into the trap of the good sense. On the contrary, the system never dies, because organisms reproduce and engender new eggs and everything starts again every time. Where a waterfall dies, a river is usually born.

NOTES

1. Of course, we are not talking about a "simple empiricism," which precisely is what Deleuze is trying to avoid: the thinking that takes things as if they were already made.

2. John Protevi has addressed this aspect of Deleuze's thought in a general way. Here, we will try to make a more precise and detailed approach to the embryological

aspects involved. See John Protevi, "Deleuze and Life," in *The Cambridge Companion to Deleuze*, ed. Daniel W. Smith and Henry Sommers-Hall (New York: Cambridge University Press, 2012), 239–64. Also, Pablo Pachilla has written about the egg and morphogenesis from Raymond Ruyer's perspective. See Pablo Pachilla, "'El mundo entero es un huevo.' Ruyer, Deleuze y la genesis ideal como embriología," in *Deleuze y las fuentes de su filosofía II*, ed. Verónica Kretschel and Andrés Osswald (Buenos Aires: RAGIF Ediciones, 2015), 43–51.

3. Gilles Deleuze, *Difference and Repetition*, trans. Paul Patton (New York: Columbia University Press, 1994), 251.

4. For this brief historical context, we follow the Denis Thieffry, "Rationalizing Early Embryogenesis in the 1930s: Albert Dalcq on Gradients and Fields," *Journal of the History of Biology* 34 (2001): 149–81.

5. See Albert Dalcq, *L'œuf et son dynamisme organisateur* (Paris: Editions Albin Michel, 1941), 194–258. All translations in this chapter are ours.

6. It is not superfluous to mention that the phases and processes that we describe are only discrete units of conceptual analysis that correspond with more or less singular and isolated moments of development. The whole process itself is a continuous variation flow.

7. Dalcq, *L'œuf et son dynamisme organisateur*, 207.
8. Deleuze, *Difference and Repetition*, 214.
9. Deleuze, *Difference and Repetition*, 216.
10. Deleuze, *Difference and Repetition*, 216.
11. Deleuze, *Difference and Repetition*, 217.
12. This point will be the object of further investigations.
13. Dalcq, *L'œuf et son dynamisme organisateur*, 208.
14. Deleuze, *Difference and Repetition*, 247.

BIBLIOGRAPHY

Dalcq, Albert. *L'œuf et son dynamisme organisateur*. Paris: Editions Albin Michel, 1941.

Deleuze, Gilles. *Difference and Repetition*. Translated by Paul Patton. New York: Columbia University Press, 1994.

Pachilla, Pablo. "'El mundo entero es un huevo'. Ruyer, Deleuze y la genesis ideal como embriología." In *Deleuze y las fuentes de su filosofía II*, edited by Verónica Kretschel and Andrés Osswald, 43–51. Buenos Aires: RAGIF Ediciones, 2015.

Protevi, John. "Deleuze and Life." In *The Cambridge Companion to Deleuze*, edited by Daniel W. Smith and Henry Sommers-Hall, 239–64. New York: Cambridge University Press, 2012.

Thieffry, Denis. "Rationalizing Early Embryogenesis in the 1930s: Albert Dalcq on Gradients and Fields." *Journal of the History of Biology* 34 (2001): 149–81.

Section II

AT THE END OF THE HISTORY OF PHILOSOPHY

Chapter 5

Deleuze's Hegel: Criticism and Praise at the Edges of Thought

Julián Ferreyra

INTRODUCTION

Hegelianism reached its peak in France in the middle of the twentieth century, when Kojève and Hyppolite were the dominant personalities of the scene; by contrast, the 1960s were characterized by a generalized anti-Hegelianism.[1] In these pages, I will analyze the criticism directed by Gilles Deleuze, one of the protagonists of this reaction against the heritage of the German philosopher, but I will not take a destructive approach. On the contrary, I will show that this moment of criticism leads to the possibility for thinking again *with* Hegel, and for retrieving the complexity and vitality of his work—against the interpretations that are washed up and dead.

Criticisms about Hegel may be found throughout Deleuze's work, and they are multiple in tone as well as in their perspective: from mockery to technical issues, from explicit to implicit arguments, from generalizations to rigorous and specific takes. My proposal is to organize and select such variety of criticisms in relation to the structure of Hegel's *Science of Logic* and addressing: (1) the Doctrine of Being and the false beginning; (2) the Doctrine of Essence and negation as the engine of movement; and (3) the Doctrine of the Concept and the identity toward which all differences are conducted by the circle of return (*Rückkehr*).[2] These criticisms are linked in an order of increasing complexity that will deepen in the dimensions of Hegelian thought. *However*, the isolated consideration of these criticisms hides the nature of the problem. Only the syllogistic relation holds the *truth* of the Hegelian ontology.[3] Being, Essence, and Concept must be conceived in a relational way, and the boundaries of the *Science of Logic* must be surpassed toward the whole system where Hegelian logic achieves a genetic character, and the Idea enlivens matter endlessly. At this point, both authors seem to enjoy a sudden complicity where Hegel, according to Deleuze, would "maximally approximate the real movement of thought" and become a "thinker of genius."[4] Nonetheless, it is also the point where Hegel will "maximally betray and distort" such real movement of thought.[5] It is a delicate conceptual equilibrium at the razor's edge, which only the interpretation may turn toward one side or the other. Interpretation is, after all, the life of a text. There is not, after all "another Hegel than the forces that take him."[6]

THE BEGINNING

Deleuze states that "the problem of the beginning has always—rightly—been regarded as a very delicate one, for beginning means eliminating all presuppositions," and some lines afterward refer specifically but not so rightly to the case of Hegel.[7] "Hegel criticized Descartes for this, he does not seem, for his part, to proceed otherwise: pure being, in turn, is a beginning only by virtue of referring all its presuppositions back to sensible, concrete, empirical being."[8] Being, pure being—without any further determination—begins the *Science of Logic* and would contain, in a slyly implicit way, empirical reality such as we experience it: the actuality (*Wirklichkeit*) would not be anything other than a tautology of vulgar experience. As I have anticipated, my exposition of Deleuze's criticisms follows an order of increasing complexity. This first one is rudimentary enough to justify the harsh accusation of Houlgate: "[Deleuze's] view of Hegel is a distortion."[9] Indeed, it is a distortion to affirm that the Hegelian beginning aims to "eliminate all presuppositions," for Being—as the development of the *Logic* will show—*is precisely a presupposition*, characterized by what it *presupposes*. "Pure Being" can be the *beginning* of the *Logic*, because it is *abstract* and it *presupposes* everything. For this reason, Hegel poses a terminological distinction between the beginning (*Anfang*) and the principle (*Prinzip*).[10] While the beginning is the most abstract, the principle is the most concrete.

If abstract being seems to be the most important principle of philosophy, it is because "the understanding tends to prefer what is abstract to what is concrete."[11] But one of Hegel's principles is that only by dispelling the illusions of the understanding can things be considered in their truth. To read the Doctrine of Being *as if* it contained all further developments of the *Science of Logic* would be like reading Marx's *Capital* as if commodities contained all the truths of Capitalism. There is therefore a fetishism of Being in the Deleuzian criticism of the beginning in Hegel.

However, to straighten out this notorious distortion it is not enough to resolve the core of the question. We still have to face the underlying criticism: is the Hegelian ontology a hypostasis of empirical reality? Is Hegel transferring the existent relations of the immediate reality such as he himself experienced it in his finitude *into* the transcendental realm, that is, into the eternal?[12] These are the questions that are crucial. Nevertheless, instead of situating them at the beginning, we should aim for the principle. But, what is the principle in Hegel? A progressive reading of the *Science of Logic*, as if the order of exposition would be one of increasing level of truth of the notions, leading to the summit of the ontology, would make us believe that the principle is the Concept (or, more precisely, the Idea). Even if this is a usual interpretation, the final pages of the *Encyclopaedia* prove it wrong. There, Hegel exposes three syllogisms (the logical, the one of reflection, and the one of necessity). The *logical* syllogism (Being–Essence–Concept) is the poorest and most immediate: mediation is just a mere *passing* (*Übergehen*).[13] Therefore, the principle is not the Concept by itself, but the Concept as a part of the complex relation that is the syllogism, and more precisely, the "syllogism of syllogisms" (the syllogism of necessity with which Hegel closes the *Encyclopedia*).

> The third syllogism is the Idea of philosophy, which has self-knowing reason, the absolutely universal, for its middle, a middle that divides into mind and nature, making mind the presupposition, as the process of the Idea's subjective activity, and nature the universal extreme, as the process of the Idea that is in itself, objective.[14]

If we interrogate the syllogism of syllogisms as a *principle*, then the question, rigorously phrased, should be whether the principle presupposes the empirical as we encounter it in our immediate consciousness. The answer must in the affirmative, for reason contains, as its presupposition, both Nature and Spirit in which it unfolds, and only thereafter it is not only a logical Idea, but the Idea "acted" as absolute Spirit.[15] As it contains Nature, it also contains the "empirical and sensible being." Deleuze is therefore right: the abstract being presupposes not only the Concept but *also* the "the Idea as being" (*die seiende Idee*) in Nature. However, this "sensible" is still an early development of the system, still abstract, and only becomes *concrete* as long as it contains ("now") the Concept.[16] Pure Being is abstract and it must become concrete. Therefore, yes, the pure beginning has *also* the empirical as its presupposition, but not as an isolated part of it but as a component of the activity of the Idea as absolute Spirit.

If we consider this problem from the standpoint of Deleuze we could reach a similar conclusion. For Deleuze, "the true philosophical beginning, Difference, is in-itself already Repetition."[17] There is a large debate in the Deleuzian studies about the articulation of the spheres of his ontology, and how the virtual, the actual, the intensive and the extensive distinguish themselves and relate to each other.[18] My position in this debate is that the difference repeats itself in each level in a different way (that there is a virtual difference, an intensive difference, and an extensive difference), and that they are all bonded by the form of the fold (folding and unfolding the produce reality). This way, the "true beginning" (Difference) supposes the relation between the empirical and the transcendental, that there is "an empiricism of the Idea" and that the Idea exists as it actualizes itself ("a multiple ideal connection, a differential relation, must be actualized in diverse spatial-temporal relationships.") and that there are always "actual intensive series which correspond to these ideal series, incarnating them."[19] From this point of view, the Deleuzian "true beginning" also has the empirical as its presupposition.

NEGATION

However, the spirit of Deleuze's objection is not aimed at the distinction between the beginning and the principle. The heart of the matter is not which element has ontological priority, or if, in the extreme, both are the expression of one eternal movement that can only be understood in an organic way. The issue is that these elements are not actually *different* but repetitions of the same. The beginning can only refer "all its presuppositions back to sensible, concrete, empirical being" insofar *pure* being and *empirical* being are the same, because they are bound by identity.[20] In the very same way, we could say, reason can only unfold in Nature *and* Spirit because they are actually *the same*. What Deleuze is arguing, after all, is that Hegelian differences are only apparent, and what drives every movement of the concept is a philosophy of *identity*, against which the philosophy of *difference* presents itself as an alternative and a radical renewal.

Deleuze does not consider the Hegelian identity to be a *simple* identity (the kind that could exist between indifferent and perfectly exchangeable elements, which Hegel doubtless fights off), but the sophisticated identity that Deleuze calls "orgiastic representation," where both extremes of the "infinitely large" coincide.[21] The point is the difference between the beginning and the principle would be so large that they come down to "the same." On this issue, Deleuze quotes the Doctrine of Essence:

> Only when the manifold terms have been driven to the point of contradiction do they become active and lively towards one another, receiving in contradiction the negativity which is the indwelling pulsation of self-movement and spontaneous activity [*Lebendigkeit*].[22]

Pure and empirical being are the same, because the vitality of the movement depends on contradiction and negativity. The problem is not the beginning (real or supposed), but the *engine* of the process. We have thus arrived at the second (and the most repeated and reproduced by scholars) of the criticisms that Deleuze addresses to Hegel: the critique of negativity.[23] However, even though Deleuze aims his criticism against "negativity" *in general*, actually his argument applies to a very determined aspect of negativity. It is neither the most developed negativity (the "*total* negativity," which is negativity in the concept)—nor the unilateral negativity of the finite—but the negativity of contradiction, that is, negativity in the Essence.[24] There is a long interpretative tradition that casts the Doctrine of Essence in the role of the *engine* of the Hegelian ontology, both as a virtue and as an insurmountable flaw.[25] Essence would be the *ground* of the system. This is the tradition that Deleuze follows, evidently on the critical line. Hegel considers that *the negative* is the engine, when actually it is not:

> It is not the negative which is the engine. Rather, there are positive differential elements which determine the genesis of both the affirmation and the difference affirmed. [. . .] Negation results from affirmation: this means that negation arises in the wake of affirmation or beside it, but only as the shadow of the more profound genetic element.[26]

We can observe how Deleuze delimits the question. Negativity as contradiction guarantees the identity of the extremes in the frame of orgiastic identity. Considered as a genetic element (as engine) it is mere poverty, abstraction, death: it produces only the same. Thought becomes only the reproduction of the empirical, while the empirical world can only be grasped by abstract and schematic forms. However, that is *exactly what Hegel has fought against*. We could argue the degree of success, but not that this has been Hegel's great goal: to fight against a thought that would only be a collection of abstract and barren schemes implicitly grounded in the immediate experience, in order to give place to a thought that allows grounding experience in all its richness and vitality. But precisely these main objectives of the great Hegelian machine are obstructed when we consider the Doctrine of the Essence—that it is only a systematization of the categories of the understanding—as the engine of the system.

The perspective of the Doctrine of the Essence sets into place a form that assassinates Hegel's spirit: a first position (the beginning), an almost-mechanic middle (negativity or contradiction), and an empirical result (identical to the beginning). The ontology is nothing else than an identical repetition of that empirical result, which is as much foreseen as foreseeable. The element in which vitality should lie (the middle) is actually something dead, mechanical and automatic. Historicism and anthropologism are nothing other than the necessary consequence of this perspective: a metaphysics that unfolds mechanically into the actual reality, conducting with necessity the becoming of nature and human history, whose point of arrival is Hegel's empirical reality: the Prussian State and his philosophy (already implicit in the beginning). Then—nothing else. End of History. Infinite boredom.

It would be so if Hegel is situated in the standpoint of reflection, a standpoint he explicitly criticizes: "When we ask about the grounds of things, this is precisely the standpoint of reflection. [. . .] We want to see the thing in question duplicated as it were: first in its immediacy and secondly in its ground."[27] Therefore, Hegel is aware that the extreme difference of contradiction "resolves difference by relating it to a ground," and thus leads difference toward *in*difference; that is: Hegel agrees with the criticism that Deleuze addresses against him.[28] And the reason for this is that Essence is not the Concept, and the negativity in Essence (that is, contradiction) is not the *total* negativity. Far from making it possible for the concept to carry out the function that Hegel sets for it, if the scheme of the negativity of Essence (reflection) *was its ground* it would make the movement of the Concept *impossible*.[29] The Concept *as such* would disappear, and we would only have *in the one hand* Being, and *in the other hand* Concept, both as appearances of the Essence, that would actually only be mechanical duplications of a sole unmoved mover.

RETURN

If we want to grasp the logic of the movement of the Hegelian thought, we shall place ourselves in the Logic of Concept. Only the *Concept* can be the engine. This does not mean, of course, that there is *no* Essence, that the Essence has no function, that Hegel could have written the *Logic* without its Book Two. Essence is the sphere where the Concept can *posit itself* as that which it *presupposes* without resorting to a logic of emanation or ontological degradation: "a series of degradations, beginning with the perfection and absolute totality [. . .] down as far as the negative, the matter, the acme of evil. In this way, emanation ends in the complete absence of form."[30] In order for the Concept not to lose itself and move away from itself toward being (pure as well as empirical), a mediation is necessary. This function of the Essence is unavoidable: it is a mediation that guarantees the return (*Rückkehr*) of the Concept toward itself. However, this return is not the mere reflection that we have criticized in the previous section. Instead, the logic of the *return* is the object of the third of the Deleuzian criticisms that we will face in these pages: "Hegel's circle is not the eternal return, only the infinite circulation of the identical by means of negativity."[31] On these pages we have been displacing the accent from one book of the *Science of Logic* to the next, trying to escape from Deleuze's criticism: criticism of the beginning has the flaw of considering the pure being as a principle, when Being presupposes explicitly the Essence; criticism of negativity is inadequate because it grounds itself in the Essence, when the truth of the Essence is the Concept. Now the problem emerges when we focus on the Concept and we find ourselves cornered in the last book of Hegel's masterpiece. We have solved nothing, because even if we consider the Concept as the axis and truth of the system, we still are forced to think the Essence as the engine or mediation (or else we fall in emanationism) and Being as the mere repetition of the same: infinite circulation of the identical through negativity. No novelty will wait for us in Nature or Spirit, only the continuity of this dead movement. Eternal return of the identical. Deleuze's third criticism would be the definitive one.

This line of thought is losing sight of the *logic of syllogism*. If we consider again the closing section of the *Encyclopedia*, we can grasp this profound movement of thought. The dynamic of the return is that of the syllogism of reflection: it now includes the thought of the Concept, but differences still reflect "into simple identity."[32] In order to be *absolute* Idea, the movement must be thought neither as a logical syllogism nor a syllogism of reflection, but as a *syllogism of necessity*: a *productive* instance that posits its own moments. No sphere of the system can be considered in an isolated way; how high its place in the ontological ladder is doesn't matter. From a syllogistic perspective, each moment is the major premiss, the minor premiss, *and* the conclusion: the premises are also conclusions; the presupposed is also posited; and to posit is to presuppose. Each *reality* is universal, particular, and singular. Thus conceived, the movement does not mean an identity of its moments, but their most profound difference:

> The Idea positing itself eternally as *purpose* and at the same time bringing forth its actuality through [its] activity.—This life, which has returned to itself from the difference and finitude of cognition, and which has become identical with the Concept through the activity of the Concept, is *the speculative or absolute Idea*.[33]

In this quotation of the exposition of the absolute Idea in the *Encyclopedia* are present both sides of the Hegelian philosophy. In the one hand, that which Deleuze attacks: the return-into-self as a dissolution of all differences, the Idea as an identity where all differences vanish into eternal stillness—"has returned to itself from the difference . . . and has become identical." *In addition to this, however*, we find the activity of the Idea that brings forth *eternally* its actuality through its activity. Each side can infect the other: if we put the emphasis in a still identity as the dissolution of all difference, *the activity of the Idea* is only a slow process of entropy, the return toward the inanimate from the swarming of the finite. If we emphasize the *eternal* positing of the

Idea, we can doubt the fact that stillness could be the end. We can think that the return, the "identical" becoming of the Idea has nothing to do with the stillness of the stars, but that, on the contrary, it is the eternal enlivening of the matter *through the activity of the Idea,* what prevents, precisely, the quiet stillness, the death, the dissolution of differences and the entropy. "God does not remain petrified and moribund however, the stones cry out and lift themselves up to spirit."[34]

From our perspective, from the standpoint of our finite knowledge, it is never possible to reduce all multiplicities to the Concept, and we must therefore "be content with the fact of that which has already come within one's grasp [*was man in der Tat bis jetzt begreifen kann*]."[35] Consequently, that which is able to *become* (in the world and history) *appears as* an infinite progress and the eternal process of the Idea *in its actualization* may seem to be a bad infinity.[36] Indeed, from the standpoint of temporal becoming the progress *is* infinite: for that very reason, there is no end of history. *Nonetheless,* the temporal perspective is one-sided and therefore lacking any truth—bad infinity is only an appearance, just the form in which the Idea *appears* in the phenomena, the finite. Given this, the activity of the Idea may seem to be a "leap," an "event" form of the perspective of the "time after time."[37] Such "leaps" express that there is not only one temporality in the phenomenal field, but a multiplicity of dimensions of the existent and finite, which manifest different aspects of the activity of the Idea. In this sense, Hegel states that that "which is finite is temporal [. . .] its time begins with it, and there is no time without finitude."[38] The actualization of the Idea in the world is thus not a transformation of the curve in a straight line as the historicism would want. Wordly time is *in each and every case* the eternity of the Idea herself.

Nevertheless, if the actualization of the Idea is not the transformation of the circle of time into a straight line, nor is it an empiricala mold in the form of a circle, as Hegel's criticism against the circular orbits of nature shows: "The circle is the curve of the understanding, and posits equality. Circular motion can only be uniform."[39] Therefore, there is neither the straight line of time nor a uniform circular motion. The circle of the *Rückkehr* is not the circle of the same, because none of its arcs, none of its curves, are ever exhausted, but eternally posited by the activity of the Concept. Deleuze's criticism ("Hegel's circle is not the eternal return, only the infinite circulation of the identical by means of negativity") vanishes into its contrary: by reason of the infinite circulation of the Idea, Hegel's circle may even be the *eternal* return, the great *fold* which goes through each layer of the ontology, repeating the difference, actualizing, intensifying, and destroying all beings in the single clamor of Being, "which displaces and disguises them and, in turning upon its mobile cusp, causes them to return."[40]

DELEUZE: "HEGEL IS A GENIUS PHILOSOPHER"

If the *Rückker* is an eternal return and not the infinite circulation of the same, if the movement of the concept is not traced after the empirical and if—far from being the guarantee of a monotonous and identical repetition—it is the genetic source of reality in an eternal production of the new, then the differences between Hegel and Deleuze seem to dissolve. As Juliette Simont proposes:

> The Hegel of a *Logic* that winds and unwinds in spirals that have no other purpose than the declination of their slight differences. [. . .] The Hegel that we try to propose, that Hegel who does not try, at all costs, in order to benefit the greatest contradiction, to discredit the series, and who speaks in a good light of the "intermediate states," this Hegel who is not obsessed by the transparent reversibility in every relation, but who knows also how to take into account a one-sideness always unbalanced through which the difference only exists as long as it *asserts* itself as such, this Hegel is maybe too Deleuzian, or that is only possible to be read through Deleuze. And it is so. However, is there another Hegel than "the forces that seize him"?[41]

According to Simont, there is "another" Hegel when we read it through Deleuze. How would it then be possible that Deleuze himself was not able to read this other Hegel? Indeed he did, but he decided to wait until the generalized anti-Hegelianism of the sixties had dispersed, until the dominance of Hyppolite and Kojève had faded, to speak about this "other" Hegel. And he did so in the "intimacy" of the classroom. Indeed, during his lectures of the May 3 and 10, 1983, Deleuze presents a peculiar interpretation of Hegel's dialectic:

> It is idiotic to say that Hegel believes that things contradict themselves, that Hegel thinks that contradiction is in the things themselves. Hegel believes that *non*-contradiction brings identity into things. Hegel is the first thinker that literally tells us that things *do not* contradict themselves. What did the others do? They said that the essences where the identical, and that the sensory world was contradictory. Hegel says, evidently, the contrary. He is the first to tell us that the world is not contradictory. Why? Because the law of the world is "A is not not-A." Therefore, those who believe that things contradict themselves are the others, not Hegel. The principle that rules existence is the principle of non-contradiction, principle that presents itself under the form of the negation of the negation. If you understand this, you have grasped everything about Hegel, his genius, and the reason why he is a great philosopher.[42]

Deleuze says, explicitly, that Hegel is a *great philosopher* and empathizes his *genius*. This quote brings down, therefore, the whole library of the Hegel-Deleuze debate that is based on a supposed Deleuzian aversion to Hegel and drives the Chilean philosopher Espinoza Lolas to leap to the other extreme and affirm that Hegel thinks "in the right way, that is, in the *same way* that Deleuze himself thinks."[43]

The lecture of May 17, 1983, structures itself around the three traditional logical principles and how they are completely subverted by their application to existence. The post-Kantians (Fichte, Schelling, and Hegel) overcome the principle of identity through the one of non-contradiction as a principle of existence:

> "I is not equal to not-I." It is amazing because it means that the I only posits itself as identical by opposing itself to a non-I. It not at all Cartesian, it is the post-Kantianist philosophy. It is Fichte's "I = I": the self-positing of the I implies the opposition of the I with a not-I.[44] The I only posits itself as I through the negation of the not-I. [. . .] The synthetic identity is the operation that raises thought to the power of the existent and takes hold of the existence. And what is the synthetic identity? It is the principle of non-contradiction. [. . .] When Hegel says that "things contradict themselves," he is saying something about things. Not only he says something about things, but about how they are born and how they develop themselves.[45]

The real genius of Hegel was not to replace the principle of identity by that of contradiction as the core of the ontology, but to achieve an identity between "logic and existence."[46] This praise is already present in the early writings of Deleuze; in 1954, he wrote that the Hegelian innovation consisted in proposing an ontology ("philosophy must be ontology, it cannot be anything else") where the sense of "this world" was not only "sufficient for us," but "sufficient by itself," and thus capable of "transforming metaphysics into logic, the logic of sense."[47] Hegel reshapes logic by making it no longer refer to the possibility of the existent (as the principle of analytic identity that only states if something is possible) but to its principle of genesis.

The lectures of 1983 restore therefore the definition of post-Kantianism that Deleuze offers in Difference and Repetition: to attain the point of view of the genesis, overcoming that of conditioning, where Kant would have remained, or, in other words, to transform the hypothetical judgment into a "thetical" judgment.[48] The post-Kantians found the logical principle of sense, that is, the genetic principle of existence in the world. "This procedure maximally approximates the real movement of thought."[49] Therefore, the genius of Hegel, although only recognized explicitly in 1983 and in the "intimacy" of a lecture, is implicit in Difference and Repetition as a part of the post-Kantianism, and in line with the review of 1954: to transform logic into metaphysics and to transform metaphysics into the principle of actuality.

CONCLUSION: THE RAZOR'S EDGE

However, we must be cautious before stating that all this evidence means, as Espinoza Lolas affirms, that Deleuze thinks matters as Hegel does. Deleuze warns about the fact that the post-Kantians, at the very same time that they approximate the real movement of thought, their philosophy "also maximally betrays and distorts this movement."[50] Deleuze bases this accusation of "betrayal" on two obscure reasons: "this conjoint hypotheticism and moralism, this scientistic hypotheticism and this rationalist moralism."[51] These two objections restore the first two criticisms that we have reviewed, and revitalize them, for they are at the core of the post-Kantianism, at the same time as its great philosophical discoveries.[52] They simultaneously approximate and betray the real movement of thought.

We are at the razor's edge. Hegel is at the same time the traitor and the genius from the Deleuzian perspective. There is not, as Simont affirmed, "another Hegel than the forces that take him."[53] We can ground in the letter of Hegel a moralist conception of the world, according to which the philosophy only repeats the state of the matter, only produces the same and only performs a dead movement. But we can also interpret the Hegelian Concept, as we did previously, as the circulation of the Idea as an eternal enlivening of matter in a circle that never closes unto itself. From this perspective, the Hegelian image of thought does not work either as a moral imperative or as an empirical being as its implicit hypothesis; instead, it affirms in each manifestation the power of the Idea, as an actual reality in which we find ourselves and where we have to carry out our real choices. According to this interpretation, which we prefer for its capacity to contribute to constructing an affirmative and vital thought, there is not thus a sole reality to which we must resign. The passing of empiric time depends on the strange temporality of the Concept that enlivens it, in the very same way that the interpretation that we give of it can make the *Science of Logic* into a dead letter, or can make it eternally enlivened by philosophical thought.

NOTES

1. "In 1945, then, all that was modern sprang from Hegel. [. . .] In 1968, all that was modern [. . .] was hostile to Hegel," Vincent Descombes, *Modern French Philosophy* (Cambridge: Cambridge University Press, 1980), 12. Deleuze pointed out that a "generalized anti-Hegelianism" was "in the air" at the end of the 1960s in the preface to *Difference and Repetition*, trans. Paul Patton (New York: Columbia University Press, 1994), xix.

2. I choose to translate *Begriff* as "Concept," even if I follow Miller's translation, who favors "Notion," for in the frame of the relation with Deleuze it is important to underline its affinity with the French "concept." The interpretative structure of

the criticisms I propose has only an organizational goal. The various studies on the Deleuze-Hegel relation have chosen other takes in the matter. Somers-Hall (*Hegel, Deleuze, and the Critique of Representation*. New York: SUNY Press, 2012) leveled three main criticisms: (1) that "Hegel misunderstood the cause of the movement of thought by continuing to represent it" (208); (2) that "this movement is always around a particular point" (208); and (3) that the idea of opposition "is too rough to provide an adequate description of the world" (209). Juliette Simont in her *Kant, Hegel, Deleuze, les "fleurs noires" de la logique philosophique* (Paris: L'Harmattan, 1997) points out (1) that dialectics rejects an intrinsic consideration of multiplicities; (2) the dissolution of the difference in a "transparent reciprocity" (p. 269); and (3) the Deleuzian accent in the temporal dimension while Hegel would "ignore time" (p. 324).

3. "It is the syllogism of syllogisms—the logical form that Hegel uses to present, at the end of the *Encyclopaedia*, his philosophical system. [. . .] The third syllogism holds thus the first two, it is a syllogism of syllogisms. [. . .] It is the true universal, the reason, that occurs endlessly," Vincenzo Vitiello, "Hegel. Lógica/Realidad: La superficie y el fondo," in *Hegel, la transformación de los espacios sociales*, ed. Ricardo Espinoza Lolas (Concón: Midas, 2012), 192–94.

4. Deleuze, *Difference and Repetition*, 197; Gilles Deleuze, *Lecture on Cinema of May 3rd, 1983*. http://www2.univ-paris8.fr/deleuze/article.php3.

5. Deleuze, *Difference and Repetition*, 197.

6. Simont, *Kant, Hegel, Deleuze, les "fleurs noires" de la logique philosophique*, 297.

7. Deleuze, *Difference and Repetition*, 129, translation modified.

8. Deleuze, *Difference and Repetition*, 129.

9. Stephen Houlgate, *Nietzsche and the Criticism of Metaphysics* (Cambridge: Cambridge University Press, 1986), 7.

10. G. W. F. Hegel, *Science of Logic*, trans. A. V. Miller (New York: Humanity Books, 1968), 67.

11. G. W. F. Hegel, *Philosophy of Nature*, trans. J. Petry and D. Phil (London: George Allen and Unwin 1970), 263.

12. Such criticism is not at all original, for it is already present in the middle of the nineteenth century, with Ludwig Feuerbach (*Manifestes philosophiques, textes choisis, 1839–1845*, trans. L. Althusser, Paris: PUF, 1960, 21–25) and Karl Marx ("Critique of Hegel's Doctrine of the State," in *Early Writings* [London: Penguin, 1992], 69–71). Feuerbach, whose influence is strong in Deleuze's criticism of the Hegelian beginning, was in force in France at the time of *Difference and Repetition*, thanks to the translation of "selected writings" that Louis Althusser had published in 1960. On the empirical inadequacy of such accusation, and the differences between the Prussian State and that of Hegel, see Eric Weil, *Hegel et l'état* (Paris: Vrin, 1950).

13. "The first appearance is constituted by the syllogism that has the logical as its ground, its starting-point, and nature as the middle that joins the mind together with the logical. [. . .] The mediation of the concept has the external form of transition, and science has the form of the progression of necessity, so that only in the one extreme is the freedom of the concept posited as its joining together with itself," Hegel, *Philosophy of Mind*, 276. "The first appearance is constituted by the syllogism that has the logical as its ground, its starting-point, and nature as the middle that joins the mind

together with the logical. [. . .] The mediation of the concept has the external form of transition, and science has the form of the progression of necessity, so that only in the one extreme is the freedom of the concept posited as its joining together with itself," Hegel, *Philosophy of Mind*, 276. This syllogism is based on the syllogism of existence: "The syllogism in its immediate form has for its moments the determinations of the Notion as immediate. Hence they are the abstract determinatenesses of form, which are not yet developed by mediation into concretion, but are only single determinatenesses," Hegel, *Science of Logic*, 666.

14. G. W. F. Hegel, *Philosophy of Mind*, trans. W. Wallace and A. V. Miller (Clarendon Press: Oxford, 2007), 276.

15. Hegel, *Philosophy of Mind*, 276.

16. "We have now returned to the Concept of the Idea with which we began. At the same time this return to the beginning is an advance. What we began with was being, abstract being, while now we have the Idea as being; and this Idea that is, is Nature," G. W. F. Hegel, *The Encyclopaedia Logic (with the Zusatze)*, trans. T. F. Geraets, W. A. Suchting, and H. S. Harris (Indianapolis, IN: Hackett, 1991), 307.

17. Deleuze, *Difference and Repetition*, 129.

18. Regarding the debate on Deleuzian ontology, Dale Clisby has reconstructed the main perspectives, which cover, by the way, *all possible combinations*: "Deleuze's Secret Dualism? Competing Accounts of the Relationship between the Virtual and the Actual," *Parrhesia* 24 (2015): 127–49.

19. Deleuze, *Difference and Repetition*, 278, 183, 280.

20. Deleuze, *Difference and Repetition*, 129.

21. "When representation discovers the infinite within itself, it no longer appears as organic representation but as orgiastic representation: it discovers within itself the limits of the organised; tumult, restlessness and passion underneath apparent calm," Deleuze, *Difference and Repetition*, 42. This logic of the "negative of opposition" (Deleuze, *Difference and Repetition*, 44, 211) must be attributed to Kojève to a greater extent than to Hegel: "Where can the homogenizing pliers of dialectics, the tactics of an infinite reaping that bounds every difference to identity, the 'uniformity of the greater contradiction' be found? Must they maybe be looked for more in A. Kojève than in the *Logic*, and the adversary of Deleuze is perhaps, more than Hegel himself, this 'hyperhegelian' reincarnation of dialectics?," Simont, *Kant, Hegel, Deleuze, les "fleurs noires" de la logique philosophique*, 274.

22. Hegel, *Science of Logic*, 442. Quoted by Deleuze in *Difference and Repetition*, 44, through the French translation of Jakélevich (Patton resorts to Miller's English translation, as we do).

23. A paradigmatic example is Michael Hardt: "[Deleuze] engaged Hegelianism not in order to salvage its worthwhile elements, not to extract 'the rational kernel from the mystical shell,' but rather to articulate a total critique and a rejection of the negative dialectical framework," *Gilles Deleuze, An Apprenticeship in Philosophy* (Minneapolis: University of Minnesota Press, 1993), x.

24. "That which is finite is transitory and temporal because unlike the Notion, it is not in itself total negativity," Hegel, *Philosophy of Nature*, 230.

25. "If we consider the general structure of the *Logic*, in the 'essence' we are certainly in a sphere still corrupted by exteriority. [. . .] *However*, its importance lies in

the fact that it is a field where we find 'the posited contradiction' [Hegel, *Science of Logic*, 431], that in the sphere of Being is only *in itself*, as the engine of the dialectical enfolding of the Idea and of the resulting 'realization of idealism'. By this reason, we consider as crucial the *reflection* and we see on it the presupposition without which it would not be possible that the *concept* could perform the function that Hegel gives to it," Jorge Dotti, *Dialéctica y derecho, el proyecto ético-político hegeliano* (Buenos Aires: Hachette, 1983, emphasis original), 100. The emphasis is in the original. Further ahead (193), the great Argentine philosopher points out that this tradition goes back to Trendelenburg, who considers that contradiction is the engine of dialectics.

26. Deleuze, *Difference and Repetition*, 55, translation modified.
27. Hegel, *The Encyclopaedia Logic*, 189
28. Deleuze, *Difference and Repetition*, 44.
29. Hegel, "The Negativity of Essence Is Reflection," in *Science of Logic*, 391.
30. Hegel, *Philosophy of Nature*, 213–14, translation modified.
31. Deleuze, *Difference and Repetition*, 50.
32. Hegel, *Science of Logic*, 695.
33. Hegel, *The Encyclopaedia Logic*, 303 (emphasis original).
34. Hegel, *Philosophy of Nature*, 206.
35. Hegel, *Philosophy of Nature*, 259.
36. Hegel, *The Encyclopaedia Logic*, 306.
37. "The old saying, or law as it is called, '*non datur saltus in natura*' is by no means adequate to the diremption of the Concept," Hegel, *Philosophy of Nature*, 214–15. These leaps must not be understood as a radical discontinuity that may justify a logic of all or nothing, without intermediate states that Simont keenly criticizes (*Kant, Hegel, Deleuze, les "fleurs noires" de la logique philosophique*, 273–74). What appears as "leaps" in our empirical reality is the *effect* of the living continuity of the movement of the Concept.
38. Hegel, *Philosophy of Nature*, 207.
39. Hegel, *Philosophy of Nature*, 270.
40. Deleuze, *Difference and Repetition*, 304. The meaning of Deleuze's reformulation of eternal return, which makes it into something different from even Nietzsche's, is the object of controversy in Deleuzian studies. Structurally, the notion appears in the development of the main concepts of the book, and in each of the five chapters: difference in itself, the synthesis of time (especially the third one), the origin of the Ideas and the constitution of an *intensive* space. In this last, Deleuze distinguishes his conception to the eternal return "as it was believed by the Ancients," that is, as a circle which repeats "the same" (242). Deleuze's eternal return is nonetheless *a circle*, but a circle that never closes into itself, and which is also "purely intensive" (243). Considering, in addition, the affinity of intensity and the form of a fold (280), I believe it is safe to affirm that the eternal return is the great fold of Being.
41. Simont, *Kant, Hegel, Deleuze, les "fleurs noires" de la logique philosophique*, 297 (emphasis original).
42. Gilles Deleuze, *Lecture on Cinema of May 3rd, 1983*. http://www2.univ-paris8.fr/deleuze/rubrique.php3. This interpretation of the principle of non-contradiction goes against the usual interpretation of Hegel (which would make most interpreters *idiots*), and even his very letter. Indeed, contradiction is the third "determination of

reflection" (Hegel, *Science of Logic*, 431–35) the "the point where the manifold terms become active and lively towards one another," as Hegel affirms in a passage of the *Science of Logic* that, as we have seen, that Deleuze himself emphasized in *Difference and Repetition*. Nonetheless, we can observe how Hegel's exposition of the principle of non-contradiction backs Deleuze's 1983 interpretation up: "[contradiction is] positing identity with itself by excluding the negative" (Hegel, *Science of Logic*, 432); if there was contradiction, the opposites would remain indifferent to each other in their exclusion; they only posit themselves by this exclusion because there is not actual contradiction.

43. "If we follow with care these words of Deleuze about Hegel, we will see that he does not see in Hegel a rival who is just wrong, but a great philosopher that thinks matters in the right way, that is, in the same way that Deleuze himself thinks them in the '80s," Ricardo Espinoza Lolas, "Repensando a Deleuze y el 'acontecimiento' desde lo 'lógico' de la *Wissenschaft der Logik* de Hegel . . . en torno al devenir cosa," in *Hegel, la transformación de los espacios sociales*, ed. Ricardo Espinoza Lolas (Concón: Midas, 2012), 156.

44. "As surely as the absolute certainty of the proposition '~A is not equal to A' is unconditionally admitted among the facts of empirical consciousness, so *surely is a not-self opposed absolutely to the self*," J. G. Fichte, *Foundation for the Entire Science of Knowledge (1794)*, trans. Peter Heath and John Lachs (Cambridge: Cambridge University Press, 1982), 104. I do not really grasp the reason why the translator shifts his translation of the German "*Ich*" from "I" to "self" from the first to the second principle of the *Foundation*. . . .

45. Deleuze, *Lecture on Cinema of May 17th, 1983*.

46. "Leibniz was the first one to identify logic and existence. The second one must have been Hegel," Gilles Deleuze, *Lecture on Cinema of May 17th, 1983*. http://www2.univ-paris8.fr/deleuze/rubrique.php3.

47. Gilles Deleuze, "Jeans Hyppolite's Logica and Existence" (1954), in *Desert Islands and Other Texts*, trans. Michael Taormina (Los Angeles: Semiotext(e), 2004), 13, 16.

48. "Just as the post-Kantians objected, Kant held fast to the point of view of conditioning without attaining that of genesis," Deleuze, *Difference and Repetition*, 170.

49. Deleuze, *Difference and Repetition*, 197.

50. Deleuze, *Difference and Repetition*, 197.

51. Deleuze, *Difference and Repetition*, 197.

52. On the one hand, the objection of "hypotheticism" goes back to the first of the criticisms that we have reviewed, the pure being (the beginning of the Logic) is only a beginning as long as it refers all its presuppositions to the empirical, sensible, and concrete being (the beginning of the *Phenomenology*, the immediate consciousness): the "thetical" would be the "pure beginning" and the hypothetical element behind it would be the empirical presupposition (in the case of Fichte, the empirical I would work behind the absolute I; in Hegel, science would suppose consciousness, and the *Logic* would secretly contain the *Phenomenology*—more precisely, the most primitive aspect of consciousness and the *Phenomenology*: its beginning, the immediate consciousness: "On Hegel and the analogous transformation, see the relation between the in-itself and the for-itself in *The Phenomenology of Mind*; the relation between the

Phenomenology itself and the Logic; the Hegelian idea of 'science,' and the passage from the empirical proposition to the speculative proposition," Deleuze, *Difference and Repetition*, 326). On the other hand, the objection of "moralism" aims at the perpetuation of the state of affairs, its continuity into infinity, in the very same way that the mechanical repetition that the negativity in the Essence supposes.

53. Simont, *Kant, Hegel, Deleuze*, 297.

BIBLIOGRAPHY

Clisby, Dale. "Deleuze's Secret Dualism? Competing Accounts of the Relationship between the Virtual and the Actual." *Parrhesia* 24 (2015): 127–49.
Deleuze, Gilles. "Jeans Hyppolite's Logic and Existence." In *Desert Islands and Other Texts*. Translated by Michael Taormina. Los Angeles: Semiotext(e), 2004.
Deleuze, Gilles. *Difference and Repetition*. Translated by Paul Patton. New York: Columbia University Press, 1994.
Deleuze, Gilles. *Lectures on Cinema of May, 1983*. http://www2.univ-paris8.fr/deleuze/rubrique.php3.
Descombes, Vincent. *Modern French Philosophy*. Cambridge: Cambridge University Press, 1980.
Dotti, Jorge. *Dialéctica y derecho, el proyecto ético-político hegeliano*. Buenos Aires: Hachette, 1983.
Espinoza Lolas, Ricardo. "Repensando a Deleuze y el 'acontecimiento' desde lo 'lógico' de *la Wissenschaft der Logik* de Hegel . . . en torno al devenir cosa." In *Hegel, la transformación de los espacios sociales*, edited by Ricardo Espinoza Lolas, 155–75. Concón: Midas, 2012.
Feuerbach, Ludwig. *Manifestes philosophiques, textes choisis, 1839–1845*. Translated by Louis Althusser. Paris: PUF, 1960.
Fichte, J. G. *Foundation for the Entire Science of Knowledge (1794)*. Translated by Peter Heath and John Lachs. Cambridge: Cambridge University Press, 1982.
Hegel, G. W. F. *Philosophy of Mind*. Translated by W. Wallace and A. V. Miller. Clarendon Press: Oxford, 2007.
Hegel, G. W. F. *Philosophy of Nature*. Translated by J. Petry and D. Phil. London: George Allen and Unwin, 1970.
Hegel, G. W. F. *Science of Logic*. Translated by A. V. Miller. New York: Humanity Books, 1968.
Hegel, G. W. F. *The Encyclopaedia Logic (with the Zusatze)*. Translated by T. F. Geraets, W. A. Suchting, and H. S. Harris. Indianapolis, IN: Hackett, 1991.
Henry Somers-Hall. *Hegel, Deleuze, and the Critique of Representation*. New York: SUNY Press, 2012.
Houlgate, Stephen. *Nietzsche and the Criticism of Metaphysics*. Cambridge: Cambridge University Press, 1986.
Marx, Karl. "Critique of Hegel's Doctrine of the State." In *Early Writings*. London: Penguin, 1992.

Simont, Juliette. *Kant, Hegel, Deleuze, les "fleurs noires" de la logique philosophique*. Paris: L'Harmattan, 1997.
Vitiello, Vincenzo. "Hegel. Lógica/Realidad: La superficie y el fondo." In *Hegel, la transformación de los espacios sociales*, edited by Ricardo Espinoza Lolas, 177–202. Concón: Midas, 2012.
Weil, Eric. *Hegel et l'état*. Paris: Vrin, 1950.

Chapter 6

Resonances of the Voice of Being: Analogy and Univocity in Deleuze and Kant

Pablo N. Pachilla

INTRODUCTION

This chapter analyzes the problem of the univocity and equivocity of being in Deleuze by contrasting the Deleuzian account with that of Kant. I will argue that univocity and equivocity are present in both philosophers' work, albeit in very different ways. Kant's point of departure is the unity of apperception, and hence, in order to relate it to the multiplicity given in sensibility, he must perform a transubstantiation of unity in the categories. In doing so, he produces a partial equivocity of being—that is, analogy—and thus generates a merely relative unity in objectivity. In this manner, there are, in Kant, two mirrored poles of unity—that of the cogito and that of the object—plus a variety of intermediary forms. Deleuze, on the other hand, avoids all mediations between unity and multiplicity, predicating only one and the same sense of being of all its individuating differences. By skipping all mediations between the extreme poles of unity and multiplicity, the voice of being is directly expressed in each occasion within the process of production of the real, the nature of which is, for Deleuze, that of becoming or differentiation.

HOMONYMY, SYNONYMY, AND ANALOGY

Dealing with the issue of univocity does not require justifications within Deleuzian scholarship. Choosing Kant as a source for dealing with that issue, however, does need a certain explanation. There is, since the Aristotelian foundation of metaphysics, a staunch enemy of univocity: analogy. If, in Medieval philosophy, the figure of Thomas Aquinas rises up as a banner of the analogical answer to the question concerning being, within Modern philosophy, Kant is doubtlessly the representative *par excellence* of this stance. Tackling the problem through Kant will henceforth be of use in order to render explicit everything against which Deleuze will rise, by exhibiting some of its problems and examining what is at stake.

The contrary of univocity is equivocity. The most pristine phrasing of ontological equivocity is the Aristotelian *dictum* "Being is said in many ways." Why is it said in many ways? Because it is said as quantity, quality, time, place, and so on. However, if all of those senses would be lost in the pure dispersion of a mere homonymy, ontology as a science would lack *one* object, and what is worse, further ahead in history, God and creation would not have a common measure. If we say that the created being *is*, and at the same time that there is no common measure between created and uncreated being, where does this leave the ontological status of divinity? Deleuze presents this problem with a sharp sense of humor in one of his lectures:

> The point of heresy within equivocity consists in the fact that those who said that being is said in many ways, and that those different senses have no common measure, ultimately preferred to say "God is not" to saying "He is," in as much as "is" was a statement that could be said of the table or the chair. Hence, given that God is completely otherwise, in a manner which is wholly equivocal and with no common measure compared to the being of the chair, or the being of man, all things considered it was better to say "He is not," which is the same as saying "He is above being." But the meanings of these puns would turn very dangerous: if they were discrete, they would say "God is superior to being," but insisting a bit on "God is not" was enough for things to turn rather bad.[1]

It was necessary to find a middle term between *synonymy* (the univocity of being that led to pantheism) and total *homonymy* (the equivocity of being that led to negative theology): being is said in many ways, but it is said primordially (*pros hen* in Aristotle, *ad unum* in Thomas Aquinas) as substance. This third way, that of *analogy*, establishes a difference but simultaneously a proportion between the different senses of being. Although being does not occur in the same manner for the finite and the infinite, for the created and the uncreated, analogy allows for the link between those different ways in which being is said, according to a first sense taken as a parameter, thus rendering possible a measurable ordering of those different senses.

These different ways in which being is said are κατηγορίαι (*katēgoriai*), a term that Aristotle adopts from juridical language, thus providing the verb used to accuse, *kategorein*, with a predicative sense. In this manner, as Athens could accuse Socrates of corrupting the youth, Aristotle can "accuse" him of being a rational animal, or "accuse" the table of being white. This peculiar juridical conception of predication will survive the Hellenic world and the Middle Ages reaching Modernity, when it will be transformed and revitalized by most eminent of the jurist philosophers. Kant will make a legal process out of philosophy, a philosophy and a concept out of a trial, and an element of judgment out of concepts in general. Kant's philosophy can be seen as a fractal object, whose basic structure is judgment repeated at different scales. The *Critique* itself is a court case where, on the one side, there is Hume's skeptical empiricism and, on the other, Wolffian dogmatic rationalism. As Deleuze writes, "Critique has everything—a tribunal of justices of the peace, a registration room, a register—except the power of a new politics which would overturn the image of thought."[2]

Concerning the doctrine of the faculties, the action proper to understanding is judging, which means, just as in Aristotle, to attribute, to predicate, to say. There are for Kant twelve ways in which the understanding must be able to judge, and in that way, constitute an object, that is, to attribute objectivity to the multiple given in sensibility. The Kantian novelty in this regard lies in his ingenious overlapping between the Aristotelian categorical doctrine and the great philosophical Cartesian invention: the cogito, through categories, brings the diversity of the given to the unity of the I think—since categories are functions of unity, but this unity is the unity of consciousness. For Aristotle this was not necessary, since categories were inherent to beings in themselves and their unity was given by the οὐσία; with the Copernican turn, on the other hand, Kant prohibits himself to find unity in things themselves. The source out of which unity will emanate will thus be found in the cogito, or, in Kantian terminology, in the transcendental apperception.

THE UNIVOCITY AND EQUIVOCITY OF BEING IN THE *CRITIQUE OF PURE REASON*

The political problem of harmony lies at the core of the question concerning being, and it is for this reason that only by being able to listen thoroughly to the relationship between unity and multiplicity that we will be able to grasp the ontological discontinuity between Kant's pacifying chords and Deleuze's bet for an agreement found only at the apex of dissonance—a project that will be later summarized—together with Guattari—in the formula "PLURALISM = MONISM."[3]

In the section called "On having an opinion, knowing, and believing" [*Vom Meinen, Wissen und Glauben*], Kant writes that truth "rests upon agreement [*Übereinstimmung*] with the object, with regard to which, consequently, the judgments of every understanding must agree [*einstimmig sein müssen*] (*consentientia uni tertio, consentiunt inter se*)."[4] The term that Guyer and Wood accurately translate as "agree" and that we could paraphrase as "be concordant with" is *einstimmig*, which also means "unison" in a musical context and "unanimous" in a political one (where it is equivalent to *ohne Gegenstimme*—without any voices against it).⁵ It is important to have in mind this double context of applicability of the terms, the political and the musical one, since both are intertwined in the Kantian statement.

The verb *stimmen* says of something that it is true or correct, accurate, such as in the common expression in the German language "*stimmt!*," which could function as exclamations such as "right!," "OK!," "agreed!" *Übereinstimmung*, on the other hand, which means "agreement" or "concordance," takes a derivative of *Stimme*, "voice": *Stimmung*, which is usually proffered to refer to "moods," and has also a musical connotation in which it means "tuning."⁶ Thus, *stimmen* also means to tune or to harmonize. To emphasize this polysemy is key to understanding what is at stake in the Kantian statement with a greater richness—to multiply its harmonics.

In §18 of *Prolegomena . . .* , Kant writes something very similar: "If a judgment agrees [*übereinstimmt*] with an object, then all judgments of the same object must also agree [*übereinstimmen*] with one another, and hence the objective validity of a judgment of experience signifies nothing other than its necessary universal validity."⁷ This is the *consentientia uni tertio, consentiunt inter se*: by agreeing with a third—the object in its truth—judgments (issued by the same subject and, most importantly, by different subjects) agree among themselves.

The passage from the *Critique* continues as follows:

> The touchstone of whether taking something to be true is conviction or mere persuasion is therefore, externally, the possibility of communicating it and finding it to be valid for the reason of every human being to take it to be true; for in that case there is at least a presumption that the ground of the agreement [*Einstimmung*] of all judgments, regardless of the difference among the subjects, rests on the common ground, namely the object, with which they therefore all agree [*zusammenstimmen*] and through which the truth of the judgment is proved.⁸

The object is—one might say—the *A* note that the first violin must provide before the commencement of a concert, and which every instrument must take as a reference: every instrument must attune to it in order to, in like manner, attune to every other instrument (by agreeing with a third, they agree among them). Tellingly, it is the same logic of the "one" of the synthesis of the multiplicity of the represented in the unity of the representer in some early-Modern theories of political representation—one can think of chapter XVI of Hobbes' *Leviathan*:

> A multitude of men, are made *one* person, when they are by one man, or one person, represented; so that it be done with the consent of every one of that

multitude in particular. For it is the *unity* of the representer, not the *unity* of the represented, that maketh the person one. And it is the representer that beareth the person, and but one person: and *unity*, cannot otherwise be understood in multitude.[9]

The relationship with a third placed on a different level is first with regard to the peer-to-peer relationship: the instruments and the first violin, the represented and the representer, the judgments and the object.

Just as the noun *Einstimmigkeit, Einstimmung* is formed by two roots: *ein-*, "one," and *stimm-*, relative to the voice (*Stimme*). *Einstimmigkeit* is the peculiarity of having *eine Stimme*, one voice: in English, the word for this would be *univocity*. And patently, if the term is even thinkable to begin with, it is because there is more than one voice: there are several voices, and that about which we are speaking is, accordingly, *harmony*. The Greek word ἁρμονία, just like the German terms *Einstimmung* and *Übereinstimmung*, means "agreement" or "concordance," and derives from the verb ἁρμόζω, which means—again just like the German terms *stimmen* and *übereinstimmen*, "to match," "to concord" or, if you will forgive the repetition, "to harmonize."

Unison (*einstimmig*) is the most basic case in the field of harmony, since every voice sings the same; however, that does not exclude a properly harmonious quality: unlike a melody sung by a single voice, unison implies a variety of voices singing the same note. There is a plurality that, by means of this harmonization, becomes community. But there will be more complex cases. In the *Critique of Power of Judgment*, Kant invents new harmonies, where the voices sing different notes: a beautiful, unfathomable harmony, like the murmur of fallen leaves in the wind; but also a sublime harmony, discordant and dissonant, that retains, however, a curious unity—and what is more—unveils a deeper unity.

The whole Kantian critical project is a monumental essay on finding a way to attune voices. It is necessary to tune the spirits or the choir for there to be harmony between the voices. The Kantian way of doing so is, first, through the delimitation of a territory. Kant being a great surveyor, he will second, demarcate domains within the territory to which he will assign different legislators. Knowledge will be ruled by the understanding; morality, by reason; the feeling of pleasure and displeasure, by the free and concordant relationship between imagination and understanding.

Given our spatial limitation, let us stick to the simplest case: that of knowledge. Let us imagine for an instant that some of us believe ourselves to be in contact with bodiless spirits, ghosts. Naturally, the rest of us would not be able to see the same phantoms, and hence, our judgments could never agree.[10] Such is the case of the Swedish theosophist Emmanuel Swedenborg—or, as Kant calls him, Herr Schwedenberg—in a precritical text, *Dreams of a*

Spirit-Seer [*Träume eines Geistersehers*], in which he already aims to draw boundaries to knowledge's pretensions or, to be more precise, to delimit a territory in which one could judge on key, and therefore, to be in tune with others. That territory, the borders of which are thoroughly drawn by Kant, will be baptized—for the bewilderment of the public—with a word otherwise already existent and referred to something completely different: *experience*. But in order to ground a rule of law in this heretofore untamed territory, Kant will first and foremost—as the good Rousseauian he is—look for a legislator. This legislator is the understanding, and it is here where we can begin to speak of equivocity.

In the famous passage about the cinnabar from the "A Deduction," Kant imagines a state of affairs where things would change in manners ungraspable and without following any logic. This would pose a serious problem because it would impede one from having knowledge. Kant modifies that passage in the second edition of the *Critique* because it can give rise to a misunderstanding: thinking that the possibility of experience depends on the stability and regularity of experience itself in a sense that would be independent from the subject, which does not seem to be what Kant had in mind.[11] However, the same problem that Kant posed in regard to the different perceptions of one and the same subject can be formulated with regard to different subjects: if X would see the cinnabar red, Z black, and Y gray, there would be no way in which they could concord among them. The voices of their spirits could never sound in unison, which would render the communitarian bond impossible.

In light of this, we must above all ask: what does "object" mean for Kant? The object is the result of the application of the categories or pure concepts of the understanding to what is given in sensibility, whose pure form constitutes the objectivity of the object. And where does the unity of the object come from, since there are twelve categories? The unity of the object is the reflection of the unity of consciousness, whereby the categories would be their emissaries.[12] But even if we were to accept that there is a unity of consciousness—that is, that it is something more than a bundle of perceptions,[13] and that this unity is transmitted to the unity of the object, between the unity of the object and that of consciousness a plurality persists, namely, that of the categories.

The understanding—whose unity is the "I think" or the transcendental apperception—predicates being in twelve ways (the categories) and in like manner constitutes the objectivity of the object. Here, *there is definitely univocity* (*Einstimmigkeit*), since being is said in one and only one way: as *object*. It is the old univocity of John Duns Scotus' *aliquid* and Ibn Sina's *quidditas* (*māhiyya*).

Two issues arise nonetheless. First, in order to reach the univocity of being as objectivity, the understanding must pass through the categorical moment, which is unequivocally *equivocal*: being as objectivity is said in twelve different ways. And second, and even more problematic, given that human understanding is finite and hence is in need of something to be given, this whole process is but an activity of the subject exerted over a vaster field *that exceeds objectivity*. The inconvenience that arises with Kant rejecting the question concerning the origin of the given through sensibility is that, by the mere fact of not calling it "experience," it will not cease to *be*: this, then, adds *another*—yet rejected—*sense* of being.

Besides the duodecimal categorical equivocity, we then have a more profound dual equivocity: being is said as noumenon and as phenomenon. The univocity gained with objectivity corresponds only to this latter sense—to being as phenomenon. In Kant, therefore, equivocity corrodes the unity of the voice of being twice.

UNIVOCITY AND ETERNAL RETURN IN DELEUZE

Analogy in judgment is for Deleuze one of the four elements of the "quadruple yoke of representation" together with the identity in the concept, the opposition in predicates, and resemblance in perception.[14] If representation is a yoke, the tamed animal is difference. In organic or finite representation, the movements of the beast are restricted to a middle range, which is why too large or too small differences turn out to be dangerous. We previously pointed out two moments of the equivocity of being in Kant: the different senses of being in categorical predication and the distinction between phenomenon and noumenon. Beyond this distinction, the real is too large to be apprehended by the concept. In the other extreme, the genetic process of the multiplicity given to sensibility remains unthinkable inasmuch as it is too small a difference. It is the aporia of organic representation: the voice of being has a limited pitch and is unable to sing the imperceptible unconscious highs that compose clear perceptions and the excessive basses of the trans-categorical.

The quadruple yoke that representation imposes upon difference entails, for Deleuze, a transcendental illusion. Analogy is, out of the four complementary types of illusion, that which properly concerns being.[15] Identity in the concept does not by itself provide a concrete rule of determination, appearing instead as wholly abstract: "The identity of an indeterminate concept; Being or I am (that 'I am' which Kant said was the perception or the feeling of an existence independent of any determination)."[16] Transcendental apperception is, actually, completely *indeterminate*. For this reason, it is necessary to put forward ultimate concepts or first *determinable* predicates that would hold an interior relation to being, in such a way that being would be analogous in their regard. "Identity must itself be represented every time in a certain number of determinable concepts": categories as emissaries of the unity of the cogito.[17]

In like manner, according to Deleuze, two limits are imposed upon difference: the Large and the Small, "the categories as a priori concepts and the empirical concepts; the originary determinable concepts and the derived determined concepts; the analogous and the opposed; *the large genera and the species*."[18] That said, this double limitation betrays, at the same time, the nature of being as collective and cardinal, that of nomadic distributions—rendering them fixed or sedentary—and that of difference as individuating.

Instead of thinking of a plurality of voices of being that delivers a monotony of what is, Deleuze holds that the voice of being is one, but that that of which it is said differs. It is of the essence to highlight the following point: being (*l'être*) is not said of beings (*les étants*). Being is said of difference, and beings are the result of this expression.

> Univocity signifies that being itself is univocal, while that of which it is said is equivocal: precisely the opposite of analogy. Being is said according to forms which do not break the unity of its sense; it is said in a single same sense throughout all its forms—that is why we opposed to categories notions of a different kind. That of which it is said, however, differs; it is said of difference itself. It is not analogous being which is distributed among the categories and allocates a fixed part to beings, but the beings which are distributed across the space of univocal being, opened by all the forms. Opening is an essential feature of univocity. The nomadic distributions or crowned anarchies in the univocal stand opposed to the sedentary distributions of analogy. Only there does the cry resound: "Everything is equal!" and "Everything returns!" However, this *"Everything is equal"* and this *"Everything returns"* can be said only at the point at which the extremity of difference is reached. A single and same voice for the whole thousand-voiced multiple, a single and same Ocean for all the drops, a single clamour of Being for all beings: on condition that each being, each drop and each voice has reached the state of excess—in other words, the difference which displaces and disguises them and, in turning upon its mobile cusp, causes them to return.[19]

The esoteric nucleus of univocity of being is for Deleuze the eternal return, and the title *Difference and Repetition* is but an allusion to this concept that the philosopher forges from Pierre Klossowski's reading of some scattered and muzzy Nietzschean passages. If we could envelope this book in one sentence, it would be: *revenir est l'être du devenir* (returning is the being of becoming).[20] One could paraphrase it with other Deleuzian expressions: returning is the One said of the Multiple, the Same said of the Different and so on. The answer to the question "what is the meaning of being?" could not be more straightforward in Deleuze: *to return*.

The question that has a less direct answer is "how?" It is worth underlining that the return is never guaranteed: one must become worthy of it. Yet, by which means? Through *hybris*, by breaching the limit that concerns us exclusively, by jumping over—like the demons—all forms that attempt to define us or, like Welles, by crossing the fence with the sign of *NO TRESPASSING*. That is the only way of being worthy of what we experience or of counter-actualizing the event: to reach and breach the limit of our own potency. That is the only tuning required by Deleuze in order to participate in the universal symphony in which each voice, by singing something different, resonates in every other voice. This harmonic modality does not presuppose the agreement with a transcendent hierarchical third, since the resonances are produced transversally among every voice without intermediaries: crowned anarchy.

The previous formulations hide nonetheless a simpler answer: if returning is the being of becoming, then the only way of being worthy of returning is precisely by *becoming*. But then, if being is the return of becoming, does that mean that when one does not become, one is not? And hence, is not being said in two different senses: when it is said of *what becomes and therefore is*, and when it is said of *what merely is but does not become*? These are tricky questions. The latter, because it assumes that being is said of something which *already is*; but one does not then see the need for being to be said of that something—ontologically speaking—since that something appears to be in no need of being in order to be. The former, because it implies that it is possible *not to become*. This point is somewhat more complex, and Deleuze never stopped dealing with the problem: How is it possible that we seem to conceive of things that are but do not become? What is the source of this transcendental illusion?

There are two important elements in the Deleuzian answer to this pressing issue. First, they do become, but we focus on a macro-level ("the molar") in which they seem stable, even as on a micro-level ("the molecular") they are always in the process of becoming, and that is why there is something in them that *is*—because it becomes, and becoming returns. Behind every Subject that utters "I think" swarms an infinity of larval subjects, changing at every moment; underneath every *Deus mortalis*, a multiplicity of forces and affects in fluctuating connections. Second, there is something peculiar about these things which leads us to think that they do not become. Deleuze calls this "transcendence." And transcendence, for Deleuze, *is not* (because it does not become, *ergo* it does not return).

The role of the eternal return as the productive principle of the univocity of being could not be overestimated. Difference must achieve being, and it only does so by *repeating itself*. According to *Difference and Repetition*'s theory of the three passive syntheses, there are three basic ways of repeating.

However, Deleuze suggests that temporal repetitions (developed in the second chapter) correspond to spatial repetitions (developed in the fifth chapter), wherewith we should think of repetition as not only engendering time but also space—albeit a nonrepresentative space. The aforementioned theory culminates with the eternal return as a synthesis, which in its temporal regard, produces the future in the manner of a generative opening to the contingency of becoming.

Analogy in judgment—the duodecimal equivocity in Kant—functions as a barrier between thinking and the real, since it applies a logic of *external* determination between concept and sensation. This logic curbs eternal return, since exteriority in the process of determination imposes limits (those of the Large and of the Small) on assemblages and hence separates beings from what they *can* (become). This is why only by reaching a logic of internal reciprocal determination between thinking and being can we become capable of thinking—and more importantly—of accomplishing univocity.

Let us end this essay with a dissonant note in regard to the argumentative path followed heretofore. In sections 24 and 25 of the *Critique*, Kant discovers a difference that is internal to the I and that simultaneously reveals its genetic potential: time introduces a fissure between the thinking I and the affected self which allows however their reciprocal determination. That moment, which according to Deleuze marks the discovery of the transcendental, opens up a new path for thinking of the mode of production of reality as a resonance between divergent series or the differentiation of difference. Kant, thus, at the same time as he builds a monumental system of analogy, creates the logic of immanent determination that Deleuze will use as one of his main instruments in the composition of his scream: "Being is univocal!"

NOTES

1. Gilles Deleuze, *Cours Vincennes*, January 14, 1974. Accessed September 18, 2019, https://www.webdeleuze.com/textes/175 (my translation).

2. Gilles Deleuze, *Difference and Repetition*, trans. Paul Patton (New York: Columbia University Press, 1994), 137.

3. Gilles Deleuze and Félix Guattari, *A Thousand Plateaus: Capitalism and Schizophrenia*, trans. Brian Massumi (London: Continuum, 2004 [1980]), 23.

4. Immanuel Kant, *Critique of Pure Reason*, trans. Paul Guyer and Allen W. Wood (New York: Cambridge University Press, 1998), 685. For all the Kant quotes, the German terms within square brackets are added, whereas the emphasis of the Latin terms is original. The original passage in German is: "Wahrheit aber beruht auf der Übereinstimmung mit dem Objecte, in Ansehung dessen folglich die Urtheile eines jeden Verstandes einstimmig sein müssen (*consentientia uni tertio consentiunt inter se*)." Kant: AA III, 532: 06–09. Kant's works in German are referenced according

to the Berlin Academy of Sciences style: AA for *Akademieausgabe*, followed by the volume in Roman numbers, the page in Arabic numbers and the lines after a colon, when necessary.

5. It is said, for instance, *etwas einstimmig beschließen* (to decide something unanimously).

6. Beyond the obvious political weight of the voice regardless of the language in question, the word *Stimme* also means *vote* in a political context (such as in the expression *ungültige Stimme*, invalid ballot).

7. Immanuel Kant, *Prolegomena to Any Future Metaphysics*, trans. Gary Hatfield (Cambridge: Cambridge University Press, 1997), 50. Kant: AA IV, *Prolegomena zu einer jeden künftigen Metaphysik, die als Wissenschaft wird auftreten können*, 298:13–4 (§18): "wenn ein Urtheil mit einem Gegenstande übereinstimmt, so müssen alle Urtheile über denselben Gegenstand auch unter einander übereinstimmen."

8. Kant, *Critique of Pure Reason*, 685. "Der Probirstein des Fürwahrhaltens, ob es Überzeugung oder bloße Überredung sei, ist also äußerlich die Möglichkeit, dasselbe mitzutheilen, und das Fürwahrhalten für jedes Menschen Vernunft gültig zu befinden; denn alsdann ist wenigstens eine Vermuthung, der Grund der Einstimmung aller Urtheile ungeachtet der Verschiedenheit der Subjecte unter einander werde auf dem gemeinschaftlichen Grunde, nämlich dem Objecte, beruhen, mit welchem sie daher alle zusammenstimmen und dadurch die Wahrheit des Urtheils beweisen werden." Kant: AA III, 532: 09–16.

9. Thomas Hobbes, *Leviathan* (New York: Collier, 1962), 127, emphasis original.

10. Significantly, in *Träume eines Geistersehers*, Kant quotes Heraclitus' fragment 89—although attributing it to Aristotle: "When we're awake we have a world in common, but when we dream each one has its own."

11. Kenneth R. Westphal, however, has defended the necessity of a transcendental affinity in a subject-independent way. See K. R. Westphal, "Affinity, Idealism and Naturalism: The Stability of Cinnabar and the Possibility of Experience," *Kant-Studien* 88, no. 2 (1997): 139–89.

12. Allison calls this correspondence between the unity of consciousness and the unity of the object the "reciprocity thesis," and the demonstration of the said thesis would constitute the goal—according to the scholar—of the first part of the Transcendental Deduction. See Henry Allison, *Kant's Transcendental Idealism: An Interpretation and Defense* (New Haven, CT: Yale University Press, 1983), 144–45.

13. "But setting aside some metaphysicians of this kind, I may venture to affirm of the rest of mankind, that they are nothing but a bundle or collection of different perceptions, which succeed each other with an inconceivable rapidity, and are in a perpetual flux and movement. Our eyes cannot turn in their sockets without varying our perceptions. Our thought is still more variable than our sight; and all our other senses and faculties contribute to this change; nor is there any single power of the soul, which remains unalterably the same, perhaps for one moment. The mind is a kind of theatre, where several perceptions successively make their appearance; pass, re-pass, glide away, and mingle in an infinite variety of postures and situations. There

is properly no simplicity in it at one time, nor identity in different; whatever natural propension we may have to imagine that simplicity and identity. The comparison of the theatre must not mislead us. They are the successive perceptions only, that constitute the mind; nor have we the most distant notion of the place, where these scenes are represented, or of the materials, of which it is composed." David Hume, *A Treatise of Human Nature*, Book I, Part IV, Section VI: "Of Personal Identity" (Oxford: Oxford University Press, 1960), 252–53.

14. Deleuze, *Difference and Repetition*, 300.

15. The other three forms of transcendental illusion correspond to thought (identity), to the sensible (similarity in perception), and to Ideas (opposition in the predicates).

16. Deleuze, *Difference and Repetition*, 269.

17. Deleuze, *Difference and Repetition*, 269.

18. Deleuze, *Difference and Repetition*, 269, emphasis original.

19. Deleuze, *Difference and Repetition*, 304, emphasis added.

20. "Revenir est l'être, mais seulement l'être du devenir." Gilles Deleuze, *Différence et répétition* (Paris: PUF, 1968), 59.

BIBLIOGRAPHY

Allison, Henry. *Kant's Transcendental Idealism: An Interpretation and Defense*. New Haven, CT: Yale University Press, 1983.

Deleuze, Gilles. *Cours Vincennes*. Accessed September 18, 2019. https://www.webdeleuze.com/textes/175.

Deleuze, Gilles. *Difference and Repetition*. Translated by Paul Patton. New York: Columbia University Press, 1994.

Deleuze, Gilles. *Différence et répétition*. Paris: PUF, 1968.

Deleuze, Gilles and Guattari, Félix. *A Thousand Plateaus: Capitalism and Schizophrenia*. Translated by Brian Massumi. London: Continuum, 2004 [1980].

Hobbes, Thomas. *Leviathan*. New York: Collier, 1962.

Hume, David. *A Treatise of Human Nature*. Oxford: Oxford University Press, 1960.

Kant, Immanuel. *Critique of Pure Reason*. Translated by Paul Guyer and Allen W. Wood. New York: Cambridge University Press, 1998.

Kant, Immanuel. *Kants Werke. Akademie Textausgabe*. Berlin: Walter de Gruyter, 1968ff.

Kant, Immanuel. *Prolegomena to Any Future Metaphysics*. Translated by Gary Hatfield. Cambridge: Cambridge University Press, 1997.

Westphal, K. R. "Affinity, Idealism and Naturalism: The Stability of Cinnabar and the Possibility of Experience," *Kant-Studien* 88, no. 2 (1997): 139–89.

Chapter 7

Time and Representation: Husserlian Resonances in the Treatment of Temporal Synthesis

Verónica Kretschel

Translated by Andrew Ascherl

THE QUESTION-PROBLEM

Edmund Husserl does not appear as a central reference in the work of Gilles Deleuze. Moreover, the few explicit references to him in *Difference and Repetition* are not related to the analysis of time but rather to the notion of multiplicity.[1] In addition, it would appear rather difficult to save Husserl from Deleuze's critique of the regressive character of transcendental philosophy in the book's third chapter, "The Image of Thought," where Deleuze explains that a logical error is involved in "discovering" the transcendental from a regressive methodological position: the conditions of possibility represent a mere hypostasis of individual subjective experience. The purification of the empirical turns it into nothing more than an empty form that is, of course, postulated as "originary." From this same perspective, in *The Logic of Sense* Deleuze poses the following question regarding Husserlian phenomenology:

> What is then the fate of philosophy which knows well that it would not be philosophy if it did not, at least provisionally, break with the particular contents and modalities of the doxa? What is the fate of a philosophy which nevertheless conserves the essential (that is the form), and is satisfied with raising to the transcendental a mere empirical exercise in an image of thought presented as originary?[2]

That said, Husserl's phenomenology does nothing other than postulating the purified empirical as transcendental. However, Deleuze's starting point is not the experience of reality. For him, there is nothing given that can serve as a platform from which we can launch our search for a foundation. He considers philosophy the art of creating concepts that are generated from a question-problem and established in a determinate plane of immanence.³ In this context, it seems rather useless to think about Husserl's presence in *Difference and Repetition*. Nevertheless, when reading the book, particularly chapter 2, "Repetition for Itself," we cannot help but detect irrepressible resonances of the phenomenologist. Something of Husserl appears in these paragraphs, where Deleuze presents his theory of temporality through the interaction of three temporal syntheses.⁴

Within this framework, I believe first of all that a comparative analysis of the synthesis of time in Deleuze and Husserl is the first point of any intersection between both authors' theories about this phenomenon. Second, we can see another relation between the two in their references to some of the same figures in the philosophical tradition regarding the question of time. In particular, Henri Bergson and Immanuel Kant appear as significant references for both Deleuze and Husserl. At a conference held in 1911 by Alexadre Koyré in Göttingen, Husserl reportedly claimed, "We are the true Bergsonians!" ("Les bergsoniens conséquents, c′est nous!").⁵ Additionally, Husserl remarked in a 1917 letter to Roman Ingarden, "It is as if I were Bergson."⁶ Much more commonly known is Deleuze's interest in Bergson, to whom he dedicated several works and occasionally discusses in *Difference and Repetition* in order to account for the influence the past has on the present. Deleuzian Bergsonism has also criticized the phenomenology of time, regarding it as an echo of an interpretation that understands the past as a mere derivative of the present; that is, it cannot be thought as a dimension of time strictly speaking, but rather as a modification of the present as an originary instance. Consequently, the limitations of Husserl's elucidation of the past make any awareness of the fundamental characteristic of time (i.e., that it passes) impossible. Regardless of the lack of precision in these criticisms, the analysis we are about to undertake will help us to understand that such an affirmation cannot be sustained.⁷

As far as Kant is concerned, the points of comparison are even more evident. Deleuze attributes him with being the first to dislodge time from its hinges in an effort to refer to the act of thinking time outside of any relation to movement. Starting with Kant, time no longer depends on any exterior phenomenon or on any world; it is not *the measure of movement*, rather, it itself determines how phenomena manifest themselves. That is to say, time unhinged refers to time that is not thought as one measure of a given world; rather, it is what establishes the frame according to which the world is given. This way of thinking time indicates a break in the notion of the subject.⁸ Deleuze writes that the subjective approach to temporality implies a subject that is ruptured by the possibility/impossibility of knowing itself. The paradox of an internal sense highlights the distance inherent to internal subjectivity and expresses the subject's lack of transparency with regard to its most essential constitution. We might say that it reveals the problems of representative thought as applied to the possibility of accessing the domain of the transcendental. In effect, Deleuze attempts to account for a time that escapes the schema of representation. Once time is liberated from the domain of space, it is necessary to establish its full potential, which entails not only going beyond the naturalist conception of time but also overcoming the limits that the theory of consciousness imposes on the notion.

Husserl also made a number of references to Kant on the question of time. First of all, in his thinking about the notion of passive synthesis, and already in the context of genetic phenomenology, Husserl referred to the Kantian concept of productive imagination as a precursor to the possibility of overcoming the comparison between activity and passivity.[9] Passive synthesis, as a pre-subjective operation—in the antechamber of the self—makes it possible to think a subjectivity that is constituted on originary levels, beyond the operations of understanding and will. Second, in addition to outstripping the activity-passivity comparison, phenomenology tries to overcome another dichotomy: the relation between forms of sensibility and categories of understanding. Again, the gradualist and levels-based approach of Husserlian phenomenology aims to expand on an experience that is shaped by very basic operations which give rise to fundamental notions of meaning. Husserl argues that Kant's problem was that he was unaware of the phenomenological method, but if we put Deleuzian concepts at the disposal of phenomenology, we can reformulate this idea and say instead that what Kant put into practice was the construction of an image of thought.[10] That is, by attributing to consciousness of the immanence of subjectivity the same nature as consciousness of the world, Kant was caught in the paradox of internal sense. Meanwhile, Husserl's gradualist, levels-based conception, according to which the consciousness of immanence operates as the foundation of the consciousness of transcendence, aims to establish a continuity between one form of consciousness and another. This serves as evidence that the image of the divided subject is not appropriate as a characterization of the Husserlian subject to which a self-transparent or omnipotent notion of subjectivity cannot be attributed; rather, this subject is shaped by the interplay between activity and passivity.

If we now turn to the issue of time, the question is whether phenomenology can perhaps also reflect on a notion of time dislodged from its hinges and, along with this, a time that surpasses the limits imposed by the theory of consciousness. Closely related to this, we must also be able to respond to the question of the relation between Husserl's theory of time and representative thought. Thus, we come to a third possible intersection between Husserl and Deleuze on the notion of time, which is expressed in the relation between the three elements of the Husserlian theory of time: first, the successive conceptual transformations presented in the theory; second, the modifications to the use of descriptive resources (formalizations, graphs, metaphors); and finally, the difficulties with accounting for the future in all its plenitude.

In general terms, it is possible to affirm that for Husserl, time is a form or structure that organizes the flow of the life of consciousness. The starting point of his investigation is the perception of an object. The question to which he attempts to respond is thus first of all, how is the unity of an object constituted when it manifests through multiple appearances. The phenomenological response places transcendent time between parentheses (objective time in the broad sense that includes both clock time and time in physics), and it addresses the immanence of consciousness seeking to elucidate the experience of time. This search finds that the phenomenon of time is the experience of duration. This necessitates a change in the central focus of the investigation, which is redirected from the perception of an object that lasts to the duration of consciousness itself. Therefore, temporality does not come from the object; rather, it is acts of consciousness, themselves temporal, which attribute time to perception. The primary questions Husserl confronts on several occasions include the temporal constitution of acts and, consequently, the characterization of an atemporal, constituent instance as its condition of possibility.

In Husserl's work on time, we can recognize three groups of texts that correspond to distinct moments in the development of phenomenology as a whole. Each one of these groups makes up a volume of the Husserliana series, in which the author's complete works are collected. The first group (Husserliana X), which includes the famous *Lectures on the Phenomenology of the Consciousness of Internal Time*, assembles writings from 1893 to 1917, and it is where we find Husserl's most well-known reflections on time. The second group (Husserliana XXXIII) is a collection of working manuscripts written in Bernau between 1917 and 1918 in which we can discern the genetic turn in phenomenology. The third group (Husserliana Materialenband VIII) is also a collection of working manuscripts, in this case drafted in the 1930s. In his earliest writings on time, Husserl studies the constitution of time in parallel with the constitution of space.[11] In this context, he develops a series of diagrams through which he seeks to represent different characteristics of the consciousness of time. This effort is continued in Husserl's work on time from 1917 to 1918, which established the framework of genetic phenomenology. However, in order to fully comprehend the relevance of this question and to what extent it constitutes part of the intersection with Deleuze's philosophy of time, we must first of all connect the moments of the development of Husserl's phenomenology of time with the conceptual tools he uses. The focus of his theory shifts from describing the temporalization of experiences based on the constitution of temporal objects (in texts related to the 1905 Lectures) to understanding time as the ultimate foundation of the life of consciousness (with the discovery, around 1910, of absolute consciousness, which is constitutive of time). In terms of descriptive resources, Husserl's attempt to graphically plot out the process of temporalization encountered difficulty in trying to apprehend the phenomenon of time in its ultimate dimension.

In the Bernau Manuscripts, we find a concerted effort to represent time in diagrams. Here, Husserl strives to make his earlier schemas more complex, and he concentrates on attempting to understand not only the way in which the present is extended due to the operation of retention as a means of maintaining in the present what was given in the past, but also how the consciousness of time is defined at the crossroads (*Verflechtung*) of retentions and protensions. The future phase of temporal consciousness, protension, which was simply copied from retention in his earlier studies, takes on a fundamental relevance in this (incipiently genetic) stage insofar as it is responsible for projecting what is retained. What is key here is that the experience of the present is the result of what has already been lived. However, in the third moment of Husserl's approach to the question of time, what stands out is the complete absence of temporal diagrams.

What I intend to show is that it is precisely in the problem of the representation of time that the intersection between Husserl and Deleuze can become more productive because if the former's efforts to account for time from a representational point of view appear to come out of a simple and self-evident perspective, the successive transformations and discoveries of his theory obliged him to confront a phenomenon that at the very least, escaped the possibilities of graphic representation and perhaps also the very limits of the vocabulary of phenomenology.[12] This path from graphs to metaphors, or the apparent lack of words when it comes to discussing the most important of all phenomenological questions leads us to ask whether the problem of time that interpellates Husserl is the same one that reveals the dynamic of time proposed by Deleuze. It is important to point out that we will not find explicit points of contact in these authors' texts, but rather we will see that the mode of Husserl's work is revealed to be sort of Deleuzian. Husserl's constant effort to describe temporal consciousness, including his insistent revision of the phenomenological framework that would make it appropriate for this task, became the organizing pattern of how he approached the phenomenon of time.

THE PLANE OF IMMANENCE

These three ways of approaching the intersection between Husserl and Deleuze on the question of temporality (the treatment of temporal synthesis, common philosophical references, and the methods used in the study of time) can be thought according to a more or less explicit order. In this case, and making explicit the exploratory character of the present text, we will begin with chapter 2 of *Difference and Repetition*, and we will develop a comparative and schematic approach to the treatment of the synthesis of time. The intention here is to show a coincidence in thinking the present–past relationship between both authors, which is to say, through the interaction between passive associative-temporal syntheses that constitute the foundation of active processes. This entails leaving aside Deleuze's analysis of the third temporal synthesis. Therefore, in order to establish the comparison, we will focus on the analysis of the first and second syntheses. What is interesting about this method of analysis is the possibility of showing that the phenomenology of time is not limited to thinking the constitution of present experience, and that it also accounts for a past that has its own ontological dignity and which allows for associations that articulate all levels of temporality.

In *Difference and Repetition*, the synthesis of time is presented through three related figures or characters. While the third synthesis appears as Thanatos or Eternal Return, the first synthesis—the synthesis of the present—is embodied in Habitus, which represents a process through which time is constituted as a succession of presents. It *establishes* time in the present and is the origin of the past and the future as modifications of this temporal instance. Deleuze turns to Hume and Bergson to explain the specific characteristics of the first temporal synthesis. In his reflections, there is first a traditional way of considering time: as an arrow whose trajectory is established from the present to the past in a succession of contained moments and which begins from the problem of the constitution of objects as they are formed in this succession. There is evidently a strong interest here in highlighting the passive character of this first synthesis insofar as the starting point of classical perspectives refer to active processes, such as understanding or memory. In contrast, Deleuze emphasizes that these processes are linked to sense-based and organic syntheses that indicate a desubjectivation of the synthetic operation. However, he also writes that "time is constituted only in the originary synthesis which operates on the repetition of instants."[13] Using as a reference Bergson's metaphor of the cone in *Matter and Memory*, this synthesis is located at the point of the cone, where the demands of life oblige the self to respond by contracting or synthesizing. This response yields a unity of sense that from a temporal perspective is nothing more than a discrete past. Thus while the analysis of time remains within this synthesis, it can only account for a disarticulated temporality for which no actual temporal relations exist.

When comparing the development of Habitus with Husserl's studies of time, we must first of all determine to what extent the terms Deleuze uses are references to the phenomenology of internal time consciousness. To discuss retention of the experienced and expected present and not mention Husserl would seem to be a founding gesture of the critique of interpretations of temporality based on the metaphysics of presence, which was begun by Heidegger and continued by Derrida.[14] On the one hand, it is clear that, when it is presented in terms of "Repetition for Itself," a consciousness of time such as Habitus is very restricted; as we will see in the following text, it is precisely the second synthesis that will come to show these limits and engender a more complex vision of time. On the other hand, it is necessary to emphasize that Husserl's analysis of the constitutive consciousness of time does not understand the past and the future as mere modifications of the present but rather as dimensions of temporality with their own characteristics. Husserl refers to an originary consciousness of the past to define retention, which points to a particular givenness of the past in consciousness, *a donation from the past as past*.[15] We understand, however, that, even if we accept this presentist interpretation of the phenomenology of time, mechanisms that complement this first instance of temporal constitution can also be found in phenomenology. Therefore, if we accept that absolute consciousness, with its triple structure, makes present experience possible, we must also refer to the analysis of association in order to account for sensible or organic syntheses. When within the framework of genetic phenomenology in *Analyses Concerning Passive Synthesis*, Husserl develops the theory of primary association as the first instance of the structuring of unities of sense in the immanence of consciousness, these unities are posited as belonging to the same consciousness, as integrated into the affectively significant conditions, and as not temporally determined.[16] For there to be a temporal order, the mechanisms of absolute consciousness must be operative. Associative synthesis, like Deleuzian contraction, produces discrete unities. These unities form part of the sense-field—consciousness as the realm of givenness—and are reciprocally constituted in the struggle to stand out and capture the attention of the ego. Only temporal synthesis makes it possible to bring together and give order to the unities of sense. Thus, we must affirm that for Husserl, temporal synthesis and associative synthesis complement each other and constitute a fully passive dimension of subjective life.

The complement of the synthesis of the present is expressed in Deleuze through the figure of Mnemosyne, the passive synthesis of the past that is the condition of possibility for memory. While memory represents concrete recollection, this synthesis, rather than contracting, contains and offers up the totality of the past to the present. Through memory, lived experience is conserved as it is given and exists as a pure past that cannot be effectively reexperienced but which can be brought to presence. Insofar as the present is thought as Habitus, the past permanently comes to presence as the habitual response to a determinate stimulus. Deleuze points out that, just as the first synthesis lays the foundation for time, the second synthesis grounds it.[17] However, between Habitus and Mnemosyne, there is yet another "character": Eros, the link that "tears" from the pure past that which must be brought to presence. Thus, in its operation, it is conditioned by the needs of the present and looks to the past for an adequate response to a given stimulus. However, Eros also accounts for the experience of remembrance. Considering in particular the examples Deleuze uses (such as Proust's *À la recherche du temps perdu*), what it "tears" from the pure past responds to a more complex articulation of experience than simply that related to vital necessities. In this sense, it is necessary to point out that the operation of the Eros-Mnemosyne articulation is made more complex by referring to Freud's works *Beyond the Pleasure Principle* and by developing a critique of the analysis of the unconscious that would allow for thinking new motivations for the present–past relationship *beyond* biological or perceptive needs.

We understand that it is possible to establish an analogy between this double function of Eros and the Husserlian synthesis of awakening (*Weckung*). In order to do so, we can make use of the definition that supports genetic phenomenology according to which the intentional consciousness becomes the waking consciousness.[18] This means that past experience permanently operates in the present. Focusing on the units of meaning in the field of the present through the operation of the mechanisms of primary association, the following level, the level of secondary association, generates processes that ensure that something which has already been lived should not be constituted again. Passively, what is given in the present is associated with what has already been lived, and it communicates the affective force of the present toward the past. The past, in turn, can awaken with a distinct level of intensity, passively aiding the experience of the present or deriving an active plenitude in the form of memory. In his early texts on time, Husserl refers to resonances as modes in which the present "remembers" the past.[19] In the genetic framework, as with everything, this idea is radicalized. The subject is now the substratum of habitualities, and this implies that awakening is occurring, motivated by that which is given in the present, bringing from the past that which is necessary to give rise to an organized experience. However like Eros, awakening is the foundation of the act of remembrance, animating what has been retained and making it present. In Husserl, the motivation of memory also originates in passive, sensorial, or corporeal strata that explain the involuntary character of remembering and of the complexity of the operations on which an activity is based. In turn, these two functions of awakening are considered through the differences in the levels of phenomenological description. For instance, the primary association operates on a lower, more fundamental level than remembrance. Thus, sometimes the past is "barely perceptible," and at other times it is remembered. Regardless, in both situations, there is a concomitant presence of the past. Although at first glance, the way in which the past exists as a whole in Husserl (as retained by the absolute consciousness and submitted to the process of retentional modification) must be differentiated from the way in which it exists in Deleuze (as a whole from a pure, unmodifiable past), we can see that both theories assign the experience of the present to a similar constitutive and fundamental position. Indeed, the modification that is produced by this retentional sinking should not be taken as a substantial transformation of the past but rather as a simple change of perspective with regard to the present, as a way of accounting for the passing of time on the level of the first synthesis.

As anticipated, the present analysis must set aside Husserl and Deleuze's characterization of the future due to the patent differences between these two philosophers' approaches to it. Husserl modified his study of the future as an instance of temporalization throughout the different periods of his work. He began by thinking of it as analogous to the phase of the past, retention; however, in the *Lectures*, protention—which is to say the phase of the constituent consciousness of time that makes possible the givenness of what is to come— is not practically described. It is only with the genetic turn in phenomenology that the operation of protentional intentionality is more carefully developed in terms of the capacity for anticipation based on lived experience. That is to say, the process of temporalization is in a reciprocal relationship with retentional intentionality. For Deleuze in contrast, the future is the realization of time, its *truth*. We could say that the third synthesis allows us to break with a schema that projects what was onto what will be. In this sense, the synthesis of the future is what opens up the horizon of time outside of representation insofar as the figures that are used to characterize it, Eternal Return or Thanatos, are proposed as an ontological instance of the disruption and generation of difference. Therefore, on a first reading, it would seem evident that the Deleuzian synthesis of the future stands in opposition to genetic phenomenology's notion of protensional intentionality. Nevertheless, we believe that an analysis that brings together and equates the developments on Eternal Return in *Difference and Repetition* and on Aion in *The Logic of Sense* as modes of addressing a time that has been dislodged from its hinges would allow us to compare Deleuze's thought more closely with the genetic phenomenology of time and its estimation of the future. The phenomenological stages of the constitution of temporality particularly resonate in Deleuze's characterization of Aion as an empty form of time, in contrast to Chronos, which is characterized as a succession of discrete presents.[20] The works on genetic experience collected in the Bernau Manuscripts make possible an analysis of a temporality that constitutes itself independently of all content and where the present is blurred in the process of passive temporalization that characterizes the interaction between retentional and protensional intentionality. Although we will not undertake such a comparison here, it is nevertheless interesting to formulate and pose the question.

CREATION OF CONCEPTS

Having arrived at this intersection, we would like to conclude by taking up two final questions. On the one hand, there are the problems that arise in the Husserlian phenomenology of time's attempt to, in Deleuze's terms, represent time. Husserl dealt with this question throughout his entire career as a philosopher and, insofar as time took on an increasingly fundamental relevance for his theory, the possibility of representation became more complicated, as time tends to evade description. In short, it seems that the phenomenological method itself, as a theory of knowledge, is unable to fully grasp the phenomenon. On the other hand, the fact that Husserl offers no conclusive analysis of the potential of the future seems to be a corollary of the first inadequacy. Genetic phenomenology's analysis of the future as a simple inversion of the past, or as a purely formal dimension that enables the projection of what has already been lived, clearly contrasts with the phenomenology of retention. The relations established here with association have a level of richness and depth that allow us to accurately describe a large part of our temporal experience. What we must therefore ask ourselves is whether it is possible to connect Husserl's inability to account for the future with his insistence on representation as a mode of accessing the question of time. Although phenomena like surprise or radical novelty can be described in the language of phenomenology, we are left with the impression that the theory of knowledge always arrives late. Now, can we think that the time that Husserl was unable to describe is that which is crystallized in the third synthesis of time in *Difference and Repetition*? The force of that temporality, we believe, is present throughout Husserl's thought and is reflected in his tireless work on the problem of time. The mode of thinking that is reflected in this interminable process of writing and rewriting indicates a temporality that goes beyond mere repetition. Difference emerges in this process, and Husserl is conscious of this fact insofar as it permeates his method of working. In this sense, we believe that a study of the description of temporality found in Husserl's most experimental texts can make the task of reading them alongside Deleuze's philosophy even more fruitful.

NOTES

1. See Andrés Osswald, "Síntesis y multiplicidad: Algunas indicaciones husserlianas sobre la ontología de *Diferencia y repetición*," in *Deleuze y las fuentes de su filosofía*, edited by Julián Ferreyra and Matías Soich (Buenos Aires: Ediciones La Almohada, 2014), 48–58.
2. Gilles Deleuze, *The Logic of Sense*, trans. Mark Lester with Charles Stivale (London: The Athlone Press, 1990), 98.

3. Gilles Deleuze and Félix Guattari, *What Is Philosophy?*, trans. Hugh Tomlinson and Graham Burchell (New York: Columbia University Press, 1994), 2.

4. This intuition that something of Husserl resonates in Deleuze, and perhaps a certain "Deleuzeanism" in the Husserlian mode of philosophy, can also be detected in Nicolas de Warren's interpretation of the relation between these two philosophers. An initial approach to this reading can be found in Warren, "La anarquía del sentido: Husserl en Deleuze, Deleuze en Husserl," *Ideas: Revista de filosofía moderna y contemporánea* 1 (2015): 52–78.

5. See Rafael Winkler, "Husserl and Bergson on Time and Consciousness," in *Logos of Phenomenology and Phenomenology of the Logos: Book Three: Analecta Husserliana (The Yearbook of Phenomenological Research)*, edited by A. T. Tymieniecka, Vol. 90 (Dordrecht: Springer, 2006).

6. See Jean Hering, "La phénomenologie d'Edmund Husserl il y a trente ans. Souvenirs et reflexion d'un étudiant de 1909," *Revue Internationale de Philosophie* 1, no. 2 (Janvier 1939): 368. Regarding whether or not Bergson is a precursor of phenomenology, see Dan Zahavi, "Life, Thinking and Phenomenology in the Early Bergson," in *Bergson and Phenomenology*, ed. Michael Kelly (New York: Palgrave Macmillan, 2010), 118–33.

7. For a specific critique of Bergsonism in relation to the phenomenology of time, and as a complement to the present essay, see Michael Kelly, "Husserl, Deleuzean, Bergsonism, and the Sense of the Past in General," *Husserl Studies* 24 (2008): 15–30. In this article, Kelly confronts the claim Husserl is unable to account for an independent notion of the past and argues that Husserlian theory is closer to Bergson than Bergsonism itself.

8. On this issue, see Andrés M. Osswald's text in the present volume, "Subject and Passivity in Husserl and Deleuze."

9. Edmund Husserl, *Analysen zur passiven Synthesis. Ausvorlesungs-und Forschungsmanuskripten (1918–1926)*, Husserliana XI (The Hague: Martinus Nijhoff, 1966), 275–6.

10. Husserl, *Analysen zur passiven Synthesis*, 171.

11. Edmund Husserl, *Zur Phänomenologie des inneren Zeitbewusstseins (1893–1917)*, Husserliana X (The Hague: Martinus Nijhoff, 1969), 5.

12. On the use of diagrams to explain the characteristics of temporality and the relation between the complexity of the phenomenological approach and the sophistication of Husserl's diagrams of time, see James Dodd, "Reading Husserl's Time-Diagrams from 1917/1918," *Husserl Studies* 21, no. 2 (2005): 111–37.

13. Gilles Deleuze, *Difference and Repetition*, trans. Paul Patton (New York: Columbia University Press, 1994), 70.

14. Even though Husserlian phenomenology is included in the tradition that Heidegger called the "metaphysics of presence" in *Being and Time*, basing this inclusion on Husserl's attribution of a certain privilege to the present as a fundamental instant over the past and the future, this same critique of time has itself been criticized for presenting a depresentialized vision of time. This reading can be found, for example, in the work of both Michel Henry and Emmanuel Levinas. I have discussed the critique of Husserlian presentism in Verónica Kretschel, "Husserl y la metafísica de la

presencia: la relación protoimpresión-retención," *Anuario Filosófico* 46, no. 3 (2013): 543–63.

15. Here again, it would be interesting to read this work alongside the text by Zahavi cited above, which addresses the originality of the temporal phases included in Husserl's earliest work on time (see Edmund Husserl, *Zur Phänomenologie des inneren Zeitbewusstseins (1893–1917)*).

16. This description can be found in "Association," the third division of *Analysis Concerning Passive Synthesis*, where Husserl begins the development of the constitution of the sense-field and establishes the relation between association and temporal synthesis. See Edmund Husserl, *Analysen zur passiven Synthesis. Ausvorlesungs- und Forschungsmanuskripten (1918–1926)*, Husserliana XI (The Hague, Martinus Nijhoff, 1966), 125 and passim.

17. Deleuze, *Difference and Repetition*, 95.
18. Husserl, *Analysen zur passiven Synthesis*, 118.
19. Husserl, Analysen zur passiven Synthesis, 118.
20. Deleuze, *The Logic of Sense*, 162–68.

BIBLIOGRAPHY

De Warren, Nicolas. "La anarquía del sentido: Husserl en Deleuze, Deleuze en Husserl." *Ideas: Revista de filosofía moderna y contemporánea* 1 (2015): 52–78.

Deleuze, Gilles and Félix. *What Is Philosophy?*. Translated by Hugh Tomlinson and Graham Burchell. New York: Columbia University Press, 1994.

Deleuze, Gilles. *Difference and Repetition*. Translated by Paul Patton. New York: Columbia University Press, 1994.

Deleuze, Gilles. *The Logic of Sense*. Translated by Mark Lester with Charles Stivale. London: The Athlone Press, 2013.

Dodd, James. "Reading Husserl's Time-Diagrams from 1917/1918." *Husserl Studies* 21, no. 2 (2005): 111–37.

Hering, Jean. "La phénomenologie d´Edmund Husserl il y a trente ans. Souvenirs et réflexions d´un étudiant de 1909." *Revue Internationale de Philosophie* 1, no. 2 (15 Janvier 1939): 366–73.

Husserl, Edmund. *Analysen zur passiven Synthesis. Ausvorlesungs-und Forschungsmanuskripten* (1918–1926), Husserliana XI. The Hague: Martinus Nijhoff, 1966.

Husserl, Edmund. *Zur Phänomenologie des inneren Zeitbewusstseins (1893–1917)*, Husserliana X. The Hague: Martinus Nijhoff, 1969.

Kelly, Michael. "Husserl, Deleuzian Bergsonism and the Sense of the Past in General." *Husserl Studies* 24 (2008): 15–30.

Kretschel, Verónica. "Husserl y la metafísica de la presencia: la relación protoimpresión-retención," *Anuario Filosófico* 46, no. 3 (2013): 543–63.

Osswald, Andrés. "Síntesis y multiplicidad. Algunas indicaciones husserlianas sobre la ontología de *Diferencia y repetición*." en *Deleuze y las fuentes de su filosofía*, Ferreyra, Julián-Soich, Matías (Eds.), 48–58. Buenos Aires: Ediciones La Almohada, 2014.

Serrano de Haro, Agustín, "Presentación de la edición española." en *Lecciones de fenomenología de la conciencia interna del tiempo*, Edmund Husserl (Ed.). Madrid: Trotta, 2002.

Zahavi, Dan. "Life, Thinking and Phenomenology in the Early Bergson." In *Bergson and Phenomenology*, edited by M. Kelly, 118–33. New York: Palgrave Macmillan, 2010.

Chapter 8

Subject and Passivity in Husserl and Deleuze: A Debate around the Contemporary Reception of Kant's Doctrine of the Productive Imagination

Andrés M. Osswald

"I am, I exist, this is certain. But for how long?" —Descartes

INTRODUCTION

Although Edmund Husserl's and Gilles Deleuze's theories on passivity are independent of one another, these two philosophers share a common background: they find in Immanuel Kant not only the most relevant influence for their own thought on this matter but also a designated target for their criticism. It is very unlikely that Deleuze was aware of the publication in 1966 of *Analysen zur Passiven Synthesis* and therefore that the eleventh volume of *Husserliana* is a key source, for the elaboration of *Difference and Repetition*, which appeared in France two years later. In general, Husserl does not play a major role in *Difference and Repetition*; he is only mentioned sporadically regarding the *Logical Investigations*.[1] By contrast, in *Logic of Sense*, published in 1969, Husserl is a more prominent reference. But in that work, Deleuze tends to present Husserlian phenomenology as an eminent representative of contemporary subjectivism and thus as one of his conceptual opponents.

However, and despite the relative distance between the two philosophers, I believe that they share a common intention, which is to overcome the rigid opposition between synthesis and passivity inherited from Kantian philosophy. Thus, it is in this context that I propose to analyze the critical interpretation of both philosophers regarding the role of the imagination in the *Critique of Pure Reason*. In this sense, I claim that the main hermeneutic difference has to be found, on the one hand, in the strong distinction that Deleuze traces—following Kant—between sensibility and understanding in his theory of passive synthesis and, on the other hand, the Husserlian reading that tends to blur such rigid difference between the faculties. Consequently, in terms of the distinction between activity and passivity, the Deleuzian interpretation separates the orders that Husserl thinks of as being nonindependent parts of a continuum. From this, a general consequence for a theory of the subject could be drawn from the foregoing: if activity and passivity are heterogeneous realms, the subject has necessarily to be divided.

If activity and passivity are not heterogeneous realms, a subject entails a unity which extends without any break between passivity and activity. The first option—one that Deleuze seems to embrace—can be traced to the so-called paradox of inner sense. The second alternative is embraced by Husserl, who claims that passive syntheses—in particular, the synthesis of immanent time—are a condition of possibility for the unity of subjectivity and as such a general condition for activity. Furthermore, the debate around the subjective unity and the character of the relationship between activity and passivity also contains consequences for transcendental philosophy. If the subject is unrestrictedly identified with active processes—such as a Cartesian Ego—and with the vague concept of person, then it has to be conceived in metaphysical terms as an "effect" of a transcendental field as defined by the passivity, a-subjectivity, neutrality, and productivity. The continuity between active and passive processes, by contrast, allows one to think that the Ego is also a founded level of subjectivity by virtue of passive syntheses that are also subjective.

SYNTHESIS OF IMAGINATION

One of the key distinctions that Kant made in the *Critique of Pure Reason* is the separation of sensibility and understanding and, correspondingly, the association of passivity with the former and activity with the latter. Kant's rigid differentiation among faculties responds ultimately to his attempt to ground knowledge in sensory representations. The inability of understanding to "produce" its objects by itself strengthens this attempt. As a result, understanding receives its material from a pure receptive sensibility, which Kant calls "passive" due to its lack of productivity. One immediate consequence of this topology of concepts is that the origin of sensory representation must be located beyond the realm of sensibility. If sensibility was able to produce its own material, it would be problematic to insist that the subject does not give itself its own object of knowledge. In other words, the pure receptivity of sensibility involves the distinction between "phenomenon" and "thing-in-itself"—which affect us and is the cause of the affection of sensibility.[2] It is also clear that in Kantian terms, the notions of "synthesis" and "passivity" are mutually exclusive; otherwise, the very distinction between knowing and thinking would collapse.

Nevertheless, Husserl finds some signs of distention in the inflexible opposition between passivity and synthesis in the role that Kant assigns to productive imagination in the "Transcendental Deduction of Categories"—above all in the first edition of the *Critique*.[3] Husserl writes in *Analyses of Passive Synthesis*: "But, in our view, that [productive imagination] is nothing other than the team-work (disclosable by our phenomenological method) of the constantly higher developing intentionalities of passive consciousness."[4] In fact, if the imagination could assemble the sensitive material in immanent time, it would be appropriate to consider here a spontaneity essentially different from the one that operates in understanding—hence the former synthesizes intuitions and the latter synthesizes concepts—such syntheses oriented to sensations that flow in time gather the two main syntheses that constitute, for Husserl, the passive life of consciousness, namely, the formal synthesis of time and the associative synthesis of sensation, which is also the leading theme of the *Analyses*.

In Husserl's terms, the Kantian doctrine of productive imagination forms a continuity between sensibility and understanding instead of a radical opposition. However, Husserl himself has a fluctuating position on this matter. In *Logical Investigation*, for instance, he defines "sensibility" as simple intuition and reserves for "understanding" the active role of synthesis. In that context, activity is identified with judgment in a broad sense: it is not only related to the predicative synthesis of propositions (judgment in a narrow sense) but also to the position (*Setzung*) entailed by perception. That is, Husserl considers that the being-character of perceptual objects depends on the judgment.[5] Around 1909 this early position starts to be relativized and he begins to consider the relationship between sensibility and understanding to be more fluid, as if they were not really two separate spheres but moments of a more profound unity.[6] Therefore, Husserlian phenomenology allows for a concept of passivity that differs from mere receptivity by means of a double procedure: on the one hand, the abandonment of the rigid opposition between sensibility and understanding and, on the other hand, the extension of the domain of intentionality. In other words, Husserl must abandon the idea that only the acts of the ego possess an intentional character. As a consequence, he has to admit that some levels of consciousness are intentional even though they do not emanate from an attentive-ego; correspondingly, they are not directed toward a thematic objectivity.

The Deleuzian interpretation of the role of productive imagination in Kant's philosophy moves in the opposite direction. In his lecture on Kant at the University of Paris VIII in Vincennes, he affirms:

> The big problem that Kant discovers is the nature of the relation between, on the one hand, the form of determination, or activity, or spontaneity, and on the other hand the form of receptivity, or form of the determinable, time. If I shift slightly, I would no longer say the form of determination and the form of determinable, but: two types of determination which are heterogeneous.[7]

The heterogeneous character of spontaneity and receptivity reflects not only the mediator role of imagination in Deleuze's account of Kant but also the nature of the relationship between activity and passivity. Furthermore, Deleuze finds in this distinction a key element for his theory of subjectivity. In fact, the difference between the determination and the determinable introduced here explains both the contrast between the Cartesian and the Kantian cogito and the novelty involved by the transcendental character of time.

SELF-KNOWLEDGE

As has been frequently noted, there exists a hiatus between the certainty of the Cartesian cogito—if I think, I must necessarily exist—and the determination of being as substance—I am a thing that thinks. Deleuze returns to this subject and claims:

> It is as though Descartes's Cogito operated with two logical values: determination and undetermined existence. The determination (I think) implies an undetermined existence (I am, because "in order to think one must exist")—and determines it precisely as the existence of a thinking subject: I think therefore I am, I am a thing which thinks.[8]

According to this, Descartes moves too fast when he tries to define an undetermined existence—I am—by means of a determination revealed as indubitable—I think—because he does not explain how thinking determines being; he just considers that each act of thinking is an attribute of the substance that I am. In other words, from the act of thinking it does not follow that only a substance can think. By contrast, Kant would provide an appropriate solution to the Cartesian precipitation through the introduction of a mediating element between being and thinking. Deleuze writes:

> My undetermined existence can be determined only within time as the existence of a phenomenon, of a passive, receptive phenomenal subject appearing within

Concurrently, in transcendental philosophy, sense would express an order articulated by the guiding principle. Outside the scope of the principle, nonsense would possess only a negative character: beyond order, there is an undifferentiated depth, an abyss without properties, an uninformed nonbeing.

By contrast, Deleuze tries to characterize nonsense positively and that means that he must avoid, above all, the dead-end toward which both transcendental philosophy and metaphysics would lead. Then, nonsense would be less an uncrossable boundary for thought than precisely what is has to be thought. If from a static point of view it is easy to establish a clear distinction between the order of sense—and with it the metaphysical essence and the transcendental subject—and nonsense—the undifferentiated depth—a genetic perspective shows not only a progressive relaxation between the realms but, even more important, it brings to the foreground the productive character of nonsense. Moreover, and given that the genetic question reveals transcendental subjectivity as a mere image of thought, a proper transcendental perspective could be maintained only by means of the abandonment of the subjective anchoring. That is, transcendental philosophy has not been able until now to leave behind the tendency of common sense that tends to trace the empirical level onto transcendental structures. As Deleuze points out:

> What is evident in Kant, when he directly deduces the three transcendental syntheses from corresponding psychological syntheses, is no less evident in Husserl when he deduces an originary and transcendental "Seeing" from perceptual "vision."[21]

A transcendental field purified of all subjective remain becomes an impersonal, neutral, and dynamic space inhabited by singularities:

> We cannot accept the alternative which thoroughly compromises psychology, cosmology, and theology: either singularities already comprised in individual persons, or the undifferentiated abyss. Only when the world, teaming with anonymous and nomadic, impersonal and pre-individual singularities, opens up, do we tread al last on the field of transcendental.[22]

At this point, we can ask: what does it mean to be a subject in *Logic of Sense*? First, it has to be said that Deleuze does not there carry out his theory of the subject, but uses the concept to characterize the position of his conceptual adversaries. In this sense, he tends to identify without further restriction the notion of the subject with the concepts of consciousness, I, Ego, human person, and cogito.[23] However, in his own theory of the subject—mostly developed in the second chapter of *Difference and Repetition*—he acknowledges that this higher dimension of subjectivity (assimilated here with the active Ego of a human person) is founded on a passive synthesis that ultimately depends on temporal syntheses. Despite the apparent proximity to Husserl's own appraisal of the fundamental character of temporality, the Deleuzian temporal syntheses play a quite different role in that context. For Deleuze, time not only does not provide a transcendental unity for consciousness—as a matter of fact, the "synthesis of the future" blocks any chance of subjective unification—but also subjectivity in itself is conceived as an effect of syntheses instead of its agent.[24] Deleuze writes:

> There is a self [*moi*] wherever a furtive contemplation has been established, whenever a contracting machine capable of drawing a difference from repetition functions somewhere. The self does not undergo modifications, it is itself a modification—this term designating precisely the difference drawn.[25]

In other words: if an Ego exists, that is because there are syntheses and not the other way around. In this context, the skeptical appraisal of the Sartrean attempt to nihilise the phenomenological consciousness has to be taken into account:

> This field [regarding the transcendental field] cannot be determined as that of a consciousness. Despite Sartre's attempt, we cannot retain consciousness as a milieu while at the same time we object to the form of the person and the point of view of individuation. A consciousness is nothing without a synthesis of unification, but there is no synthesis of unification of consciousness without the form of the I [*Je*], or the point of view of the Self [*moi*].[26]

Two general conditions of the Deleuzian description of classic subjectivity can be drawn from this passage: (i) a subject entails a synthesis of unification and (ii) a subject always imply a point of view. Deleuzian philosophy, for its part, could be negatively described as an attempt to abandon these two conditions in the definition of the transcendental field. On the one hand, while a subject unifies the transcendental field around a central element—the I or *je*—Deleuze wants to think a transcendental field without a center, inhabited by nomadic singularities that organize themselves in series by means of an "auto-unification": a synthesis does not need an agent separated from the elements—an I, for instance.[27] On the other hand, if the subject is completely constituted—that is what means to be "an effect"—the transcendental field must lack any privileged point of view, or positively speaking, it has to be neutral. Neutrality and impassiveness define the Event that happens beyond the subject. Therefore, the subjective perspective entails a denaturation of ontology. Following the appendix of *Ethics* I, Deleuze writes: "To grasp whatever happens as unjust and unwarranted (it is always someone else's fault) is [. . .] what renders our sores repugnant—veritable *ressentiment*, resentment of the event."[28] In short, if the subject is only an effect, then it necessarily lacks of any productive potency—everything what constituted its reality was created behind its back—or, conversely, the transcendental synthesis is not subjective.

The unrestricted identification between, on the one hand, subject and person and, on the other hand, the transcendental field and passivity is not valid for Husserlian phenomenology. Genetic inquiry leads Husserl to deepen the notion of subject by acknowledging the passive dimensions of subjectivity. In such a context, activity—associated with the superior levels of consciousness— and personal existence are also founded in syntheses that do not emanate from an awaken I—and this is precisely what defines them as passive—but this does not entail, in Husserl's terms, the splitting between subjectivity and transcendental field. Such a conclusion could only be reached if beforehand passive productivity and subjectivity had been artificially opposed. Hence, the anti-subjectivism defended by Deleuze is less rather a result of the analysis than more a departure point from it, and therefore, it constitutes his own image of thought.

From my understanding, here also lies the key to the dispute over Cartesianism: while Deleuze can only think that the cogito is an empirical phenomenon—a form of self-knowledge—Husserl holds that the self-appearance of consciousness is not primarily empirical. If that were the case, that is, if a subject only could be self-aware of itself by means of an explicit act of reflection, then self-appearance would lead inexorably to an infinite regression. In effect, the act of reflection can only make conscious an elapsed and objectified consciousness, while the present act of reflection would remain unconscious. Such a reflective act would become conscious retroactively insofar as it is intended by a new act of reflection and so on.

In temporal terms, that implies that the present of consciousness is unconscious. But Husserl explicitly rejects such a possibility: "It is just nonsense to talk about an 'unconscious' content that would only subsequently become conscious. Consciousness is necessarily *consciousness* in each of its phases."[29] Furthermore, a pure empirical interpretation of self-awareness would become an unthinkable reflection in itself. That is, inasmuch reflection is an act, it lasts—it involves a certain amount of time—an infinite number of acts would involve an infinite time as well. The very possibility of reflection involves therefore a pre-reflective and passive self-awareness that Husserl finds in the ultimate coincidence between the constituent and the constituted in the absolute flow of time. According to this, a subject is not only (i) a synthesis and (ii) a point of view, but these two conditions depend on a third one: (iii) a subject should experience itself pre-reflectively. Against Kant, Husserl does not believe that the possibility of experience of a representation as our own depends on the syntheses of consciousness but, on the contrary, he thinks that those syntheses presuppose the self-appearance of subjectivity in the stream of immanent time. In technical terms, that means that the transcendental apperception entails a passive cogito.

Deleuze, like Kant and the early Husserl, remains blind to such originary self-experience, and consequently, he would try to define subjectivity from a third-person perspective, as if a subject were just a thing among things, "like a house or a tree."[30] In this regard, Deleuze asserts: "The universal Ego is, precisely, the person corresponding to something = x common to all worlds, just as the other egos are the person corresponding to a particular thing = x common to several worlds."[31] According to this, a particular subject could be defined as the individual case of the set of all properties that only belong to it and, correspondingly, the universal subject—the transcendental Ego—would be the intersection of the set of the whole of subjective properties. From this point of view, self-appearance could be apprehended ony as an abstract phenomenon that no one experiences, instead of the unique and radically singular experience that everyone has of oneself, whether it be active or passive.

CONCLUSIONS

While Deleuze finds in the discovery of passivity to be not only the main reason for the fragmentation of subjectivity but also a key argument for the abandonment of the subjective character of the transcendental field, Husserlian passivity ensures at the same time the unity of subject and gives a transcendental role to self-experience. Regarding the former, the splitting of the subject reflects the classical opposition of transcendental philosophy between the constituted and the constituent but now within subjectivity. Such a conclusion is a corollary of the broader critique of modern subjectivism, which would have fallen into the trap of understanding the transcendental subject as a purified double of a concrete, empirical subject. Consequently, this modern image of thought would confuse personal subjectivity—defined as human, rational, transparent, and reflective—with the transcendental field. In order to remedy this misunderstanding, the transcendental field should be purified of all subjective remains or, positively stated, it has to be defined as impersonal, neutral (without any privileged point of view), productive and virtual. Deleuze affirms that between the virtual and the actual, there is no similarity or opposition but difference and, therefore, its synthesis is asymmetrical. Husserl, on his behalf, critiques the modern identification between subject and person and, just like Deleuze, rejects the personal character of the transcendental subject. A person is a worldly object and, as such, a constituted phenomenon. However, this does not imply the disengagement between subjectivity and the transcendental field but, on the contrary, it leads to a deepening of the notion of subject.

In this regard, it has to be mentioned that the Husserlian enlargement of the concept of subjectivity covers not only humans but also animals and plant life. Husserl defends in this sense a gradualness of subjective immanence, which although it is passively founded has also recognized the productive role of activity: categorial objects, for instance, are the correlative object of an active categorial intuition. On the contrary, in this instance, Deleuze seems to draw an uncrossable border between activity and passivity, which marks at once the limit between the empirical and the transcendental dimensions of ontology.

Given this, I think that the Deleuzian criticism of Husserl in *Logic of Sense* must be taken cautiously because it is based on a false premise, namely, that the subject is always a human person. Deleuze seems to remain conditioned by that image of thought. But despite their differences, Husserl and Deleuze share a fundamental insight into the relevance of Kant's doctrine of productive imagination in the contemporary theory of passive synthesis. They also agree that the modern theory of subjectivity must be surpassed by a comprehensive analysis of the passive dimension of subjectivity and ontology. Both philosophers also show that the thought of passivity raises anew the question: what is a subject?

NOTES

1. It has to be mentioned in the first place the positive appraisal of Husserl's treatment of the concept of "multiplicity" in the IV chapter of *Difference and Repetition*, trans. Paul Patton (New York: Columbia University Press, 1994), 182.

2. See Immanuel Kant, *Critique of Pure Reason*, trans. Paul Guyer and Allen W. Wood (New York: Cambridge University Press, 1998), 305, 435 (190, A 387).

3. Edmund Husserl, *Analyses Concerning Passive and Active Synthesis: Lectures on Transcendental Logic*, trans. Anthony J. Steinbock (Dordrecht/Boston/London: Kluwer, 2001), 410.

4. Husserl, *Analyses Concerning Passive and Active Synthesis*, 411.

5. See Iso Kern, *Husserl und Kant. Eine Untersuchung über Husserls Verhältnis zu Kant und zum Neukantianismus* (Den Haag: M. Nijhoff, 1964), 63.

6. This Husserlian thesis is however not new. In fact, a similar interpretation can be traced back to the early reception of the *Critique of Pure Reason*. In his 1789 *Versuch über die Transcendentalphilosophie*, Salomon Maimon—whom Deleuze holds in high regard—asserts: "Kant claims that sensibility and understanding are two completely different faculties. But I argue that an infinite thinking being must think them as one and the same power [*Kraft*] despite the fact that we must represent them as two different faculties in I us, and that for us sensibility is incomplete understanding." Salomon Maimon, *Essay on Transcendental Philosophy*, trans. Nick Midgley, Henry Somers-Hall, Alistair Welchman, and Merten Reglitz (New York: Continuum, 2010), 181. The German term within square brackets is added.

7. Gilles Deleuze (1978, March 28), *Cours Vincennes*. Retrieved from https://www.webdeleuze.com/textes/68.

8. Deleuze, *Difference and Repetition*, 85.

9. Deleuze, *Difference and Repetition*, 86.

10. See Claudia Jáuregui, *Sentido interno y subjetividad. Un análisis del problema del auto-conocimiento en la filosofía trascendental de Kant* (Buenos Aires: Prometeo, 2008), 73.

11. Gilles Deleuze (1978, March 21), *Cours Vincennes*. Retrieved from https://www.webdeleuze.com/textes/67.

12. Deleuze (1978, March 21), *Cours Vincennes*.

13. Husserl, *Analyses Concerning Passive and Active Synthesis*, 171.

14. Jáuregui, *Sentido interno y subjetividad*, 87.

15. Husserl, *Analyses Concerning Passive and Active Synthesis*, 171.

16. In recent years, an intense debate on the objective character of immanent time has toke place among the Husserlian scholars. See Dan Zahavi, *Self-Awareness and Alterity: A Phenomenological Investigation* (Evanston, IL: Northwestern University Press, 1999) and John Brough's *Notes on the Absolute Time-Consciousness* (in Dieter Lohmar and Ichiro Yamaguchi (Comp.), *On Time—New Contribution to the Husserlian Phenomenology of Time*, Dordrecht, Heidelberg, New York: Springer, 2010). There is also a special issue of *Husserl Studies* on this subject: Volumen 27, N° 1 (2011).

17. Edmund Husserl, *On the Phenomenology of the Consciousness of Internal Time (1893–1917)*, trans. John Barnet Brough (Norwell, MA: Kluwer Boston, 1991), 84.

18. Husserl, *On the Phenomenology of the Consciousness of Internal Time*, 89.

19. Gilles Deleuze, *Logic of Sense*, trans. Mark Lester (London: Athlone Press, 1990), 106, emphasis original.

20. Deleuze, *Logic of Sense*, 106.

21. Deleuze, *Logic of Sense*, 98.

22. Deleuze, *Logic of Sense*, 103.

23. With regard to the identification between cogito and consciousness: "We cannot think of the condition in the image of the conditioned. The task of a philosophy which does not wish to fall into the trap of consciousness and the cogito is to purge the transcendental field of all resemblance" (*Logic of Sense*, 123); on the identification among person, consciousness and subject: "an impersonal transcendental field, not having the form of a synthetic personal consciousness or a subjective identity—with the subject, on the contrary, being always constituted" (ibid., 98/99); and, finally, with respect to the human character of subject: "As for the subject of this new discourse (except that there is no longer any subject), it is not man or God, and even less man in the place of God" (ibid., 107).

24. See in this volume Verónica Kretschel's "Time and Representation: Husserlian Echoes in the Development of the Temporal Synthesis."

25. Deleuze, *Difference and Repetition*, 78–79. The French term within square brackets is added.

26. Deleuze, *Logic of Sense*, 102. The text within square brackets is added.

27. Deleuze, *Logic of Sense*, 103.
28. Deleuze, *Logic of Sense*, 103.
29. Husserl, *On the Phenomenology of the Consciousness of Internal Time*, 123.
30. Edmund Husserl, *Logische Untersuchungen. Zweiter Teil. Untersuchungen zur Phänomenologie und Theorie der Erkenntnis. In zwei Bänden* (The Hague: Martinus Nijhoff, 1984), 363.
31. Deleuze, *Logic of Sense*, 115.

BIBLIOGRAPHY

Deleuze, Gilles. *Cours Vincennes*. Retrieved from https://www.webdeleuze.com.
Deleuze, Gilles. *Difference and Repetition*. Translated by Paul Patton. New York: Columbia University Press, 1994.
Deleuze, Gilles. *Logic of Sense*. Translated by Mark Lester. London: Athlone Press, 1990.
Husserl, Edmund. *Analyses Concerning Passive and Active Synthesis*: *Lectures on Transcendental Logic*. Translated by Anthony J. Steinbock. Dordrecht/Boston/London: Kluwer, 2001
Husserl, Edmund. *On the Phenomenology of the Consciousness of Internal Time (1893–1917)*.Translated by Barnett Brough. Norwell, MA: Kluwer Boston, 1991.
Jáuregui, Claudia. *Sentido interno y subjetividad. Un análisis del problema del autoconocimiento en la filosofía trascendental de Kant*. Buenos Aires: Prometeo, 2008.
Kant, Immanuel. *Critique of Pure Reason*. Translated by Paul Guyer and Allen W. Wood. New York: Cambridge University Press, 1998.
Kern, Iso. *Husserl und Kant. Eine Untersuchung über Husserls Verhältnis zu Kant und zum Neukantianismus*. The Hague: M. Nijhoff, 1964.
Lohmar, Dieter and Ichiro Yamaguchi, eds. *On Time—New Contribution to the Husserlian Phenomenology of Time*. Dordrecht, Heidelberg, New York: Springer, 2010.
Maimon, Salomon. *Essay on Transcendental Philosophy*. Translated by Nick Midgley, Henry Somers-Hall, Alistair Welchman, and Merten Reglitz. New York: Continuum, 2010.
Zahavi, Dan. *Self-Awareness and Alterity: A Phenomenological Investigation*. Evanston, IL: Northwestern University Press, 1999.

Section III

AT THE END OF LANGUAGE

Chapter 9

Double Death and Intensity in *Difference and Repetition*

Solange Heffesse

INTRODUCTION

Maurice Blanchot (1907–2003) and Gilles Deleuze (1925–1995) are two of the most prominent figures of contemporary French thought. As diverse as they are with regard to their styles of writing and methodological approaches to philosophy, nonetheless their works share some vital philosophical concerns. Throughout his fragmentary works, his theoretical writings, and his fiction, Blanchot, a thinker of silence, impossibility, and disaster, reflects on the being of language and on the bond between writing literature and the experience of death. Deleuze comments that on those pages "you live in the irrespirable. Hence, Blanchot's fascination with the madness of Hölderlin, with Artaud, etc."[1] Perhaps that is why Deleuze gives the impression of stressing the distance between them (he being so often labeled as a thinker of merry affirmation and joy).[2] "I don't think we'll stay here for very long because it would be extremely sad. . . . But after all, Blanchot is not very cheerful,"[3] Deleuze jokes during his lessons on Foucault. In line with this comment, we can say that submerging in Blanchot's writings is an experience that confronts the reader with the irrespirable. Still, beyond that divergence of tonalities, there's no doubt that Blanchot's work is a reference for Deleuze, at the very least in terms of his critique of subjectivity.[4]

Deleuze highlights two of Blanchot's central concepts: on the one hand, the notion of the Outside, an image through which Blanchot points to the intrinsic relation—or non-relation—of thought with the unthought (which Deleuze turns into an image for the transcendental field in *Foucault* and in his works on Cinema).[5] On the other hand, there is Blanchot's development of the notion of death as *double*, presented in *The Space of Literature* (1955) and recovered by Deleuze in *Difference and Repetition* (1968).[6] This last point is important because it reveals the closeness between these two authors when it comes to the configuration of a non-personological philosophy in the French intellectual context of the time.[7] But it is also important because it proves how Blanchot makes an essential contribution to Deleuze's own views on death—which is a central problem in his work as well.[8] In Blanchot's texts, Deleuze finds a way to inquire about death that does not necessarily compromise him with Heideggerian approaches or categories (which have been determinant for the history of philosophy concerning that matter). We will examine the alliances that can be traced between both thinkers, focusing on Blanchot's discovery of death as double, and on how Deleuze integrates the alternative theorization of death into his ontology, especially in his characterization of the role of intensity.

The explicit references to *The Space of Literature* in *Difference and Repetition* are found in two sections of chapter IV, "The Work and Death's Space," where, according to Deleuze, Blanchot's core argument can be found. First, "Art, Suicide," where Blanchot shows how the suicide reveals that the desired death never coincides with the one that actually arrives, and second, "The Secret of Double Death" (the proper exposition of the impersonal death). In *Difference and Repetition*, the quotation can be found in chapter II, "Repetition for Itself," in the context of an argument against Freud on the death instinct and the bond between Eros and Thanatos, where Deleuze works his way toward the third synthesis of time, which is the mysterious synthesis of the future and the Eternal Return. The matter will be taken up again toward the end of chapter V, "Asymmetrical Synthesis of the Sensible," where Deleuze exposes the case of individuation in psychic systems. In this last section of chapter V, the notion of *intensity* takes on a double character. There is a tendency toward entropy and the canceling out of the characteristic differences of the extension, the visible face of death; and also, "the liberation and swarming of little differences" that intensity holds in an implicit state because in this individuation, death shows its invisible face.[9]

THE DOUBLE DEATH IN *THE SPACE OF LITERATURE*

Blanchot's work defies our thinking by creating and supporting a logic of impossibility that affirms the coexistence of heterogeneous ideas in order to deactivate every one of the mechanisms of dialectical opposition (presence/absence, inside/outside, etc.). The tensions between these concepts will be sustained and never annulled by means of a third "person" that is impersonal or neutral. This mark of style is present in the construction of *The Space of Literature*, a work that in an elliptic, progressive, and fragmentary way, "asks itself about the conditions of possibility of experience in writing."[10] Foucault traces the genesis of this thought of the impossible back to the paradox of Epimenides, which accounts for the fact that in Western literary fiction, language operates as "a passage to the 'outside,'" when it "escapes the mode of being of discourse—in other words, the dynasty of representation" and confronts Western philosophy with its own risk.[11] In Foucault's own words:

> The "subject" of literature (what speaks in it and what it speaks about) is less language in its positivity than the void that language takes as its space when it articulates itself in the nakedness of "I speak." . . . "I speak" runs counter to "I think." "I think" led to the indubitable certainty of the "I" and its existence; "I speak," on the other hand, distances, disperses, effaces that existence and lets only its empty emplacement appear. Thought about thought, an entire tradition wider than philosophy, has taught us that thought leads us to the deepest interiority. Speech about speech leads us, by way of literature as well as perhaps by other paths, to the outside in which the speaking subject disappears. No doubt, that is why Western thought took so long to think the being of language: as if it had a premonition of the danger that the naked experience of language poses for the self-evidence of "I think."[12]

Blanchot's thought is, according to Foucault, a thought of the Outside that evades the trap of interiority, and dismisses the traditional forms and categories of the Western philosophical reflection by standing "outside subjectivity, setting its limits as though from without, . . . and that, at the same time, stands at the threshold of all positivity . . . in order to regain the space of its unfolding, the void serving as its site, the distance in which it is constituted."[13]

Blanchot's point of departure in *The Space of Literature* can also be characterized by this sort of paradoxical movement of exclusion that is exposed to the void. He begins with the principle that "he who writes the work is set aside" from "his" work, toward which he irremissibly tends.[14] What the work as such requires of the writer is "that he loses everything he might construe as his own 'nature,' that he loses all character and that . . . he becomes the empty place where the impersonal affirmation emerges."[15] This requirement slowly approaches the topic of death. Blanchot will trace a parallel between the writer's relation with his work and man's relation with death, both imbued with that simultaneously impossible and irresistible tension. Writing and death will never cease to be inseparably united. On this ground, the experience of the creative process will find itself bonded to the vital dispositions of the writer toward death. In chapter IV of *The Space of Literature*, Blanchot examines the experiences of Kafka, Rilke, and Mallarmé under this light.

In the first of the sections quoted by Deleuze ("On suicide"), we again find the parallel between writer-work and man-death. According to Blanchot, what defines suicide is that it is about "a strange and contradictory undertaking," an "effort to act where immeasurable passivity reigns, this striving to maintain the rules . . . to fix a goal in a movement that escapes all aims and all resolution."[16] However, this tension between extreme passivity and demand—which tends to turn death into an act—leads at the same time to a transfiguration of action, "as if to reduce death to the level of a project were a unique opportunity to elevate the project toward that which exceeds it."[17] Such madness, says Blanchot, is only shared by that of the artist, who can be said to be "linked to the work in the same strange way in which the man who takes death for a goal is linked to death."[18] The work and the projected death are instances that imply the *I* at the same time that they radically exclude it. And in the very same way that the one who writes is thus expelled from the work, we cannot die death, which is made explicit by the fact that no one can say about himself "I die." The Blanchotian ambiguity of the "double death" is already operating in this analysis of suicide: the substantive, "death," as a fatal event that takes place in time, is distinguished from the verb "to die," which designates the aspect of death that cannot be appropriated, which can never be said to be "mine."

From that, tension between activity and passivity derives the critique of the notion of possibility. Blanchot says that both movements—that of the suicidal man and that of the author—"involve a power that wants to be power even in the region of the ungraspable, where the domain of goals ends."[19] How can this act be described in terms of action or activity when dying is an endless movement by which death never ceases to arrive? It happens that suicide shows an unfolding of the *I*: that *I*, which acts sovereignly to conjure and exclude death from future uncertainty, confuses visible death with invisible death by ignoring that "the one who is thus struck is no longer I, but another."[20] This means that death, even wanted and sought death, death in its empirical aspect (its visible face: the physical disappearance of the person), in the end "always comes from without."[21]

Here Blanchot criticizes the idea of death as man's "ownmost" or most extreme "possibility": a structural moment that, in some way, would arrive to complete life, closing its sense as a whole. This is the discussion with Heidegger. There are certainly many affinities between them, but here Blanchot tries to take his own mortuary philosophy away from the issue of authenticity. And Deleuze will quote, precisely, two sections where Heidegger is called into question. In contrast with this idea of possibility, Blanchot's writing will gradually construct a lattice of notions connected with the idea of *impossibility*, in order to describe the non-relation that is characteristic of dying:

> The act of dying itself constitutes this leap, the empty depth of the beyond. It is the fact of dying that includes a radical reversal, through which the death that was the extreme form of my power not only becomes what loosens my hold upon myself by casting me out of my power to begin and even to finish, but also

becomes that which is without any relation to me, without power over me—that which is stripped of all possibility—the unreality of the indefinite. I cannot represent this reversal to myself, I cannot even conceive of it as definitive. It is not the irreversible step beyond which there would be no return, for it is that which is not accomplished, the interminable and the incessant.[22]

I quote this long fragment because it constitutes the first part of the quotation that Deleuze takes up.[23] According to Blanchot, the uttermost form of my power is at the same time what has the least relation to me in a reversal that transforms a power that is "mine" into a force or potency that excludes the *I* and eludes any form of representation. Whereas for Heidegger, *Dasein* can understand itself as open and "pure possibility" only insofar as its existence is correlative with an authentic or "proper" death, the impossible of Blanchotian impersonality turns life and death into something indiscernible, as it makes death enter life as a *power* or potency that transmutes action and transforms or contaminates life, and not like a mere external "possibility."[24] On the other hand, the unfathomableness of dying, its impossibility, Blanchot says, lies not in a future and unknown "beyond," but in that leap which is in itself a void. In temporal terms, it would be that which lacks presence: it is not an event in the world and it has no duration at all. Dying is what is not accomplished, "the unreality of the indefinite," "the part of this event which its accomplishment cannot realize," is the invisible face of death.[25]

The second section Deleuze cites is framed by Blanchot's analysis of the life and work of Rilke (1875–1926), which we will briefly retrieve. For Blanchot, Rilke's work presents a transit between two stances: from "dying faithful to oneself" to "dying faithful to death." At first, Rilke commits to the search for an authentic death, a death that singles out the man who lives immersed in the anonymity of the great cities: a death that "makes sense" at a personal level with the lived life. But this way, where art is presented as "the road toward myself," will progressively turn, in his late production, toward a "point where, within myself, I belong to the outside . . . where I am no longer myself, where if I speak it is not I who speak."[26] From that point onward, a different kind of closeness with death is established. "Dying . . . will be to escape death," a transmutation accomplished in us by death itself.[27] Dying brings into play a power of metamorphosis that operates in us when we adopt a negligent attitude toward death, in which we set apart everything we are supposed to do before it (fear it, cling to things, etc.).[28]

According to Blanchot, this second moment in Rilke's work is characterized by the introduction of the impersonal, which must not be understood as something *improper*—as that anonymous death Rilke initially avoided. "The impersonality toward which death tends . . . is ideal. It is above the person: not the brutality of a fact or the randomness of chance, but the volatilization of the very fact of death."[29] Blanchot will then claim that Rilke's strategy looks for the invisible or impersonal death as if it were a "pure death," by establishing a parallel with the ecstatic experience of the artist's gaze: a disinterested gaze in regard to things.[30] The effort "to raise death to itself, to make the point where it loses itself within itself coincide with the point at which I lose myself outside of myself," coincides with the work of the poet, who, by depriving things of their utility, wants to "raise things themselves to a point of greater reality and truth."[31]

The question that governs Rilke's efforts after his embrace of the notion of impersonal death would be: "What must one do to die without betraying this high power, death?"[32] One possible path is to start from things themselves, since it is "by turning authentically toward them that we learn to turn toward the invisible."[33] However, it seems that to "turn toward the intimacy of things—to 'see' them truly, with the disinterested gaze of him who does not cleave to himself" one must depart from the profundity of death.[34] But then again, how is it possible to render impersonal death as a point of departure? It is at this point that Blanchot picks up the idea of a volatilization that Rilke performs in his attempt to purify death of its brutality: death turns into the invisible, the absolute indetermination. The Rilkean disposition of acceptance or poetic opening toward death is usually linked to Heidegger's philosophy, a link that Blanchot finds in the use of the image of the anemone as a symbol of the Open—that privileged field of manifestation or access to the truth of being in its purity (in contrast to which the Blanchotian notion of the Outside seems to be forged).[35] According to Blanchot, this is, however, a very comfortable idea, a tranquilizing promise "which takes such care not to threaten our faith in the oneness of being," and which still remains between the poles of the authentic and the inauthentic.[36]

The unexpected twist is that even despite the tranquilizing promises of Rilke himself, in his work one is confronted by the dreadful "death as abyss . . . absence and the loss of all foundation."[37] Death is purified from the random character of a brutal event, and unfolds into "that which is not even an event," the invisible part of the event "which its accomplishment cannot realize."[38] We once again find the Blanchotian challenge of holding us in the line of impossibility, since the "doubleness" of death does not deny either of its meanings, but rather affirms them simultaneously. Hence, the connection between contraries with which Blanchot closes this section, holding that the perspective of the double death admits of no "being *for* death," since "it does not have the solidity which would sustain such a relation."[39] Rilke's impersonal death ultimately expresses the profundity by which it is "not the term, but the interminable, not proper but featureless death, and not true death but, as Kafka says, 'the sneer of its capital error.' "[40]

But let us go back to a previous fragment, in which Blanchot reintroduces the temporal dimension of the problem by expanding on the idea of the impersonal death as a part of the event "which its accomplishment cannot realize."[41]

> When the force upon which he makes everything depend is detached from the moment when it has the reality of the last instant, it escapes him and escapes us constantly. It is inevitable but inaccessible death; it is the abyss of the present, time without a present, with which I have no relationships; it is that toward which I cannot go forth, for in it I do not die, I have fallen from the power to die. In it *she* dies; *she* does not cease, and *she* does not finish dying.[42]

When citing this text, Deleuze introduces a subtle modification: where Blanchot writes *elle* (for "death"), Deleuze put into brackets *lui*, "him."[43] Who? Time. That is what Deleuze's emphasizes. Which sort of time? One that is detached from the time of the instant, the time without present to which Blanchot refers: "neither present nor past but always coming, the source of an incessant multiple adventure in a persistent question."[44] With this torsion of the text, Deleuze allows himself to transfer the features of Blanchotian impersonality into the third synthesis of time: synthesis of the future detached from the course of time (neither destiny nor the "living present" which follows in the succession of presents); the pure form of time abstracted from every content, the time of the ungrounding, of Thanatos and the Eternal Return. The Rilkean time of dying is, for Blanchot, a threshold through which the impersonal transmutes life by depersonalizing it, the Eternal Return will be for Deleuze a power that affirms "only the excessive and the unequal," "the secret coherence which establishes itself only by excluding my own coherence, my own identity, the identity of the self, the world and God."[45]

THE TWO FACES OF DEATH IN *DIFFERENCE AND REPETITION*

Death unfolds into a personal and an impersonal face, one that is visible and one that is invisible, "two incommensurable faces" that cannot coincide even in suicide.[46] Deleuze recovers Blanchot's proposal in two discussions at two different moments of *Difference and Repetition*, and around two concepts in his ontology: the third synthesis of time and the concept of *intensity*. The first of these discussions goes against the Freudian conception of the death drive. Deleuze is interested in recovering the approach to death as an "instinct"—Thanatos, a figure which presides over the third synthesis—but he thinks that Freud was wrong in not considering the double sense of death discovered by

Blanchot. Freud conceives of death only as a return to inanimate matter, as "the personal disappearance of the person, the annihilation of *this* difference represented by the I or the ego," that is, the death which comes from the outside and is empirical, representable, calculable.[47] Second, Deleuze discusses common sense as established by thermodynamics, which institutes entropy as the only figure of death.[48] In this discussion, Deleuze pretends to "rescue" intensity—"the form of difference in so far as this is the reason of the sensible"—from this supposedly fatal destiny of entropy.[49]

Deleuze turns to the empirical principles of thermodynamics as a way to approach the sense that intensity will have in his ontology. He will face the problem of entropy that, by its own nature, tends to nullify every difference.[50] However, Deleuze will try to show that entropy is only the visible face of death, and that intensity is not reducible to the qualities and extensions it creates. Intensity "explicates," it unfolds itself in order to create them, but some of its potential always remains "unexplained." This is the second movement of intensity, movement of implication by which it "remains implicated in itself and continues to envelop difference."[51] Deleuze will then say: "The essential process of intensive quantities is individuation. Intensity is individuating, and intensive quantities are individuating factors."[52] Following Simondon's theory, Deleuze describes individuation as the process of actualization of a potential by which every individual remains "attached to a pre-individual half which is not the impersonal within it so much as the reservoir of its singularities."[53] Individuation is the act or the process that intensity moves through. In these processes, entropy operates as an empirical principle of degradation. "The law of explication remains the cancellation of productive difference," but only of explication, as entropy can never account for the creation or evolution of a system of individuations.[54] Deleuze develops this idea through the exposition of what would be the "result" of individuation (the physical, biological, and psychic "systems").

It is not a coincidence that the reference to Blanchot's double death reappears during the analysis of the individuation of psychic systems.[55] In accord with the Blanchotian spirit, the theory of individuation shows that the psychic has little to do with the I—the *Je*, as "the quality of human being as a species," "the universal form of psychic life" crystalized in identity—or with the Self—the *Moi*, "the properly psychic organism," "the universal matter of that form [. . .] constituted by a continuity of resemblances."[56] It does not have to do with the *moi* either, that is, the set of thousands of larval, passive *I*'s, that in contracting habits lay at the basis of the temporal passive synthesis.[57] Those are forms that imprison the power of individuating elements. In psychic individuation, we find two deaths. Death as entropy, accidental and violent: "the cancellation of difference in a system of explication, or the degradation which compensates for the processes of differentiation."[58] It is

Spinoza's external death, the empirical death of that which exists in extension. The other face is death as "a 'death instinct,' an internal power that frees the individuating elements from the form of the I or the matter of the self in which they are imprisoned."[59] That second death is Thanatos: impersonal death as a transcendental instinct, immanent drive, internal to the processes of individuation which liberate that which is implicated in intensity, ungraspable by the universal form of the I and by the matter of the Self, which are in turn dissolved to give place to individuations. Thus, the elements of Blanchot's theory that we have seen are gathered in an original Deleuzian synthesis:

> It would be wrong to confuse the two faces of death, as though the death instinct were reduced to a tendency towards increasing entropy or a return to inanimate matter. Every death is double, and represents the cancellation of large differences in extension as well as the liberation and swarming of little differences in intensity. Freud suggested the following hypothesis: the organism wants to die, but to die in its own way, so that real death always presents itself as a foreshortening, as possessing an accidental, violent and external character which is anathema to the internal will-to-die. There is a necessary non-correspondence between death as an empirical event and death as an "instinct" or transcendental instance. Freud and Spinoza are both right: one with regard to the instinct, the other with regard to the event. Desired from within, death always comes from without in a passive and accidental form. Suicide is an attempt to make the two incommensurable faces coincide or correspond. However, the two sides do not meet, and every death remains double. On the one hand, it is a "de-differenciation" which compensates for the differenciations of the I and the Self in an overall system which renders these uniform; on the other hand, it is a matter of individuation, a protest by the individual which has never recognized itself within the limits of the Self and the I, even where these are universal.[60]

Entropy is no longer the tragic universal destiny because there is always "a 'one dies' more profound than 'I die,'" that tingling of little differences as intensive power of transformation and dissolution of forms.[61] In individuation, the death of the "one" enters life as a power of transformation.

The web of notions that we have been studying show the fruitful relation between Deleuzian and Blanchotian thoughts, and reveal at least one point where each approach, each with his own style, a thought of the Outside. This Outside no longer asks about the conditions of enlightenment or access to the truth of being of entity. It does not search for the way of preserving faith in the unity of being and leaves behind the anxious and, in the end, humanist mood of the Heideggerian question of authenticity. Blanchot's Outside is a wandering word. It begins by considering the being of a language that abolishes itself in literature, pointing out the failure of Western metaphysics; later, it is associated with the obscurity, the night, the inaccessible, the impossible. . . . That which goes away from the lighting of truth. Deleuze's interpretation is based in this inversion made by Blanchot, since the Outside for him is also partly a mortal line. But the question is, can one conceive some other movement which moves away from that of mortality? Can the Outside be something that drives thought toward a way of thinking that for Blanchot remained unthinkable?

NOTES

1. Gilles Deleuze, "Lecture of April 22th, 1986," http://www2.univ-paris8.fr/deleuze/article.php3.
2. See Andrew Culp, *Dark Deleuze* (Minneapolis: University of Minnesota Press, 2016), 1–8.
3. Gilles Deleuze, "Lecture of April 22th, 1986."
4. If we can say that Deleuze could be confused with a priest of joy, as Peter Pál Pelbart puts it (*Filosofía de la deserción. Nihilismo, locura y comunidad*, trans. S. García Navarro and A. Bracony, Buenos Aires: Tinta limón, 2016, 8), Blanchot in turn is death's herald, and his writing style reflects the density of that irrespirable atmosphere, a ceaseless, anguished movement through which the ideas he poses are progressively constructed—in an entirely different style from Deleuze's.
5. For an incisive analysis of Deleuze's use of the Blanchotian image of the Outside in relation to cinema, see Marie-Claire Ropars Wuilleumier, "Image or Time? The Thought of the Outside in The Time-Image (Deleuze and Blanchot)," in *Afterimages of Gilles Deleuze's Film Philosophy*, ed. David Rodowick (Minneapolis: University of Minnesota Press, 2010), 5–30.
6. Maurice Blanchot, *The Space of Literature*, trans. Ann Smock (Lincoln: University of Nebraska Press, 1989). Gilles Deleuze, *Difference and Repetition*, trans. Paul Patton (New York: Columbia University Press, 1994).
7. Deleuze deals with this issue in his lessons on Foucault, differentiating between a current of thought that leads toward a "personology," and another one where the impersonal, the neuter, the ungraspable aspects of experience, eluding the categories of representation, become a point of departure. Blanchot, Foucault, and Deleuze himself belong to this second current. Deleuze points out that Blanchot is the first to initiate a double reaction against the dominant "personology" of his contemporaries. Blanchotian developments on the French pronoun *On*, the neuter and the third person/non-person as irreducible to the defined pronoun counteract the personalistic tendency that Deleuze paradigmatically finds in Benveniste and in psychoanalysis. According to Deleuze, Foucault would deal with the impersonal at the three dimensions in which his work can be divided: knowledge, power, and subjectivation. One could say that they refer to different effectuations of the pronoun *On*: *on parle, on voit, on lutte, on résiste, on meurt*. See Gilles Deleuze, "Lecture of April 22th, 1986."
8. For instance, this is pointed out by David Lapoujade, who characterizes Deleuze's thought as a vitalism with a mortalistic background (*Deleuze, les mouvements aberrants*, Paris: Minuit, 2014).
9. Deleuze, *Difference and Repetition*, 259.

10. Anna Poca, "Prólogo a la edición española: de la literatura como experiencia anónima del pensamiento," in *El espacio literario*, by Maurice Blanchot, trans. V. Palant and J. Jinkis (Buenos Aires: Paidós, 1969), 15.

11. Michel Foucault, "The Thought of the Outside," in *Aesthetics, Method, and Epistemology* (Essential Works of Foucault 1954–1984, Vol. 2), ed. James D. Faubion, trans. Robert Hurley (New York: The New Press, 1998), 148–49. This article was originally published in 1966, and it is very likely that it acted as mediation in the Deleuzian interpretation of Blanchot.

12. Foucault, "The Thought of the Outside," 149.
13. Foucault, "The Thought of the Outside," 150.
14. Blanchot, *The Space of Literature*, 20.
15. Blanchot, *The Space of Literature*, 54.
16. Blanchot, *The Space of Literature*, 104.
17. Blanchot, *The Space of Literature*, 104.
18. Blanchot, *The Space of Literature*, 104.
19. Blanchot, *The Space of Literature*, 105.
20. Blanchot, *The Space of Literature*, 106.
21. Deleuze, *Difference and Repetition*, 113. Deleuze retrieves the Spinozist view of death as always being the result of a "bad encounter" that decomposes an individual's characteristic relation.
22. Blanchot, *The Space of Literature*, 105.
23. Deleuze, *Difference and Repetition*, 112.
24. See Noelia Billi, "'Quien muere en el mundo sin razón . . .' Lecturas blanchotianas en torno a la muerte en Rilke," *Daimon. Revista Internacional de Filosofía* 57 (2012): 35–50.
25. Blanchot, *The Space of Literature*, 154.
26. Blanchot, *The Space of Literature*, 155.
27. Blanchot, *The Space of Literature*, 145, 147.
28. Blanchot, *The Space of Literature*, 146.
29. Blanchot, *The Space of Literature*, 148.
30. Blanchot, *The Space of Literature*, 148.
31. Blanchot, *The Space of Literature*, 149.
32. Blanchot, *The Space of Literature*, 127.
33. Blanchot, *The Space of Literature*, 152.
34. Blanchot, *The Space of Literature*, 152.
35. In regard to this image, Cragnolini holds that there is, in the Heideggerian conception of being-toward-death ("the existenciary that points towards the most proper property of Dasein"), a point in which the Heideggerian pretension of overcoming Western metaphysics as centered in the subject reveals its shortcomings, by affirming a privilege of one's own death over the death of the other: "We could say that Dasein, as openness, is the anemone that needs to return to its own shell so that it can—in that domain of 'return to itself'—assume its own finitude. In that 'closing,' the other seems annulled, forgotten, and the death that one must assume is one's own." Mónica Cragnolini, "Temblores del pensar: Nietzsche, Blanchot, Derrida," *Pensamiento de los Confines*, Buenos Aires, n° 12, junio de 2003, 11–119.

Last accessed April 15, 2017. http://redaprenderycambiar.com.ar/derrida/comentarios/temblores.html.

36. Blanchot, *The Space of Literature*, 153.
37. Blanchot, *The Space of Literature*, 153.
38. Blanchot, *The Space of Literature*, 154.
39. Blanchot, *The Space of Literature*, 154.
40. Blanchot, *The Space of Literature*, 154.
41. Blanchot, *The Space of Literature*, 154.
42. Blanchot, *The Space of Literature*, 153–54 (translation modified).
43. "It is inevitable but inaccessible death; it is the abyss of the present, time without a present, with which I have no relationships; it is that toward which I cannot go forth, for in it I do not die, I have fallen from the power to die. In it they die; they do not cease, and they do not finish dying." Deleuze, *Difference and Repetition*, 112.
44. Deleuze, *Difference and Repetition*, 112.
45. Deleuze, *Difference and Repetition*, 115, 90–91.
46. Deleuze, *Difference and Repetition*, 259.
47. Deleuze, *Difference and Repetition*, 113, emphasis original.
48. Entropy is the universal tendency to the annihilation of the differences of intensity that lay as the basis of physical phenomena: an irreversible process of degradation of energy in time that follows the paradigm of caloric energy. "This is the most general content of the principles of Carnot, Curie, Le Chatelier, *et al.*: difference is the suffcient [*sic*] reason of change only to the extent that the change tends to negate difference [. . .], like an 'arrow of time,' from more to less differenciated, from a productive to a reduced difference, and ultimately to a cancelled difference" (Deleuze, *Difference and Repetition*, 223).
49. Deleuze, *Difference and Repetition*, 222.
50. See Deleuze, *Difference and Repetition*, 223.
51. Deleuze, *Difference and Repetition*, 240.
52. Deleuze, *Difference and Repetition*, 246.
53. Deleuze, *Difference and Repetition*, 246. Deleuze seems to establish a distinction between the pre-individual, which is virtual, with respect to the impersonal, which as we have seen relates to intensity.
54. Deleuze, *Difference and Repetition*, 255.
55. This is a moment in which Deleuze comes back to the critic to the subject from the perspective of the sensibility-intensity, having already gone through that theme in previous chapters of the book from multiple viewpoints (for example, time, the Idea, or the Image of thought).
56. Deleuze, *Difference and Repetition*, 257.
57. See Deleuze, *Difference and Repetition*, 78–79.
58. Deleuze, *Difference and Repetition*, 259, emphasis added.
59. Deleuze, *Difference and Repetition*, 259.
60. Deleuze, *Difference and Repetition*, 259.
61. Deleuze, *Difference and Repetition*, 113.

BIBLIOGRAPHY

Billi, Noelia. "'Quien muere en el mundo sin razón . . .' Lecturas blanchotianas en torno a la muerte en Rilke." *Daimon. Revista Internacional de Filosofía* 57 (2012): 35–50.

Blanchot, Maurice. *The Space of Literature*. Translated by Ann Smock. Lincoln: University of Nebraska Press, 1989.

Culp, Andrew. *Dark Deleuze*. Minneapolis: University of Minnesota Press, 2016.

Deleuze, Gilles. "Lecture of April 22th, 1986." http://www2.univ-paris8.fr/deleuze/article.php3.

Deleuze, Gilles. *Difference and Repetition*. Translated by Paul Patton. New York: Columbia University Press, 1994.

Foucault, Michel. "The Thought of the Outside." In *Aesthetics, Method, and Epistemology* (Essential Works of Foucault 1954–1984, Vol. 2), edited by James D. Faubion. Translated by Robert Hurley. New York: The New Press, 1998.

Lapoujade, David. *Deleuze, les mouvements aberrants*. Paris: Minuit, 2014.

Pál Pelbart, Peter. *Filosofía de la deserción. Nihilismo, locura y comunidad*. Translated by S. García Navarro and A. Bracony. Buenos Aires: Tinta limón, 2016.

Poca, Anna. "Prólogo a la edición española: de la literatura como experiencia anónima del pensamiento." In *El espacio literario*, by Maurice Blanchot. Translated by V. Palant and J. Jinkis. Buenos Aires: Paidós, 1969.

Ropars Wuilleumier, Peter. "Image or Time? The Thought of the Outside in the Time-Image (Deleuze and Blanchot)." In *Afterimages of Gilles Deleuze's Film Philosophy*, edited by David Rodowick. Minneapolis: University of Minnesota Press, 2010.

Chapter 10

Indirect Discourse and Ideology: Bakhtin in *A Thousand Plateaus*

Santiago Lo Vuolo

Translated by Emilio Vergara

Language is a form of expression that fulfills a social function: to transmit order-words (*mot d'ordre*, slogans). That is the thesis defended by Deleuze and Guattari in the fourth chapter of *A Thousand Plateaus*, "Postulates of Linguistics."[1] According to the authors, the various trends of Linguistics would have overlooked this simple fact and, therefore, reproduced the myth of representation in different ways. But the linguistic act, referring to social obedience, does not respond to an informative or communicative intention (the characteristic modes of representation in language). Enunciations, as order-words, are linked like voices within other voices, collective compositions that respond to *what is said* in a given social field. Given this condition, free indirect discourse (or free indirect style) is not just another linguistic type but the "first determination of language." In fact, in the form of this discourse, in which different enunciations come into relation, the authors find the law of the "translative movement proper to language"; its condition, the modality of all speech.[2] The privilege of representation in language fades: its pattern will never be given to us by a designation of states of things or by a structured meaning that we should locate somewhere "before" practice itself, in an objective or subjective instance that would explain the pragmatic one. A pragmatics of language implies the suppression of transcendent instances: there is, in the first place, no subject or interiority that expresses itself through signs. Neither are there linguistic forms available as codes for empirical use. There is only a relational flow of discursive practices (*statements-acts*), assemblages that determine *subjectivations of enunciation*.

Deleuze and Guattari consider the work *Marxism and the Philosophy of Language* to be a fundamental contribution to thinking language in a pragmatic way.[3] It is a work published in 1929 under the name of Valentin Voloshinov but later attributed to Mikhail Bakhtin.[4] The social approach to phenomenon, the critique of individualist perspectives, both those of the German school of idealistic subjectivism and those of the school based on Ferdinand de Saussure's ideas, and the thematization of the autonomy of free indirect discourse are the three elements that Deleuze and Guattari emphasize.

First of all, we will recover the meaning of the text by Bakhtin/Voloshinov as a source of *A Thousand Plateaus*. We will then see a point of confrontation between the two theories, which the French authors themselves discern, although they do so in an enigmatic way that is up to us to reconstruct.

THE LINGUISTIC FORM OF EXPRESSION IN BAKHTIN/VOLOSHINOV

Voloshinov starts with a simple question: is ideology a phenomenon of consciousness, a "false consciousness," as Marx and Engels postulate in some texts? To answer this, he considers that if the ideological circulates in the word, ideology is an objective structure, not a subjective one. It is a material instance. The irreducibly social nature of ideology prevents it from being limited to the psychological sphere. Consciousness is, rather, an effect of language, since it appears after, and not before the semiotic material.[5] It is in the social interaction—in the ideological content that circulates—that consciousness becomes consciousness. The affirmation does not avoid the circular paradox: language makes social interaction; social interaction makes language.

Voloshinov considers that in the main trends of Linguistics, and in the Marxist theory of ideology, there is a predominance of a subjectivist position. We therefore lose sight of the material and objective nature of language. This is the case with the explicitly subjectivist theories of Vossler, Spitzer, and others, which postulate as the foundation of language "the individual and creative act of discourse" and describes the movement of language as a sort of expression of the interior in the exterior.[6] It is a remnant of German romanticism that cannot account for the priority of the social over the private.

On the other hand, in the first decades of the twentieth century, de Saussure's abstract objectivist theory gained ground. Objectivism is in this case *abstract* and not *material* because it is based on the determination of an object of study that is in itself abstract: the system of language "as a system of phonetic, grammatical and lexical forms."[7] These forms are constructed as objects of study by abstracting the social life of language, which Voloshinov calls "discursive interaction." The act of enunciation is thus lost. Saussure determines *la Langue* and not *le Parole* as object of study. Moreover, in pure abstract objectivity, signs are conventional and arbitrary: there is no necessary relationship between meaning and signifier. But from the historical materialist point of view, for the social approach of Marxism, the sign is not arbitrary: it is determined in the enunciation as the basis of the generation of discourse, in the flow of linguistic interrelation, in the continuous dialogue that is the experience of language.

This criticism gains strength when it becomes a demonstration of the potential of the focus on the social dimension of language, on collective enunciation. And its application will be an exercise in the study of syntax.

TRANSMISSION OF ANOTHER SPEAKER'S SPEECH SYNTAX

In the syntax, the irreducibility of language to internal elements of language, or to internal characters of the subject that expresses itself, becomes especially evident. Voloshinov asserts that "traditional principles and methods in linguistics" cannot deal with the syntax of enunciation.[8] Linguistics can study, at most, the syntax of a sentence, but not of the enunciation, which is a living phenomenon linked to social, dynamic circumstances of verbal interaction. This entire aspect is only seen in enunciation, which leads us to linguistic limits, to the consideration of *extraverbal* elements.

To illustrate the "elementary" character of all linguistic categories, Voloshinov says, "One need only take any finished utterance [. . .] consisting of a single word": what happens is that, if we make use of the linguistic categories, we will be able to define the word as an element of the language, characterizing it phonetically, morphologically and even syntactically as a sentence, but we will not be able to realize what makes that word a complete enunciation.[9] Certainly, what makes it a meaningful enunciation and gives it its syntactic form is not something found in the abstract system of language, but rather in discursive interaction. This instance is described by Voloshinov as an extraverbal situation in which the word is connected with a social totality. It is something that is outside the limited, elementary, linguistic approach, and is therefore considered to be something supplementary, aggregate. Deleuze and Guattari, we will see later, take this criticism and reformulate it in their own terms: linguistics, searching for constants in a system of signs, cannot account for these variables, that is, for the variations that make up the sense of an enunciation. These variations are not elements of language, and yet they are the basis of the syntax of the enunciation. Voloshinov would say that the social approach to language can indeed account for the instance that, in the linguistics of the elements of language, would be a mystery, an *aporia*, an empty place of theory.

This proposal becomes effective in the study of reported or transmitted speech. The method is thus applied to the problem of syntax, since reporting the word of another requires performing connections of subordination, coordination, and so on.

Voloshinov describes styles of transmission of another's discourse and even different models (direct, indirect, free indirect, or quasi-direct discourse) and modalities of those models. Each of these forms responds to ideological questions: modes of social behavior, historical trends, and attitudes toward the other. Certainly, the way in which we structure our discourse always responds to the consideration we have of our listener/reader; whether we report their discourse or whether we aim to be clear, convincing, and so forth.

Voloshinov distinguishes two styles of transmission of the word of the other, characteristic of certain periods of Russian literature, in which influences from other cultures are revealed:[10]

- A *linear* style, which focuses on conveying the theme of someone else's discourse, and therefore makes use mostly of direct discourse, that is, of textual quotation.
- A *picturesque* style, which emphasizes the form of the reported discourse. Here the contours between the author's discourse and the other's discourse become less clear. Indirect discourse forms are used to convey not only the content of his words but the emotional, aesthetic, and so on, background of his discourse. In this style, a different form from the previous ones may appear, although it is frequently confused with some of them: *free indirect discourse*.

THE AUTONOMY OF FREE INDIRECT DISCOURSE

This third model of transmission of another speaker's discourse is a literary style that can reach high degrees of experimentation, but is also formulated in simple ways, and its peculiarity can be unnoticed. Let's look at an example:

> I told her that this trip was dangerous and that his behavior was risky. But she was not born yesterday, she would avoid all dangers, she would know how to take precautions. I wasn't convinced by all her arguments.[11]

Following Voloshinov's analysis, it should be noted, first of all, that here both author and character are speaking at the same time. The voice of the narrator incorporates the voice of another character without introducing a direct quotation or indirectly expressing what has been said or thought by the other. Rather, we are faced with "a single linguistic construction within which the accents of two differently oriented voices are maintained."[12] How do we understand this conjunction of diverse orientations? Some studies reviewed by Voloshinov have tried to simplify their specificity, considering that it is a simple mixture or sum of forms. However, what is important for Voloshinov is that we are being witnesses of "a completely new, positive tendency in active reception of another person's utterance, a *special direction* in which the dynamics of the interrelationship between reporting and reported speech moves."[13] It is, as we said, a new form of transmission of the discourse of the other, and therefore of the perception of his or her voice, and his or her orientation. In this style, it is frequent for the narrator to introduce or let slip his own valuations—of contempt or suspicion, of relativization—when transmitting the perspective of the character.

On the other hand, it may help to accentuate the peculiarity of free indirect discourse by noting the difficulty in transmitting it phonically, with our voice.[14] The evaluative interference, so common in the new narrative—Dostoyevsky as the greatest exponent—is impossible to transmit phonically. A silent reading becomes the new register of prose: "Only this 'silencing' of prose could have made possible the multi-leveledness and voice-defying complexity of intonational structures that are so characteristic of modern literature."[15] Certainly, it becomes very difficult to intone with expressive value the permanent sway between the axiological (evaluative) horizon of the author and the horizon of the character, and inversely.

For Voloshinov it is crucial to understand that, although there are recognizable syntactic marks and other formal linguistic elements that intervene in these cases and could characterize free indirect discourse, this phenomenon of the influx of voices leads us to discover an extrinsic factor: the social device that demands that the contours between one enunciation and the other are not so clear, that they can be interfered with, intermingled with, or articulated with a certain resistance (without losing their autonomy). That element is what sociolinguistics (the "organic approach") gives us.

BAKHTIN/VOLOSHINOV IN THE PRAGMATICS OF DELEUZE AND GUATTARI

Deleuze and Guattari defend a pragmatics of language that has *Marxism and the Philosophy of Language* as a key ally. This pragmatics, presented through remnants that we will try to reconstruct in its points of greater contact with Bakhtin/Voloshinov, is defined by several concepts. The first says: "The elementary unit of language—the statement—is the order-word."[16] This means that the orders that are transmitted as order-words are based on other orders and not on previous information or a communicative intention. Thus, language always seems to presuppose language, because it always goes from something that is said to something that is said. A second key concept is that of indirect discourse: all discourse is indirect discourse. More specifically, free indirect discourse is *the first determination of language*. That is, there is no language before its pragmatic instance, and acts of language are based only on other acts of language. Indirect discourse—as we saw in Voloshinov's analysis—shows this exemplarily. It is a discourse composed of voices that we cannot reduce to previous instances. According to Deleuze and Guattari, this means that the subjects of enunciation result from an indirect and free relationship. It would seem that it is the phenomenon of relating voices that creates forms of subjectivation.[17] Voloshinov says, in fact, that the phenomenon is not a mixture of direct and indirect forms, or of forms previously available to the act of mixing them. Thus, it is not a question of preestablished voices that enter into a relationship alluding one another. It is a composition made up of voices that only take shape in the tension in which they enter.

Finally, the transmission of order-words as enunciations implies that language is not closed into itself. Variables of expression—external, social circumstances—give sense to the enunciation. These factors "*establish a relation between language and the outside, but precisely because they are immanent to language*," that is, intrinsic to enunciation.[18] As we said previously, the problem with linguistics is that it loses sight of these variables of enunciation by focusing on the search for grammatical constants.

EXPRESSION AND CONTENT: THE PROBLEM OF THE IDEOLOGICAL HYPOTHESIS

The conception of language as a chain of discourses within discourses is followed, in "Postulates of Linguistics," by the problematization of the relationship between enunciations and things of the world (the *woof of bodies* or the *form of content*). Indeed, if the warp of speeches responds to social slogans and not to objective instances (information) or subjective instances (communication), the problem is how to think the relation language-world.

One way of approaching that relationship in the tradition that considers the linguistic phenomenon linked to its social function, that is, Marxism, is to sustain what Deleuze and Guattari call an ideological conception of the statement. Language would form part of a society's ideology insofar as it is determined by economic bases, or social modes of production. It is a thesis that reduces the form of expression to an effect of the form of content. The form of expression would thus become a function of representation in language based on three elements: the causation that goes from the content to the expression, the reflection of the content in the expression, and the passivity of the expression that this relation supposes. Deleuze and Guattari's rejection of this postulation is easy to understand. But it is also interesting the critique that they elaborate on what appears to be a *new* way of thinking about language within Marxism. I'm referring to the theory of Mikhail Bakhtin and the essay on linguistics by Josef Stalin.[19]

In his famous intervention on the problems of linguistics and Marxism, Stalin postulates that language as an ideological phenomenon *par excellence* is not relative to each social class: in that case, we should accept that there are as many languages as there are ideological positions. Language is in itself neutral. Stalin considers, therefore, that the word is a means of communication, a common good to the nation, which includes the various classes. Moreover, it has an active force on its own structural basis: it is an instrument for the revolution.

Deleuze and Guattari assert that in *Marxism and the Philosophy of Language*, a stance equivalent to that of Stalin is maintained.[20] What they say explicitly is: "Even Bakhtin defines language as the form of ideology, but he specifies that the form of ideology is not itself ideological."[21] The substance is for Bakhtin ideological, while the form is independent. We have to immerse ourselves in *Marxism and the Philosophy of Language* to justify this interpretation, because Deleuze and Guattari do not indicate how this "de-ideologization" of the form is presented in Bakhtin.

But it is not difficult to find the answer. Returning to the first chapter of Voloshinov's book, we see that, after affirming that the ideological is not a phenomenon of subjective consciousness but is an objective instance that circulates in language, the question arises: why does the ideological circulate in the word? The answer is that the word is neutral in itself. Its form is independent of its content. That is why the same word receives different valuations according to the ideological orientation. There are disputes over the meaning of words, and for this reason, the statement refracts the existence, while it does not merely reflect it. Now, this refraction is what reverses the process of causation: no longer simply from economic content to ideology, but from ideology to the economic bases. If language was relative to each social class, it would be a faithful reflection of the modes of production (the economic base). But since language is *one* for the various expressions of class (*word neutrality thesis*), there is ideological refraction. Thus, for Voloshinov, as for Stalin, the ideological is the effect, not the cause. The medium is not ideology. And that is why there are ideologies. This means of communication that is the word, added to the class situation of each statement, gives us the phenomenon of ideological refraction in each case.

This thesis could be taken as an isolated fact within the book, as a moment that does not agree with the development of the conception of language that unfolds throughout the chapters. But it finds its continuity in an observation of another order by Voloshinov: the diagnosis of a loss of social determination of language in the avant-garde use of free indirect style by some modern writers.

FREE INDIRECT DISCOURSE AS IDEOLOGICAL WEAKNESS

At the very end of his book, Voloshinov maintains that free indirect discourse has become nothing more than a case of ideological weakness, a subjectivist relativism characteristic of a singular time in history. By not expressing a strong position, this style does not represent true attention to the other. It is, in his opinion, a bourgeois expression of inner doubt and lack of clarity to expose oneself to the world of enunciations: "The victory of extreme forms of the picturesque style in reported speech is [. . .] explainable in terms of the general, far-reaching subjectivization of the ideological word-utterance."[22] When, in the transmission of the word of others, the contours between the author's context and the reported speech become so fragile that the author's assessment of what is transmitted in their discourse cannot be perceived, we are, in Voloshinov's opinion, in a decadent epoch. Thus, "a revival of the ideological word [. . .]—the word with its theme intact, the word permeated with confident and categorical social value judgment, the word that really means and takes responsibility for what it says" becomes necessary.[23]

According to this perspective, the author who creates this free conjunction of voices may be falling into a way of avoiding the responsibility of taking position with respect to the values that these voices express. The use of free indirect discourse can be reduced to a mere "doxology":

> Verbal expression in literature, rhetoric, philosophy and humanistic studies has become the realm of "opinions," of out and out opinions, and even the paramount feature of these opinions is not *what* actually is opined in them but *how*—in what individual or typical way—the "opining" is done.[24]

Voloshinov's diagnosis is impeccable and is still extremely relevant, but we have to ask ourselves why he formulates it at the close of his study on free indirect discourse. Is there something in the nature of this discourse that leads directly to an omission of ideological responsibility? Voloshinov is not categorical in this respect, but we can maintain, within the framework of his concepts, the following thesis: this type of discourse hides something of the being of language, something fundamental to recover the "socially critical valuation" and abolish the *abourgoisment* of linguistic expression.

Recovering a fundamental concept from the book, we can develop something implicit in Voloshinov's diagnosis and say that, in this kind of speech, the author's own voice will never pass through the phases of social objectivity. And so, free indirect discourse is an expression that cannot produce changes in reality.

In order to explain this statement, we must begin by pointing out that it is not that free indirect discourse lacks the necessary neutrality to dilute the multiple accentuations: this is typical of the conservative character. The problem is that this discourse does not allow us to notice that if there is voice-crossing in speech, it is because ideological orientations are crossing. Now, the crossing of ideologies refers to a nonideological instance in itself: that of the language that exceeds the speeches. A writer who structures their discourse in the free indirect style is someone fascinated by the crosses without being able to see that this is a derived phenomenon, not the primordial one. It is an exaggerated attachment to the empirical character of the word, to its contingency. It lacks the totality of the relationships with which every enunciation is in contact. Under the dominion of this form of language, it becomes impossible to notice that not every refraction of the being has the same worth. It becomes impossible to make the leap to a type of refraction that *can* modify the being.

We must recognize, says Voloshinov, that this awareness of the ideological character of enunciation is characteristic of the capitalist man, let's say the *entrepreneur*, who always shows a growing interest in the diversity of things in the world and ends up transforming it; while the man of feudalism—a conservative legacy present in the Russian world—remains in a much narrower view of the world. Voloshinov's unique observation serves to show the way in which different interests ideologically expressed can change the world. But what does not make sense is to be fascinated by the flow itself, by mere fiction.

Deleuze and Guattari do not analyze the negative judgment of the Russian text on the literary style that has characterized free indirect discourse—they do not need to do so. From here, our task is to show that the judgment on free indirect discourse—its weak, relativistic, bourgeois character—is linked to the ideological conception of the statement that they consider proper to the book.

THE IDEOLOGICAL CONCEPTION OF THE STATEMENT

The classical reduction of the statement to ideology consists in making the discursive expression relative to the economic base: the statement would be causally determined by the base of the society, that is, by its mode of production, its economy. It is the classical Marxist version of the relation between base and superstructure. Certainly, Voloshinov said in the

Introduction of his book that there is a version—the dominant one so far—of the base/superstructure relationship that is pre-dialectical, insofar as it does not dialectize the facts: it does not take them in relation to the dynamics of history, and remains tied to a mechanistic logic.[25] It is a relation of equilibrium from one isolated point of the mode of production (emergence of a new relationship between Work and Capital) to another isolated point of the superstructure (emergence of such a type of character in the novelistic form of an epoch). The relationship between the economic cause and the ideological superstructural effect would be that of a reflection: one represents the other. But Voloshinov warned that in the sign, in the dimension of ideology, there is no reflection of being but rather *refraction*. The interesting thing is that when he asks the question: "How is this refraction of existence in the ideological sign determined?" he answers: "By an intersecting of differently oriented social interests within one and the same sign community, i.e., by the class struggle."[26] Thus, in this statement, we are a step further than the Marxist axiom of the determination of the economic base. Here, we find recognition of the class struggle as determinant, or at least a phenomenon of its own: that of the refraction of being. But if one takes into account the justification of this ideological phenomenon, that is, the reconsideration of the instance of struggle, one observes the exercise in an indeterminate way: it is the confluence of diverse orientations in the same language what produces the phenomenon of the characteristic refraction of ideological products.

> Class does not coincide with the sign community, i.e., with the community, which is the totality of users of the same set of signs for ideological communication. Thus various different classes will use one and the same language. As a result, differently oriented accents intersect in every ideological sign. Sign becomes an arena of the class struggle.[27]

Certainly, in the passage of "Postulates of Linguistics" to which we allude, Deleuze and Guattari make an explicit relation between the causal determination of the content over the expression (classical ideological version) and the version that grants to the expression the power to act actively on the enunciation. In Voloshinov's reasoning, if language was relative to each social class, it would be a faithful reflection of the modes of production (the economic base). But since language is *one* for the various expressions of class (*word neutrality thesis*), there is ideological refraction. Thus, for Voloshinov, as for Stalin, the ideological is the effect, not the cause. The medium is not ideology. And that is why there are ideologies. This means of communication that is the word, added to the class situation of each statement, gives us the phenomenon of ideological refraction in each case.

Read as a source for Deleuze and Guattari, the Russian text becomes ambiguous. The thematization of free indirect discourse seems characteristic of the social and critical approach that they are defending against the abstract linguistics of their time, because only in the social study of syntax, of the transmission of another speaker's speech, can we characterize this discourse as the influx of voices that in their irreducible tension form a new enunciation. However, the sociolinguistic instrument does not serve, in this case, to find a revolutionary value in modern literature, a path to follow, but—in the last instance—to denounce the bourgeois character of that style and that literature.

The Russian text shows that in discourse there is a crossover of ideological orientations, and that in free indirect discourse, there is also a crossover of orientations. However, this discourse does not give us the guidelines for the functioning of language itself: it is a case of ideological weakness. It is a style in which the characteristic crossing of linguistic expression is noticed, but instead of taking it to an objective instance, it remains in the mere conflict, without resolving it, without taking a position.

In this sense, Deleuze and Guattari's operation becomes relevant if we focus on its contrast. In effect, it elevates to the first determination of language—that is, to a transcendental instance—the phenomenon of free indirect discourse, which starts to be considered a sufficient condition of the political character of the discourse. This rejects Bakhtin/Voloshinov's own transcendental scheme, which considered the neutrality of the word as a condition of the ideological sense of the statement.

The social conception of language, the focus on the flows of enunciations and discursive practices, allows Voloshinov to realize the complexity of free indirect discourse. But this does not eliminate the ideological conception of the statement, the supposed neutral character of the word, which precludes us from seeing in this discourse something more than a mere case, a fact of sociolinguistic analysis. If language is that neutrality in which the slogans of different orientations are crossed, the place of the movement, of the first determination, is occupied by the means of communication and not by the force of transmission.

FREE INDIRECT DISCOURSE IN THE PRAGMATIC POLITICS OF LANGUAGE

For Deleuze and Guattari, Stalin and Voloshinov's model of language neutrality brings many complications:

> First, although it may be possible to conceive of a causal action moving from content to expression, the same cannot be said for the respective *forms,* the

form of content and the form of expression. We must recognize that expression is independent and that this is precisely what enables it to react upon contents. *This independence, however, has been poorly conceived*: If contents are said to be economic, the form of content cannot be said to be economic and is reduced to a pure abstraction, namely, the production of goods and the means of that production considered in themselves. Similarly, if expressions are said to be ideological, the form of expression is not said to be ideological and is reduced to language as abstraction, as the availability of a good shared by all. Those who take this approach claim to characterize contents and expressions by all the struggles and conflicts pervading them in two different forms, but these forms themselves are exempt from struggle and conflict, and the relation between them remains entirely indeterminate.[28]

The independence of expression and content is a fundamental thesis of the logic of *A Thousand Plateaus*. But that independence is misconceived if it is based on an illegitimate abstraction: an independence founded on the assumption that each form is beyond the events it comprehends. The independence postulated to think the reverse influence of the expression on the content ends up making it impossible to determine the very relationship between the two instances.

On the one hand, the economic contents suppose a form in itself not economic. We can think that certain production tools or techniques are directly economic, directly productive, tied to contingencies and use and that the form of production is an organization of a superior type: as if the industrial mode of production was not in itself capitalist but could also be a form of development of the proletariat. If, on the other hand, we have to assume that the statements have an ideological charge but the language itself does not, then we also have to assume an abstract form of expression. Indeed, Stalin says:

> While it differs in principle from the superstructure, language does not differ from instruments of production, from machines, let us say, which are as indifferent to classes as is language and may, like it, equally serve a capitalist system and a socialist system.[29]

The assumption of two abstract forms—expression and content, linguistic and economic—and the recognition of their independence allow us to postulate that expressions can act on content. But then the relation between both instances is only conceived in an indeterminate way.

The proposal of Deleuze and Guattari is that this relation is determined by the points properly "ideological" and properly "economic": by the struggles and conflicts that cross the statements and the machines of social production. More precisely, it is not the points of conflict but the *lines of flight* what connect and articulate.

Language as *la Langue* or as a "mother tongue" does not exist. What there is, according to Deleuze and Guattari, is a collective agency of enunciation, an expression machine whose variables determine the use of the elements of language. There is no neutral instance, that is to say, words without conflict, without conflictive load, without "class struggle." The unity of language depends on a "power takeover by a dominant language."[30] The mixture of bodies is not neutral either; it is loaded with attractions and repulsions, penetrations and expansions, which are those that affect all kinds of bodies related to each other. Each of these forms or aspects of agency has deterritorialization movements that enter into a mutual relationship. Certainly, the articulation of these forms of expression and content takes place in the relationship in which their deterritorialization movements enter.

In "Postulates of Linguistics" appears a very eloquent example on the financial and monetary system: the devaluation of money in the circumstances of interwar Germany reaches a point in which it is decided to cancel it and create a new one. This operation of devaluation of the monetary body connects with a semiotic operation: the creation of a new sign. One would say, then, that there is no "money" as a neutral form: there are instances of monetary processes that cross thresholds and connect with a crossed threshold at the level of enunciations.

The preeminence of free indirect discourse and jargon and dialects explains better the social dynamics in which language is inscribed. And the interesting thing is that social dynamics is what Voloshinov wanted to explain, appealing to a kind of responsible conscience about one's own voice as an author or as a partner in social dialogue. But seriousness and responsibility are not, from Deleuze and Guattari's perspective, attributes of a subject who decides to take charge of the dialogical dimension. From their perspective, as I interpret it, ethics in writing means following the flight lines in their machinic and semiotic connections. The task is to express these transformations, these events, even at the price of depersonalization. Deleuze and Guattari seem to worry more about attending the crossing of thresholds, about not denying them, than about being faithful to the dialectical dialogue of the semiotic totality.

We see something has changed in the thinking of culture along the decades of the twentieth century: from the concern in the first decades of Marxism of reversing the tendency toward individualism to the urgency of creating new ways of minority expression in the late 1960s and 1970s. In the twenty-first century, we need to recover that ethics of dialogue and the global perspective for the creation of culture and rethink its meaning in the politics of minorities and the aesthetics of pure events. The cross between *Marxism and the Philosophy of Language* and *A Thousand Plateaus* is one of the most outstanding places to evaluate it. But the answer is yet to be created and the problem must be posed in new terms.

NOTES

1. Gilles Deleuze and Félix Guattari, *A Thousand Plateaus: Capitalism and Schizophrenia*, trans. Brian Massumi (London: University of Minnesota Press, 1987), 75–110.
2. Deleuze and Guattari, *A Thousand Plateaus*, 77
3. Valentin Voloshinov, *Marxism and the Philosophy of Language*, trans. Ladislav Matejka and I. R. Titunik (New York: Seminar Press, 1973).
4. When Bakhtin's work was recovered from oblivion a few years before his death in 1975, it was considered that the works published under the names of his "Circle" (Kanaev, Medvedev, and Voloshinov) were in fact works written by him, but disguised with other names to avoid censorship. In the edition of this book read by Deleuze and Guattari, a collection directed by P. Bourdieu, Bakhtin is considered the author.
5. Voloshinov, *Marxism and the Philosophy of Language*, 11.
6. Voloshinov, *Marxism and the Philosophy of Language*, 48.
7. Voloshinov, *Marxism and the Philosophy of Language*, 52.
8. Voloshinov, *Marxism and the Philosophy of Language*, 109.
9. Voloshinov, *Marxism and the Philosophy of Language*, 110.
10. Voloshinov, *Marxism and the Philosophy of Language*, 119–23.
11. This example of free indirect discourse is given by Deleuze in his lecture on cinema and Bergson's philosophy. Gilles Deleuze, "Lecture of December 1st, 1982," Université Paris 8, accessed September 22, 2019, http://www2.univ-paris8.fr/deleuze/article.php3. It is a useful example for us given the resemblance to one of the examples of Voloshinov: "En vain il (le colonel) parla de la sauvagerie du pays et de la difficulté pour une femme d'y voyager: elle (Miss Lydia) ne craignait rien; elle aimait par-dessus tout à voyager à cheval; elle se faisaift une fête de coucher an bivac; elle menaçait d'aller en Aise-Mineure. Bref elle avait réponse á tout, car jamais Anglaise n'avait été en Corse: donc elle devait y aller. (P. Mérimée, *Colomba*)" (Voloshinov, *Marxism and the Philosophy of Language*, 142).
12. Voloshinov, *Marxism and the Philosophy of Language*, 144.
13. Voloshinov, *Marxism and the Philosophy of Language*, 142.
14. Voloshinov, *Marxism and the Philosophy of Language*, 156.
15. Voloshinov, *Marxism and the Philosophy of Language*, 156.
16. Deleuze and Guattari, *A Thousand Plateaus*, 75.
17. "[T]he statement is individuated, and enunciation subjectified, only to the extent that an impersonal collective assemblage requires it and determines it to be so. It is for this reason that indirect discourse, *especially 'free' indirect discourse*" (Deleuze and Guattari, *A Thousand Plateaus*, 80, emphasis original).
18. Deleuze and Guattari, *A Thousand Plateaus*, 82, emphasis original.
19. Josef Stalin, *Marxism and Problems of Linguistics*, Moscow: Foreign Languages Publishing House. Online Version: Stalin Reference Archive (marxists.org), 2000.
20. For a totally opposite position, which defends the absolute divergence between Bakhtin and Stalin, see Ponzio, A., *La revolución bajtiniana*, Madrid: Cátedra, 1998, 132–46.

21. Deleuze and Guattari, *A Thousand Plateaus*, 525.
22. Voloshinov, *Marxism and the Philosophy of Language*, 158.
23. Voloshinov, *Marxism and the Philosophy of Language*, 159.
24. Voloshinov, *Marxism and the Philosophy of Language*, 159 (emphasis original).
25. This section has been deleted in the 1973 English edition; I do not know the reason. The Spanish version does include it: *El marxismo y la filosofía del lenguaje*, trans. Tatiana Bubnova (Buenos Aires: Godot, 2009).
26. Voloshinov, *Marxism and the Philosophy of Language*, 23.
27. Voloshinov, *Marxism and the Philosophy of Language*, 23.
28. Deleuze and Guattari, *A Thousand Plateaus*, 89 (emphasis added).
29. Stalin, *Marxism and Problems of Linguistics*, first question.
30. Deleuze and Guattari, *A Thousand Plateaus*, 101.

BIBLIOGRAPHY

Bakhtin, Mikhail (V. N. Voloshinov). *Le marxisme et la philosophie du langage*. Translated by Marina Yaguello. Paris: Les Editions de Minuit, 1977.

Deleuze, Gilles and Félix Guattari. *A Thousand Plateaus: Capitalism and Schizophrenia*. Translated by Brian Massumi. London: University of Minnesota Press, 1987.

Deleuze, Gilles. "Lecture of December 1st, 1982." Accessed September 22, 2019. http://www2.univ-paris8.fr/deleuze/article.php3.

Evans, Fred. "Deleuze, Bakhtin and the 'Clamour of Voices.'" *Deleuze Studies* 2, no. 2 (2009):178–88. Accessed September 19, 2019. https://www.euppublishing.com/doi/abs/10.3366/E1750224108000275.

Gardiner, Michael. *The Dialogics of Critique: M. M. Bakhtin and the Theory of Ideology*. London: Routledge, 1992.

Lecercle, Jean-Jacques. *Deleuze and Language*. New York: Palgrave Macmillan, 2002.

Ponzio, Augusto. *La revolución bajtiniana*. Madrid: Cátedra, 1998.

Stalin, Josef. *Marxism and Problems of Linguistics*. Moscow: Foreign Languages Publishing House. Online Version: Stalin Reference Archive. Accessed September 19, 2019. https://www.marxists.org/reference/archive/stalin/works/1950/jun/20.htm.

Voloshinov, Valentin. *El marxismo y la filosofía del lenguaje*. Translated by Tatiana Bubnova. Buenos Aires: Godot, 2009.

Voloshinov, Valentin. *Marxism and the Philosophy of Language*. Translated by Ladislav Matejka and I. R. Titunik. New York: Seminar Press, 1973.

Chapter 11

Gustave Guillaume's "Obverse Causation": An Invocation to Deleuze from Linguistics

Matías Soich

INTRODUCTION

The French linguist and professor Gustave Guillaume (1883–1960), author of a vast body of work still not widely known in either the Spanish-speaking or the English-speaking world, is mainly remembered as the father of psycholinguistics, due to his complex psycho-mechanical theory of language.[1] The term "psycho-mechanical" refers both to a theory and to a technique of analysis whose aim is to reveal the deep tensions and dynamic mechanisms that underlie each language and explain the production of its distinctive morphology and syntaxes.

Guillaume also belongs to the constellation of "esoteric" authors that people the pages of *Difference and Repetition*. More precisely, he makes his entrance in chapter four, where Deleuze elaborates on the internal logic of the Idea in its double aspect, as differentiation in the virtual (*différentiation*) and in the actual (*différenciation*). According to the thematic index of authors at the end of the book, Guillaume serves as a source for the subject of "the logic of difference in language."[2] Deleuze values this linguist's theory as an example of how difference can be subtracted from its oppositional and negative conception in structuralism, and also as a "technical model" appropriate for showing how the logic of the virtual and the actual operates with regard to one of the many existing Ideas: the linguistic Idea.[3]

In this chapter, I will try to explain, in a general way, how Guillaume conceives of the operational field of linguistics. The focus will be on his linguistic theory, with the aim of gradually showing, throughout the sections that follow, its affinity with certain aspects of the Deleuzian theory of the Ideas. The Guillaumean texts that mainly support this exposition are two, and identically titled *Observation and Explanation in the Science of Language*. They are two different versions of the same work: a first version, unpublished in its time, and the final version, published in 1958 in *Les Études Philosophiques*. Both are compiled as chapters of the 1964 book *Langage et Science du Langage*, and henceforth will be, respectively, referred to as OE1 and OE2.[4]

With the exception of their identical opening sentences, the form and content of each text are very different, although they share their basic underlying ideas as well as the intricacy of their syntax. In both texts, Guillaume presents what can be considered a normative epistemology of linguistics. Aimed at a philosophical audience, their goal is, on the one hand, to define—in terms that we could call ontological—what linguistics can and should study; and on the other hand, to establish what are the more adequate methods and kinds of knowledge to do so.

THE THREE FIELDS OF LINGUISTIC CAUSALITY AND "OBVERSE CAUSATION"

Guillaume's normative epistemology is based on the distinction among three fields of linguistic causality. Table 11.1 shows this threefold distinction.

The point of departure is shared with traditional linguistics: it is the *caused construction* (*causé construit*), identified by Guillaume with *language* (*langue*): "A work constructed in thought on which a work constructed in signs is superimposed."[5] This implies the existence of two moments in the genetic process of language: a *tempus primum* where language is a construction elaborated in thought and only in thought; and a *tempus secundum* where

Table 11.1 Three Fields of Linguistic Causality. Adapted from OE1 and OE2.

Causation I: obverse causation	The caused construction	Causation II: reverse causation
Mental causation of language (language does not exist yet; it is not constructed as such)	Language (langue) (not yet in use)	Discourse (language in use)
Narrowing and limiting movement with relation to the caused construction	Tempus primum: language constructed in thought	Tempus secundum: language constructed in thought and in signs	Widening and diversifying movement with relation to the caused construction

it is also a construction elaborated in signs. From the caused construction, two causalities, or more precisely two *causations* (Fr. *causations*), unfold in opposite directions: causation I, inchoative, which goes up from the caused construction to the conditions whence it emanates (*émane*); and causation II, conclusive, which emanates from the caused construction as its effect.[6] Guillaume calls causation I *obverse* or "upstream" (*obverse, amont*); and causation II, *reverse* or "downstream" (*déverse, aval*).[7]

Whereas the caused construction is identified with language (*langue*), Guillaume identifies the "downstream" causation with *discourse*, that is, with the concrete uses that fully coat language in physical existence. On the other hand, following the "upstream" causation, we arrive at an exclusively mental field that lacks physical existence and upon which language is constructed. The relation between these three instances of causality—whose combined extension amounts, for Guillaume, to linguistic reality—is described as follows:[8]

> Causation I obverse . . . , generator of the caused construction, fragments it into a series of cases of itself [of the caused construction], limited in relation to its [the caused construction] total extension: it is a narrowing [*étrécissante*] causation. Starting from these fragmentary individuated cases, causation II extracts from each of them—from each case's unity—numerous different consequences: it is a widening [*élargissante*] causation, spreading across a large possibility of diversity [*un large possible de diversité*].[9]

Guillaume describes obverse causation as a *virtual* field, a term that understandably attracts our Deleuzian attention.[10] Although on a terminological level, Guillaume associates the virtual with the *possible* and the *potential*, setting it against the *real* (two movements that Deleuze strongly opposes), on the conceptual level his use of the term *virtual* matches its Deleuzian counterpart.[11] To back this statement, in the following sections we will show that obverse causation is a *genetic* and *non-empirical* field, with *no resemblance* to its productions in language (*langue*) and discourse.

OBVERSE CAUSATION AND GENESIS

The construction of language takes place in the depths of pure thought, where obverse causation constitutes the *site of differentiation* of the genuinely explanatory linguistic facts, prior to their physical covering in signs. "The explanatory linguistic facts upon which we have turned our attention are only accessible to a linguistics that knows how to take its observation to the field of the obverse causation, site of their differentiation [*différenciation*]."[12] In this quote, "differentiation" refers to the process that connects linguistic facts with the field of obverse causation. As readers of *Difference and Repetition*, this term also captures our attention and, in the same way as "virtual," predisposes us to find more explicit links with the Deleuzian work. However, at least in the two texts we are considering here, Guillaume does not elaborate any further on this notion of differentiation—a fact that does not restrain us from delineating the conceptual paths that join these two authors. Obverse causation, a site of *differentiation*, is also the *virtual* site where concrete facts of language (its daily uses, but also its grammatical structures) appear to us in a certain *order*. In Guillaume's words:

> The merit of our observation—which leans on obverse causation, by rising counter-current (from downstream to upstream) in the causation of language—is, by dispelling the night of entangled (not ordered) facts in the *real*, which can only be disentangled (ordered) by their transportation to the *virtual*, to contribute a clear and complete vision ... of that mechanism.[13]

For Deleuze, the virtual is far from being an undifferentiated chaos (the black nothingness or the white nothingness of indifference).[14] On the contrary, it is the field where differential relations and singular points constitute a *completely determined structure*:

> The reality of the virtual is structure ... far from being undetermined, the virtual is completely determined ... [virtuality] is not some confused determination but the completely determined structure formed by its genetic differential elements, its "virtual" or "embryonic" elements.[15]

Therefore, far from leading determinations to an incoherent proliferation where all cows are black, the process of differentiation—whose two sides, the virtual structure and its actualization, co-operate in what Deleuze calls the dramatization of the Idea—"integrates and welds together the *differenciated*."[16]

As a scientific source of Deleuzian ontology, Guillaume's conception illustrates, in the domain of the linguistic Idea, how the comprehension of (linguistic) facts in their actualized state demands an order that can only be attained by going "counter-current" toward the virtual, represented in this case by obverse causation as site of the truly explanatory (linguistic) differentiations. This marks a strong point of confluence with Deleuze: the virtual as a productive, differentiating, and ordering field; as well as a point where Deleuze went further. Indeed, while Guillaume considers real (having read *Difference and Repetition*, we would say "actual") linguistic facts as "entangled," Deleuze sees order and determination not only as traits of the virtual but also of actualization. In this regard, the entire fourth chapter of *Difference and Repetition* focuses precisely on explaining the double logic of different/ciation as a process where the actual and the virtual are determined according to an order of relations.

Another important aspect in which Deleuze's conception of the virtual seems to differ from Guillaume's is the breadth ascribed to the virtual in relation to the actualized. For Guillaume, obverse causation represents a "narrowing" movement that fragments the caused construction (language, *langue*) into a series of cases, each of them limited with respect to its full extent—and the obverse causation's explanatory power is apparently derived from this very fact—while, on the other hand, reverse causation represents a "widening" movement that expands each "case" of the language into a vast array of actual discursive facts. For Deleuze, on the contrary, the virtual or ideal "half" of an object has a transcendent aspect with respect to its actual "half" (and accordingly, the virtual problematic has a transcendent aspect in relation to its actual solutions). Thus, the virtual persists in the actual and the actual can never exhaust the virtual, for "the virtual structure that underpins the actual world necessarily implies ruptures and discontinuities not deducible from that world."[17] In the Deleuzian virtual, divergent series and extra-propositional singularities coexist—or, as Santaya puts it, *co-insist*—in such a way that no actualization or resolution can fully express them.[18] Thus, it would be very difficult to see in the Deleuzian virtual the limiting movement that Guillaume attributes to obverse causation with respect to the field of language (*langue*) as a constructed system. However, one thing is certain: both authors saw in virtuality a great genetic power (*puissance*).

THE OBVERSE CAUSATION AND THE (IN)VISIBLE

For Guillaume, the epistemological conquest of the purely mental, where obverse causation takes place, requires pursuing a methodological path of Platonic echoes. It involves inverting the order of the cause–consequence relation between *seeing* and *understanding*. According to him, traditional linguistics has only explored the relation that goes from the former to the latter; therefore, it only understands language through the empirical observation of the variety of its physical facts (in reverse causation). His own approach to linguistics, on the other hand, seeks to exploit the opposite and complementary relation, that is, the one that goes from understanding toward seeing. Along this path, the comprehension of the mental dynamisms that generate linguistic structures (in obverse causation) produces a new type of seeing that is no longer sensible: it is the sight of *spiritual, mental eyes*. "Visible to the eyes of the spirit, which are the eyes of its order, mentalism, wherever it is summoned by itself, without being covered by any natural physical semiotic, is invisible to any eyes that are not exclusively those of the spirit."[19]

The exercise of departing from empirical seeing to arrive at understanding is called by Guillaume "verification sight" (*voir de constatation*). The

Table 11.2 Seeing and Understanding

SEEING$_1$ ➔ UNDERSTANDING (verification sight)	UNDERSTANDING ➔ SEEING$_2$ (comprehension sight)
PHYSICAL	MENTAL/SPIRITUAL

exercise of departing from understanding in order to arrive at a spiritual seeing is called "understanding sight" (*voir de compréhension*).[20] The first applies to the *acryptic plane*, that is, the plane where linguistic structures and facts are "un-hidden" (reverse causation and *tempus secundum*); the second applies to the *cryptic plane*, where linguistic structures and facts remain hidden to the sensible eye (obverse causation and *tempus primum*). Table 11.2 illustrates these two forms of knowledge.

Table 11.2 reminds us of the Platonic allegory of the line with its division between the sensible and the intelligible. According to Plato, the geometrist relies on visible figures that he considers to be images of the intelligible. However, if one is to go beyond the realm of geometric knowledge, then it is necessary to ascend from those figures to the intelligible principles, leaving the visible behind.[21] For Guillaume, the linguists that confine their research to the field of reverse causation are like the geometrist, destined to descend "downstream" instead of rising "counter-current" to reach the fundamental principles of language. The Guillaumean linguists, on the contrary, act like philosophers: after having ascended to the knowledge of the mechanisms that produce language in pure thought, they exert "understanding sight" to cast light upon the concrete facts of discourse.

This diagram also shows that, for Guillaume, the most relevant part of linguistics deals with the plane of the mental/spiritual. Both the first and the final version of this text (OE1 and OE2) begin with the same exact words: "We explain according to what we have been able to understand. We understand according to what we have been able to observe."[22] The link between *observation and explanation in the science of language* is then clear: it comes down to being able to rise above the common vision of discursive facts until we reach the understanding of their deep linguistic structure. Since this structure produces those facts, once we have understood the structure we do not need any more discursive facts to illustrate its functioning. The understanding sight is a sight that has been emancipated from the empirical observation that was initially necessary and which, ultimately, it improves. Put in Deleuzian terms, here it is not the case that we understand because we have seen the actual; rather, we only understand the actual once we have "seen" the virtual.

In this sense, Guillaume considers that the scarce advance of traditional linguistics has been the result of a fundamental and selective blindness or more precisely, of an improperly exclusive use of the verification sight. Indeed, this science has focused its analysis on the products of reverse causation, without going beyond the *tempus secundum* where language still dons a physical existence. Due to this epistemological bias, which Guillaume calls "positivism of easiness" (*positivisme de facilité*) and which is contrary to the "true realism" of the mental, most linguists have lingered over the study of the "entangled" facts of discourse, where the multitude of real (actual) variations *wrap* the deep structures from which they emanate, hiding them from the understanding sight.[23]

> In the caused construction and in reverse causation, the mentalism of language covers itself in physism [*physisme*]: (speaking, writing, pictography, gesture) which expresses the sight of it [of the mentalism]. . . . In the obverse causation, this physism is no longer summoned [*s'évoque*], it is only invoked [*invoqué*], sought, looked for by the mentalism that requires it for externalizing.[24]

Not even the study of the caused construction seems enough to grasp the fundamental explanatory field of language as, with respect to the movement of obverse causation, even the *tempus primum* (language/*langue* as a construction in thought) forms a "medium" that hinders the full comprehension of its genetic process. To describe this hindering of our cognition of linguistic causation, Guillaume speaks of a certain "refraction," and consistently appeals to other terms connected with light and optics that set up a complete web of metaphorical meanings, such as "source," "propagation," "stasis" (a state of things marked by immobility), and "refringent" (what causes refraction):

> Departing from a potential lucidity [*lucidité puissancialle*] . . . which is its source, the obverse causation propagates, at an increasing distance from that source, with a progressively decelerating speed, and in this deceleration it reaches a state of refringent semi-stasis where the incident obverse causation is refracted. The refringent semi-stasis is the caused construction. The refraction of the obverse causation is here effected in two moments: in the first moment, the formation of language [*langue*] as a work constructed in thought takes place; in the second moment, the formation of language [*langue*] as a work constructed in signs.[25]

This process is illustrated in Table 11.3.

From an ontological and epistemological point of view, this "natural refraction" of obverse causation means that the very process of the emergence of language—its passage from a purely mental field to another where physical signs are attached to thought, opening up the varieties of discursive use—retrospectively "blocks" our intellective sight of the primary genetic field.

Table 11.3 Refraction of the Obverse Causation. Adapted from OE1.

		REFRINGENT SEMI-STASIS = THE CAUSED CONSTRUCTION = LANGUAGE (*LANGUE*)		
POTENTIAL LUCIDITY ("source of the obverse causation")	INCIDENCE OF THE OBVERSE CAUSATION ⎯⎯→	First moment of refraction: language as a work constructed in thought = mentalism of signification	Second moment of refraction: language as a work constructed in signs = physism of representation	DECADENCE OF THE REVERSE CAUSATION ⎯⎯→

This has several implications. First, that for Guillaume the virtual and the real oppose each other not only ontologically but also regarding our knowledge: the farther we get from obverse causation into concrete linguistic facts, the less we are able to "look back" into that field through the understanding sight. Second, that throughout the different fields of linguistic causation there is a directly proportional relation between virtuality and acceleration: the greater the virtuality (that is, the closer to the field of the obverse causation), the greater the acceleration in the movements of the genetic process and vice versa. And third, that the mental/virtual tends to lose its natural acceleration as it flows into the real, producing its own refraction along the way.

These three points allow an interesting contrast with Deleuze's views regarding the role of the virtual in the ongoing genesis of the world. For a start, while Guillaume poses a strong dual opposition between the virtual and the real, in which the presence of the latter progressively hinders the development (as well as our understanding) of the former, Deleuze conceives the relation between the virtual and the actual in a more complex and dynamic way, as a ceaseless and disparate communication, a "distorted mirror" where the elements of the virtual and the actual "halves" of each thing, being or phenomenon correspond to each other without any kind of resemblance.[26]

As we will see in detail in the next section, neither Deleuze nor Guillaume thinks that the virtual can be accessed by a mere "tracing" from actual/real forms. Both of them completely reject any resemblance of the virtual to the actual (in the case of Guillaume, of the purely mental structures of obverse causation to the physical signs of the *tempus secundum* and the real facts of discourse). But in the case of Deleuze, that does not mean that the virtual is absent or lost in the actual world; quite the contrary, the possibility of change and renewal comes from the actual always being "gravid" with the virtual (here the role of the centers of envelopment, as representatives of the persistence of problems throughout the explication process, is crucial).[27] Finally, while the Guillaumean virtual tends to lose its inherent acceleration as it becomes real (thus producing its own refraction), Deleuze separates the theme of speed and slowness from the virtual structure—the Ideas being elements of a *static* genesis—and assigns it instead to the spatiotemporal dynamisms of intensive individuation, which guide the actualization process.[28]

Going back to the Guillaumean notion of *refraction* and considering it in Deleuzian terms, we could say that this inevitable hindering of our comprehension of the genetic mechanisms describes a *transcendental illusion* characteristic of the linguistic Idea, insofar as that "intellective blockage" arises when we observe obverse causation from the point of view of reverse causation. We are predisposed to conceive the field of pure mentalism through concepts that, imbued with "physism," contradict the former's invisibility and thus misrepresent its nature.[29]

This refraction can also be connected with the Deleuzian paradox that states that the intensive becomes accessible to us at the price of canceling itself out as intensity. In this regard, the "positivism of easiness" that Guillaume saw in traditional linguistics runs parallel with the tendency to consider the intensive as an empirical concept, denounced in the following quote from *Difference and Repetition*:

> We know intensity only as already developed within an extensity, and as covered over by qualities. Whence our tendency to consider intensive quantity as a badly grounded empirical concept. . . . In truth, our epistemological tendency to be suspicious of the notion of intensive quantity would prove nothing were it not linked to this other tendency on the part of differences of intensity to cancel themselves out in qualified extended systems. Intensity is suspect only because it seems to rush headlong into suicide.[30]

The epistemological suspicion about intensive quantity is similar to the situation of the positivist linguists who, according to Guillaume, doubt the deep mental mechanisms that produce language and deny the scientific validity of obverse causation because it "seems to rush headlong into suicide," "canceling itself out" in the physism of representation in signs and in the products of the reverse causation. The merit of Guillaumean linguistics would be, precisely, not to be contented with "easy" explanations where the physism of representation hides the distinctive mentalism of signification, as the positivist linguists do when they reject the study of the obverse causation in favor of the products of the reverse causation.[31] However, from a Deleuzian perspective, we could also say that, in this regard, Guillaume tends to fall toward the opposite extreme: instead of rejecting obverse causation because of its invisibility (like the positivists), he judges, from the fact that obverse causation "cancels itself out" in the reverse causation, that the former leaves no trace in the latter. As a result, the first extreme leads to rejecting the invisible virtual altogether, while the second leads to distrusting the visible actual in the name of the invisible virtual: two sides of an unsatisfactory Platonic dilemma.[32]

OBVERSE CAUSATION AND (NON)RESEMBLANCE

So far, I have tried to show that, for Guillaume, the fundamental explanatory element of language is a genetic field that produces the diversity of language (*langue*) and its discursive uses and is epistemologically invisible to the empirical eye. The invisibility of the dynamisms of obverse causation results in a lack of resemblance between its products and those of reverse causation. This becomes manifest in Guillaume's use of the term *calque* ("carbon copy" or "tracing"), a term that will be dear to Deleuze when it comes to denouncing the reconstruction of the virtual on the basis of the actual, or of the transcendental on the basis of the empirical:

> We always find the two aspects of the illusion: the natural illusion which involves *tracing* [*décalquer*] problems from supposedly pre-existent propositions, logical opinions, geometrical theorems, algebraic equations, physical hypotheses or transcendental judgements; and the philosophical illusion which involves evaluating problems according to their "solvability"—in other words, according to the extrinsic and variable form of the possibility of their finding a solution.[33]

For Deleuze, it is both a scientific and a philosophical mistake to trace problems from the entities (propositions, opinions, etc.) that actually constitute those problems' resolutions. Additionally, scientific and philosophical problems should not be evaluated in terms of their possibility of finding a solution (which would fall into a vicious circle, insofar as problems are traced from those solutions). The reason for this lies precisely on the lack of resemblance between the virtual and the actual: problems, which Deleuze closely connects with the Ideas as differen*t*iated virtual structures, become solved through their actualization (differen*c*iation).[34]

> The actualisation of the virtual . . . always takes place by difference, divergence or differenciation [*différenciation*]. *Actualisation breaks with resemblance as a process* no less than it does with identity as a principle. *Actual terms never resemble the singularities they incarnate.* . . . For a potential or virtual object, to be actualised is to create divergent lines which correspond to—*without resembling*—a virtual multiplicity. The virtual possesses the reality of a task to be performed or a problem to be solved: it is the problem which orientates, conditions and engenders solutions, but these *do not resemble the conditions of the problem.*[35]

Thus, conceiving the virtual field from the model of actualized entities is the same mistake as posing problems on the basis of their solutions: it implies imposing, on the relation between the virtual and the actual, a principle of resemblance that is only valid for our perception of actual entities. We will return to this at the end of this section.

Going back now to Guillaume, he asserts that the physical sign (*tempus secundum*) always functions between a maximum and a minimum of convenience with the mentalism of signification (*tempus primum*), which exists in itself and is expressed by the physical sign. Therefore, "the physism invented in order to signify the mental is in a way its *carbon copy* [*calque*]."[36] To better understand this, we can consider the Guillaumean distinction between psycho-systematics and psycho-semiology. This distinction addresses a crucial element of language.

> The absolutely universal fact that language [*langage*] is intrinsically, and cannot be otherwise, the connection between a construction performed in thought, and solely in thought, and the invention (the finding)—among that which appears to be least inconvenient—of a sign, charged with taking on the seizure, bearing and transportation of that which thought has previously edified inside of itself.[37]

In this arrangement, psycho-systematics, related to the *tempus primum* of language (*langue*), deals with "constructing in thought, and solely in thought, that which we later attach to a sign," while psycho-semiology, related to the *tempus secundum*, deals with "choosing, in thought, a sign that is charged with bearing and transporting that which has been constructed in thought."[38] The law of psycho-systematics is the law of *coherence*, rigorous, and unique: as a mental structure, language cannot be internally incoherent. The law of psycho-semiology, on the other hand, is flexible: it is about the *expressive convenience* that physical signs must maintain, to some degree, in relation to the mental structures they translate. Between both laws, the psycho-systematic law of coherence and the psycho-semiological law of expressive convenience, there is the following disparity: while psycho-semiology aims at expressing psycho-systematics by means that faithfully reflect its internal coherence, this faithfulness is neither inevitable, nor strictly necessary, nor historically complete. Instead, the semiotic expression of mental structures is always achieved "as faithfully as possible."[39] That is why, with regard to (non-) resemblance, "psycho-semiology tends—and in the long run, in the favorable cases of a happy 'finding,' it achieves—to be *a carbon copy* [*calque*] of psycho-systematics."[40] Given the different laws (coherence/convenience) that rule them, the resemblance between the products of psycho-systematics and psycho-semiology assumes the character of a ("happy") possibility, but not a necessity.

Additionally, the criterion of resemblance seems to be valid for Guillaume only in the empirical uses of "actualized" language (reverse causation). As part of the range of possible consequences of the linguistic system, the different discursive uses of a language unit may or may not resemble one another:

> An observation whose interest focuses on the relation between language [*langue*] and discourse ... discovers that the permanent device [*dispositif*] of this relation is a fan-like device, according to which a language unity (a term) may [have], under a certain form, numerous discursive consequences that, owing to their different position in the deployment of the range of authorized consequences, *may or may not be alike.*[41]

The relation of resemblance only appears then as an intrinsic possibility of the fields of language (*langue*) in the *tempus secundum* and of discourse. The observation of the obverse causation, however, is a different matter: there, bordering "the narrow liminal field of the separation between the physical and the mental," the eyes of the spirit see something that only they can see, something that almost completely excludes the possibility of figurations or comparisons with the physical.[42]

Here Guillaume's thought connects again with Deleuze's through the former's description of obverse causation as a *virtual* and differentiating field. Indeed, just as the "actual terms never resemble the singularities they incarnate," and the actual solutions never resemble the virtual problems that condition them, the actual (in Guillaume's terms, real) linguistic signs, through which language (*langue*) appears in the physical world, have no (necessary) resemblance to the purely mental and virtual potentiality whence they emerge. In Guillaume's view, resemblance can only be strictly applied to the relations of the real/actual products of the reverse causation (discursive uses) among themselves; it applies less strictly to the relation of the physical signs, produced in the *tempus secundum*, with the mental structures of the *tempus primum*—in which case, resemblance appears only as a "happy finding" of the law of expressive convenience, with no intrinsic necessity; and finally, it does not apply at all to the virtual field of the obverse causation. This "gradual validity" of the principle of resemblance is directly aligned with the process of "refraction" of the obverse causation, which we saw in the previous section: the further we go "upstream" in linguistic causality (away from the concrete discursive uses toward the virtual mental structures), the less resemblance there is and, consequently, the more erroneous it is to conceive each linguistic field by taking its successor as a model.

OBVERSE CAUSATION AND BINARY TENSIONS
(UNIVERSAL/SINGULAR, SPACE/TIME)

In one of the previous quotes from Guillaume, he refers to linguistic causation as a *mechanism* that can be clarified by transporting the linguistic facts in the direction of the virtual.[43] In his view, the science of language is essentially mechanic.[44] This means that genesis—of language in general and of each particular language—consists of a "game" of movements, tensions, and directions that take place in thought itself.[45] For example, the specific productive power of human language derives, according to Guillaume, from the mechanic play of *a tension between two tensions*:

> The singularity of human language is to submit its constitution to the opposite mechanical possibilities of two tensions, one of which, that we will call *tension A*, is *oriented towards the effect*, and gives language the intermittence of *discourse*, alternatively present or absent; while the other [tension], *oriented towards power* [*puissance*] and here termed *tension Ω*, gives language [*langage*] the ceaseless presence, without intermittence, of language [*langue*].[46]

Human language is produced between *tension A*, which is oriented toward the expanded range of the real (actual) effects that are the uses of discourse (reverse causation) and *tension Ω* which, being oriented toward the power of the obverse causation, gives language the solid structure of the caused construction (*langue*). According to this, it can be said that for Guillaume, the full realization of our linguistic experience is only possible on the basis of the constant dynamic interplay of a tension toward the virtual (tension Ω) and a tension toward the real (tension A), or—in Deleuze's terms—the dynamic tension between the virtual and the actual. Despite the differences already noted in their conceptions of the virtual, it is clear that Guillaume's theory represented to Deleuze a satisfactory (linguistic) model of the basic ontological movement of reality. With regard to this, it is worth noting that in opposing *power* and *effect* Guillaume is also implicitly equating *power* and *cause*, which has an undeniably Spinozist flavor.

In Guillaume's view, this kind of distinction ultimately comes down to two dualities that are nested deep in the origin of language. The first is the dual relation between the human being and the universe or, more philosophically, between the singular and the universal. For Guillaume, the truly explanatory relations, given in obverse causation, correspond to the relation of the universal and the singular in thought (which can be associated with tension Ω); whereas reverse causation corresponds to intra-singular relations, that is, to the uses of discourse that emerge from the social bond between human beings (which can be associated with tension A). Only the first type of relations can explain the differentiation processes that produce the singularity of a language and its uses.

> Reverse causation concerns the man/man social rapport. Obverse causation [concerns] the universe/man rapport, which is no longer social. It is necessary to question this rapport, and not the man/man social rapport, to understand what the architecture of language is. Starting from the universe/man rapport we can find, in the science of language, the paths that language has taken to be constructed and easily derive, from this rapport, the entire system of parts of discourse of a language such as French. Also, with identical easiness, we can derive from the same rapport the amorphogenic system of Chinese.[47]

The duality of the universal and the singular is closely connected with a second duality, distinctive to language's psycho-mechanical workings: the duality of space and time, which make up what Guillaume calls the "radical binary tensor." The space/time tensor makes it possible to systematize the relation between the human being and the universe. Its two components, space and time, are the folds a "void" universe effects upon itself; without them, there would be no possibility of making any contrasts nor, therefore, of producing any thought. The universe only becomes representable "through a contrast that results from that which the void universe, keeping its emptiness, opposes to itself under the double species of the universe-space and the universe-time."[48] Given their key role in the constitution of thought, space and time are of course operative in any grammatical system and language. Their centrality in the genesis of language—which we can only mention here—evokes a deep resonance with Deleuze's concept of the dramatization of the Idea, where spatio-temporal dynamisms have a leading role in the actualization of the virtual. "The virtual . . . is the characteristic state of Ideas: it is on the basis of its reality that existence is produced, in accordance with *a time and a space immanent in the Idea*."[49] Space and time are immanent in the Idea and, consequently, in the linguistic Idea. Thus, Guillaume's radical tensor can testify this Deleuzian ontological claim from the technical model of a specific theory of language.

SOME FINAL WORDS

Throughout this chapter, we have seen that Guillaume conceives of linguistic reality as composed of three operative fields: obverse causation, the caused construction with its two moments, and reverse causation. The obverse causation is characterized as a purely mental and invisible field, site of virtual movements and dynamisms from which the whole diversity of expressed, spoken and written forms of language are progressively differentiated, as obverse causation decelerates itself and creates the caused construction of language (*langue*) with its mental structures and physical signs. Deployed in concrete discourses, these forms' actuality wraps the dynamic tensions whence they emerged, and this explains the prevailing of linguistic positivism, whose adherents believe that it is sufficient to compare the similarities and dissimilarities between discursive uses. We have seen that in relation to the Deleuzian ontology exposed in *Difference and Repetition*, Guillaume's linguistic theory presents several affinities—which account for its use as a scientific source of the linguistic Idea—as well as some important conceptual divergences. Concerning their affinities, the traits attributed by Guillaume to the obverse causation make it an ideal candidate to illustrate the functioning of the virtual and the actual in the Deleuzian linguistic Idea: a site of purely mental linguistic differences, organized in an interplay of tensions among which space and time, the universal and the singular, are central; a site that explains the apparently chaotic array of the actual linguistic individuals by relating them to an invisible and productive order to which they have no resemblance. Concerning their divergences, we have seen that Deleuze's conception of the relation between the virtual and the actual goes beyond Guillaume's more rigid dualism of the virtual and the real, as the former asserts the immanence of both ontological planes *as well as* their difference in nature (while for Guillaume, both claims seemed incompatible, the obverse causation only relating to the reverse causation in a more transcendent fashion). Despite these divergences—or because of them—Guillaume's theory remains a complex and intriguing source of the Deleuzian system.

On two occasions, Guillaume regrets the following circumstance of the scientists of language: that they have lacked the time and disposition to pose linguistic problems in the right terms, before committing to the search for their solutions.[50] Ten years after the second version of *Observation and Explanation in the Science of Language* was published, Deleuze would write: "A solution always has the truth it deserves according to the problem to which it is a response, and the problem always has the solution it deserves in proportion to its *own* truth or falsity—in other words, in proportion to its sense."[51] Guillaume could only agree. In the preliminary version of *Observation and Explanation in the Science of Language*—aimed, lest we forget, at a philosophical audience—he predicted that, if it posed its problems correctly, linguistics would then become the monarch of human sciences and earn the passionate interest of philosophy.[52] In the final version of that text, he turned that prediction into an explicit invocation:

> One of the tasks of linguistics, its ultimate and most elevated task, already advanced among the Guillaumeans, *for whose accomplishment the collaboration*

of an adjusted philosophy will be precious, is to find, under that which is in the language of the formal expressible [*dicible*]—of structure and architecture— *that which was, in the depths of thought, the point of departure.*[53]

In light of this statement, I think that Deleuze rose to the occasion and answered Guillaume's invocation of an "adjusted philosophy," not only because of the affinities between his concept of the virtual and the linguistic role of the Guillaumean obverse causation, but also because he found in *difference* that which "was, in the depths of thought, the point of departure," not only of the linguistic Idea but of the entire world's inexhaustible genetic process.

NOTES

1. See Pablo von Stecher, "La lingüística de Gustave Guillaume. De la lengua al discurso," *Onomázein* 25 (2012): 163–80.

2. Gilles Deleuze, *Difference and Repetition*, trans. Paul Patton (New York: Columbia University Press, 1994), 338.

3. See Pablo Pachilla, "La diferencia estructural con la diferencia deleuziana," in *Deleuze y las fuentes de su filosofía*, ed. Julián Ferreyra and Matías Soich (Buenos Aires: La Almohada, 2014), 115–27. This book, which can be freely downloaded from http://www.deleuziana.com.ar, also contains Pachilla's Spanish translation and prologue to Guillaume's conference "*Comment se fait un système grammatical*" (Ferreyra and Soich, *Deleuze y las fuentes de su filosofía*, 128–50). See also Pablo Pachilla, "Lenguaje, tiempo y diferencia en Deleuze, Guillaume y Ortigues," *Cuadernos del Sur-Filosofía* 41 (2012): 285–310.

4. Gustave Guillaume, *Langage et Science du Langage* (Paris-Québec: Libraire A.-G. Nizet and Presses de l'Université Laval, 1964), 25–45 (OE1), 272–86 (OE2).

5. Guillaume, *Langage et Science du Langage*, 277 (OE2). All translations of Guillaume's texts are my own.

6. When used to talk about verbs, *inchoative* (which here translates the French adjective *inceptif,-ve*) means "denoting the beginning of an action, state, or occurrence" ("Inchoative 2," Merriam-Webster Online Dictionary, accessed September 5, 2019, https://www.merriam-webster.com/dictionary/inchoative). As we will see shortly, this meaning adjusts well to the Guillaumean notion of the obverse causation as an ontologically "first" power that sets in motion the genetic process of the structures of language and their subsequent unfolding in discourse.

7. Guillaume's own comments on the terms *obverse* and *déverse* do not add more specific information, though they emphasize each causation's direction: "*Obverse* here means simply: *going towards* the production of the caused construction, and *déverse*: *departing from* the construction left by the first causation" (Guillaume, *Langage et Science du Langage*, 25). While the French word *obverse* is a synonym of *face* (the obverse or "heads" side of a coin), *déverse* refers to the verb *déverser*, meaning "to pour" and "to discharge." The latter is coherent with the aquatic and

fluvial metaphors frequently used by Guillaume to talk about causality in linguistics: according to him, *obverse* and *déverse*, respectively, describe an "upstream" and "downstream" causation. He also applies this orientational metaphor of the course of water to the *observation* of both causalities: see Gustave Guillaume, *Essai de mécanique intuitionnelle I. Espace et temps en pensée commune et dans les structures de langue* (Québec: Les Presses de l'Université Laval, 2007), 3. According to this, *causation déverse* could then be translated as "poured/discharged causation." Nevertheless, for the sake of semantic coherence and to maintain the sense of complementary opposition between these two fields of linguistic causality, I have decided to stick to the image of the two sides of a coin, thus translating *causation obverse* and *causation déverse*, respectively, as *obverse causation* and *reverse causation*.

8. Guillaume, *Langage et Science du Langage*, 32 (OE1).
9. Guillaume, *Langage et Science du Langage*, 26 (OE1). Emphasis added.
10. Guillaume, *Langage et Science du Langage*, 29 (OE1).
11. Deleuze, *Difference and Repetition*, 208–14. "The only danger in all this is that the virtual could be confused with the possible. The possible is opposed to the real. . . . By contrast, the virtual is not opposed to the real; it possesses a full reality by itself" (211).
12. Guillaume, *Langage et Science du Langage*, 36 (OE1). Emphasis added. In *Difference and Repetition*, Deleuze makes a crucial philosophical point of the distinction between the French terms *différencier* (with the everyday meaning of "making or recognizing a difference" and with the technical, biological meaning related to the development of an organ) and *différentier* (with the technical, mathematical meaning of "calculating a differential"). In the English translation, Patton reflects this by distinguishing between *to differentiate* and the neologism *to differenciate*. Here, to avoid anachronism, I have translated Guillaume's *différenciation* as *differentiation*, which—as I will soon emphasize—also matches his concept of the obverse causation in its specific resonance with the Deleuzian *différentiation* as a virtual process of determination.
13. Guillaume, *Langage et Science du Langage*, 42 (OE1). Emphasis added.
14. Deleuze, *Difference and Repetition*, 28.
15. Deleuze, *Difference and Repetition*, 209.
16. Deleuze, *Difference and Repetition*, 217. Emphasis added.
17. Gonzalo Santaya, *El cálculo trascendental. Gilles Deleuze y el cálculo diferencial: ontología e historia* (Buenos Aires: RAGIF Ediciones, 2017), 170. On the inexhaustible character of the virtual structure, see also pages 208–17 of the same book, where Santaya casts invaluable light on the Deleuzian theory of the Idea by exposing the mathematical theories that inspired Deleuze's conception of the triple aspect of the Idea in its genetic process.
18. Santaya, *El cálculo trascendental*, 181.
19. Guillaume, *Langage et Science du Langage*, 32 (OE1).
20. Guillaume, *Langage et Science du Langage*, 42 (OE1).
21. Plato, *The Republic*, trans. Allan Bloom (New York: Basic Books, 1968), 191 (510d).
22. Guillaume, *Langage et Science du Langage*, 25 (OE1), 272 (OE2).

23. Guillaume, *Langage et Science du Langage*, 45 (OE1).

24. Guillaume, *Langage et Science du Langage*, 32 (OE1). Emphasis added. Though, as far as I know, they are not Guillaumean technical terms, the counterpoint between what is *summoned* and what is *invoked* is interesting when we examine their meanings more closely. While all entries of *évoquer* refer to some degree to a *making* that has manifest results ("making spirits appear," "making someone remember," "making someone dream," "giving rise to a mental representation in someone," "alluding to something"), *invoquer* refers to a call for help aimed at something superior (natural or supernatural) without necessarily having concrete results. In this sense, one can better understand why, from the point of view of reverse causation, the physical concretion of signs is *summoned*: not just "called out to come" but also expected to have concrete results regarding the practical needs of communication. On the other hand, from the point of view of obverse causation, the physical concretion of signs is just *invoked*: "called out to come" only in relation to a need for materialization that is alien to the field of the purely mental. Regarding the term *physisme* that appears in this quote (and its derived words, like the verb *physifier*), it is a French neologism seemingly created by Guillaume to indicate the physical character of the representation conveyed by linguistic (written, spoken, gestured, etc.) signs. In the genetic process of language, pure "mentalism" comes first (as a sort of thought without images), and in a second moment, it is covered and expressed by the "physism" of representation.

25. Guillaume, *Langage et Science du Langage*, 32–33 (OE1). Emphasis added. On the expression "*lucidité puissancielle*," Guillaume comments that it does not refer to "knowledge" (*savoir*) but to "power" (*puissance*) (*Langage et Science du Langage*, 29).

26. Deleuze, *Difference and Repetition*, 183–89, 212. "The virtual structure does not refer to an original world set apart from the empirical [world], but intertwines with it in each of its points. And in each and every one of them, the actual world condenses the indefinite genetic potentiality of the virtual, which propels it toward its constant transformation, populates it with tasks to be fulfilled or problems to be solved. From the world of things to virtuality . . . and from this again to the world—or to a new world—the actual and the virtual refer to each other as two disparate sides of a distorted mirror." Santaya, *El cálculo trascendental*, 216.

27. "The centres of envelopment still testify to the persistence of the problems or the persistence of the values of implication in the movement which explicates and solves them." Deleuze, *Difference and Repetition*, 281. See also pages 47, 255–61.

28. Deleuze, *Difference and Repetition*, 183. Santaya's *El cálculo trascendental* unfolds the triple aspect of the Idea as the transcendental principle of the static genesis.

29. On the term "physism," see note 24.

30. Deleuze, *Difference and Repetition*, 223–24. In physics and in chemistry, "intensive" refers to properties and magnitudes that do not depend on a substance's quantity or a body's size (by contrast, "extensive" refers to those properties and magnitudes that do). For Deleuze, intensive quantity "includes the unequal in itself. It represents . . . that which cannot be cancelled in difference in quantity." Deleuze,

Difference and Repetition, 232. On intensive quantity and intensity, see Rafael McNamara's chapter in this book. Numerous chapters on these topics can also be found in the following books in Spanish, all of which can be freely downloaded from http://deleuziana.com.ar/: Verónica Kretschel and Andrés Osswald, eds., *Deleuze y las fuentes de su filosofía II* (Buenos Aires: RAJGIF Ediciones, 2015); Julián Ferreyra, ed., *Intensidades deleuzianas. Deleuze y las fuentes de su filosofía III* (Adrogué: La Cebra, 2016); Rafael Mc Namara and Gonzalo Santaya, eds., *Deleuze y las fuentes de su filosofía V* (Buenos Aires: RAGIF Ediciones, 2017); Solange Heffesse, Pablo Pachilla and Anabella Schoenle, eds., *Lo que fuerza a pensar. Deleuze, ontología práctica 1* (Buenos Aires: RAGIF Ediciones, 2019).

31. Guillaume, *Langage et Science du Langage*, 282 (OE2).

32. As I understand it, this dilemma emerges from a rigid dichotomous view of the relation of the virtual and the actual. Therefore, its solution may be attained by dissolving the strict barriers that separate these two ontological planes (which is not the same as conflating them or making them undistinguishable). In relation to linguistics, my research on transgender people's life stories from the combined methodological frame of Critical Discourse Analysis and Deleuzian philosophy has shown that some concrete discursive forms, like abstract and general nouns, "mitigated" verbs and "empty" pronouns (all of them, in Guillaumean terms, empirically observable as products of the reverse causation) can function as discursive markers of an intensive and imperceptible process of becoming that permeates the construction of subjectivity. The implication of this is that neither the virtual nor the intensive completely "cancel themselves out" in actualized language; rather, discourse bears the marks of the other side of the "distorted mirror." On this subject, see Matías Soich, "Los *devenires* y la identidad de género: hacia un análisis lingüístico-crítico y conceptual de la construcción de representaciones discursivas sobre la identidad de género en historias de vida de personas trans de la Ciudad de Buenos Aires (2013–2015)" (PhD diss., University of Buenos Aires, 2017), available at http://repositorio.filo.uba.ar/handle/filodigital/10007; Matías Soich, "De la esencia al proceso. Análisis lingüístico de la construcción de representaciones discursivas sobre la identidad de género en historias de vida de personas trans," *Romanica Olomucensia* 30, no. 1 (2018): 21–42; and Matías Soich, "Sobre los índices discursivos del devenir-molecular de la sexualidad," in *Lo que fuerza a pensar. Deleuze, ontología práctica 1*, ed. Solange Heffesse, Pablo Pachilla, and Anabella Schoenle (Buenos Aires: RAGIF ediciones, 2019), 299–311.

33. Deleuze, *Difference and Repetition*, 161. Emphasis added. For more examples of this use of *calquer*, see pages 135, 143, 151, 156–58, 160, 164, 192.

34. About the close relation between problems and Ideas, see, for example, Deleuze, *Difference and Repetition*, 146, 162, 168, 244.

35. Deleuze, *Difference and Repetition*, 212. Emphasis added.

36. Guillaume, *Langage et Science du Langage*, 33 (OE1). Emphasis added.

37. Guillaume, *Langage et Science du Langage*, 241. Syntax and punctuation have been slightly modified for the sake of clarity, and emphasis has been added.

38. Guillaume, *Langage et Science du Langage*, 242.

39. "While it is historically pressing that what has been constructed in thought be attached to a semiology, it is less pressing that this semiology be perfect. Thus,

practically, it is only demanded that it be sufficient." Guillaume, *Langage et Science du Langage*, 243.

40. Guillaume, *Langage et Science du Langage*, 277 (OE2). Emphasis added. Punctuation has been slightly modified for the sake of clarity.

41. Guillaume, *Langage et Science du Langage*, 45 (OE1). Emphasis added.

42. Guillaume, *Langage et Science du Langage*, 32 (OE1).

43. Guillaume, *Langage et Science du Langage*, 42 (OE1).

44. "The essential, in linguistics, is always and everywhere mechanic." Guillaume, *Essai de mécanique intuitionnelle I*, 1.

45. "In a general way, a deep study of the psycho-systematics of languages leads to the clear vision of this fact: that, everywhere and always, thought prolongs a movement inherent to itself through an identical movement inversely oriented. So that if thought goes from the wide towards the narrow, it will keep on going, in answer, from the narrow to the wide; departing from infinitude to arrive at finitude, it will respond to itself by going from the obtained finitude to a second infinitude that is not the first one—from which finitude was subtracted. There is *a game of very simple movements that condition thought and determine its power*. The study of these movements, conducted with a method, becomes a very special branch of analysis that we could call intuitional mechanics." Gustave Guillaume, *Leçons de l'année 1948–1949*, B series, *Psycho-systématique du langage. Principes, méthodes et applications I* (Québec-Paris: Valin-Presses de l' Université Laval-Klincksieck, 1971), 200. Emphasis added.

46. Guillaume, *Essai de mécanique intuitionnelle I*, 1. Emphasis added. Punctuation has been slightly modified for the sake of clarity.

47. Guillaume, *Langage et Science du Langage*, 44 (OE1). Punctuation has been slightly modified for the sake of clarity.

48. Ronald Lowe, "Avis aux lecteurs," in *Essai de mécanique intuitionnelle I. Espace et temps en pensée commune et dans les structures de langue*, by Gustave Guillaume (Québec: Les Presses de l'Université Laval, 2007), xiv. The translation is my own.

49. Deleuze, *Difference and Repetition*, 211. Emphasis added.

50. Guillaume, *Langage et Science du Langage*, 42 (OE1), 283 (OE2).

51. Deleuze, *Difference and Repetition*, 159.

52. Guillaume, *Langage et Science du Langage*, 42 (OE1).

53. Guillaume, *Langage et Science du Langage*, 284–85 (OE2). Emphasis added.

BIBLIOGRAPHY

Deleuze, Gilles. *Difference and Repetition*. Translated by Paul Patton. New York: Columbia University Press, 1994.

Ferreyra, Julián, ed. *Intensidades deleuzianas. Deleuze y las fuentes de su filosofía III*. Adrogué: La Cebra, 2016.

Guillaume, Gustave. "Cómo se hace un sistema gramatical." Translated by Pablo Pachilla. In *Deleuze y las fuentes de su filosofía*, edited by Julián Ferreyra and Matías Soich, 128–50. Buenos Aires: La Almohada, 2014.

Guillaume, Gustave. *Essai de mécanique intuitionnelle I. Espace et temps en pensée commune et dans les structures de langue.* Québec: Les Presses de l'Université Laval, 2007.
Guillaume, Gustave. *Langage et Science du Langage.* Paris-Québec: Libraire A.-G. Nizet & Presses de l'Université Laval, 1964.
Guillaume, Gustave. *Leçons de l'année 1948–1949*, B series, *Psycho-systématique du langage. Principes, méthodes et applications I.* Québec-Paris: Valin-Presses de l'Université Laval-Klincksieck, 1971.
Heffesse, Solange, Pablo Pachilla and Anabella Schoenle, eds. *Lo que fuerza a pensar. Deleuze, ontología práctica 1.* Buenos Aires: RAGIF Ediciones, 2019.
Kretschel, Verónica and Andrés Osswald, eds. *Deleuze y las fuentes de su filosofía II.* Buenos Aires: RAJGIF Ediciones, 2015.
Lowe, Ronald. "Avis aux lecteurs." In *Essai de mécanique intuitionnelle I. Espace et temps en pensée commune et dans les structures de langue*, by Gustave Guillaume, i–xxv. Québec: Les Presses de l'Université Laval, 2007.
Mc Namara, Rafael and Gonzalo Santaya, eds. *Deleuze y las fuentes de su filosofía V.* Buenos Aires: RAGIF Ediciones, 2017.
Merriam-Webster Online Dictionary. "Inchoative." Accessed September 5, 2019. https://www.merriam-webster.com/dictionary/inchoative.
Pachilla, Pablo. "La diferencia estructural con la diferencia deleuziana." In *Deleuze y las fuentes de su filosofía*, edited by Julián Ferreyra and Matías Soich, 115–27. Buenos Aires: La Almohada, 2014.
Pachilla, Pablo. "Lenguaje, tiempo y diferencia en Deleuze, Guillaume y Ortigues." *Cuadernos del Sur-Filosofía* 41 (2012): 285–310.
Plato. *The Republic.* Translated by Allan Bloom. New York: Basic Books, 1968.
Santaya, Gonzalo. *El cálculo trascendental. Gilles Deleuze y el cálculo diferencial: ontología e historia.* Buenos Aires: RAGIF Ediciones, 2017.
Soich, Matías. "De la esencia al proceso. Análisis lingüístico de la construcción de representaciones discursivas sobre la identidad de género en historias de vida de personas trans." *Romanica Olomucensia* 30, no. 1 (2018): 21–42.
Soich, Matías. "Los *devenires* y la identidad de género: hacia un análisis lingüístico-crítico y conceptual de la construcción de representaciones discursivas sobre la identidad de género en historias de vida de personas trans de la Ciudad de Buenos Aires (2013–2015)." PhD diss., University of Buenos Aires, 2017.
Soich, Matías. "Sobre los índices discursivos del devenir-molecular de la sexualidad." In *Lo que fuerza a pensar. Deleuze, ontología práctica 1*, edited by Solange Heffesse, Pablo Pachilla and Anabella Schoenle, 299–311. Buenos Aires: RAGIF Ediciones, 2019.
von Stecher, Pablo. "La lingüística de Gustave Guillaume. De la lengua al discurso." *Onomázein* 25 (2012): 163–80.

Index

Page references for figures are *italicized*.

activity, 12, 51, 87–88, 91–92, 117, 130–32, 135, 139, 141, 150
actual, 36, 42, 49–50, 56n25, 57n30, 65–66, 72, 76–79, 87–88, 140, 177, 180–89, 191, 194n26, 195n32; actualization, 36, 42, 55n19, 72, 76, 80, 92, 154, 180, 185–86, 190. *See* real; virtual
analogy, 25–26, 103–4, 109, 112
apocalypse, 1–7

Bakhtin, Mikhail, 161–62, 165, 167, 171, 174n4
being, 8, 50–51, 72, 77, 85–88, 90–92, 98nn25–26, 99n52, 103–12, 132, 152, 155, 169–70, 184, 189–90
Bergson, Henri, 116, 120; Bergsonism, 116
Blanchot, Maurice, 147–56
Book of Revelation, 3–7

capital, 170; capitalism, 169; capitalist, 172; Marx's *Capital*, 59–62, 86
Carnot, Nicolas Léonard Sadi, 20, 22
Carter, Frederick, 2
categories, 34, 43, 48, 52, 89, 103, 105, 108, 110, 117, 131, 156n7, 163

causality (linguistics), 178–79, 188, 193n7
christian(s), 3–7, 136
circle, 11, 85, 92, 95, 98n40, 186
class, 167, 170; struggle, 22, 64, 170, 173
Clausius, Rudolf Julius Emanuel, 19, 22, 23
cogito, 11, 103, 105, 110, 132, 137, 139, 140, 142n23
collective agency of enunciation, 173
combinatories, 64–65
concordance, 106–7
convergence, 10, 35, 37, 43–45, 77
cosmos, 3–8, 52
curves (mathemathics), 39, 40–43, 45–46, 49, 54n9

Dalcq, Albert, 10, 72–73, 75–76, 78–79
death, 2, 4, 21, 28–29, 60, 89, 92, 147–53, 154–56; double, 12–13, 147–56; heat, 28
degradation, 19, 26–32, 91, 154, 158
Descartes, René, 129, 132
determination, 36, 42–48, 50, 54–55n16, 61, 77–78, 109, 112,

199

132, 161–62, 166, 170–71, 180, 193n12
dialectic(al), 52, 60, 62, 65–67, 77, 93, 98n25, 148, 170, 173
difference, 19–22, 24–27, 29, 35–37, 42–43, 46, 48–49, 50–52, 59, 62, 65, 67–68, 72–73, 76, 79, 80, 87–89, 90–94, 104, 106, 109, 110, 111–12, 123–24, 129, 130, 132, 138, 140, 154, 186, 191–92; differenciation, 10, 42, 65, 72, 76–79, 80, 154–55, 177, 179, 186, 193n12; differential, 10, 21, 23, 33, 35–36, 46–57, 61–65, 72, 76–77, 80, 88, 89, 180, 193; differential calculus, 10, 35, 49, 52, 56nn22–23; differentiation, 10–11, 14, 42–43, 45–49, 54n8, 64–65, 72, 76–77, 79, 103, 112, 177, 179–80, 190, 193n12
discourse, 149, 161–66, 168, 171, *178*, 179, 182–84, 188–91, 192n6, 195n32; indirect, 13–14, 161–69, 171, 173, 174n11
dissonance, 105
dissymmetry, 20
distribution, 25, 35, 42–43, 45, 52, 65, 77, 110
divergence, 36, 52, 187, 191
dramatization, 10, 34, 53n3, 66, 72, 76, 180, 190
dynamisms, 10, 68–69n17, 72, 76–78, 80, 181, 185–86, 190

economy, 64–66, 169; economic base, 165, 167, 169, 170
egg, 72–73, 76–80, 81n2
embryology, 56n25, 71–73, 76
end of the World, 1–8
entropy, 9, 19–28, 91, 92, 148, 154, 155, 158
equivocity, 11, 103, 104, 105, 108, 109, 112
eros, 121–22, 148
event, 1, 33, 50, 92, 111, 142, 144, 150–53, 155
explication, 27–29, 154, 184

extension, 21, 23, 24, 73, 77, 78, 149, 154, 155, 179
extraverbal situation, 163

fold, 88, 92
fragmentation of subjectivity, 154–56
function: biology, 76, 78–79; mathematics, 37–39, 41–42, 44–46, 48–50
future, 7, 21, 112, 117, 119, 120–21, 123–24, 138, 148, 150–51, 153

gastrulation, 73, 75
genesis, 29, 35, 48, 60–62, 64–65, 73, 94, 149, 184–85, 189–90, 194n28; genetic, 19–20, 51–52, 89, 109, 112, 179; genetic phenomenology, 117; genetics, 77–78, 80
god, 3, 4, 5, 7, 8, 57, 92, 104, 136, 142, 153
good sense, 9, 19, 21, 22, 27, 29, 55, 80
ground, 89–90; unground(ing), 27, 79, 153
Guillaume, Gustave, 14, 177, 180–81, 184–85, 188–89, 191–92

habitus, 120–22
harmony, 7, 105, 107
Hegel, Georg Wilhelm Friedrich, 85–100; Hegelianism, 60
Heidegger, Martin, 121, 125n14, 148, 150–52, 155; Heideggerian, 157n35
historicist, 60–62, 64
homonymy, 103, 104
Husserl, Edmund, 115–19, 120–24, 120, 130–31, 133–37, 139–41
Hyppolite, Jean, 85, 93

idea, 35, 42, 46–47, 50–53, 55n19, 57nn30–34, 62, 72, 76–78, 88, 98n40, 177, 180, 185–86, 190, 193n17, 194n28, 195n34; Hegelian Idea, 85, 87, 91–92, 95, 97n16, 98n25; Kantian Idea, 51–52, 114n15; linguistic Idea, 14, 177, 180, 185, 190–92; Platonic

Idea, 50, 136; social Idea, 59–61, 63–67
identity, 35, 88–89, 91, 94, 109, 110, 114, 142, 153, 154, 186
ideology, 19, 63, 64, 161–63, 166–67, 169, 170
illusion, 27–28, 109, 111, 114n15, 185–86
impersonal, 136–37, 140, 148–49, 151–55, 156n7, 158n53, 174n17
implication, 27–29, 154
impossibility, 116, 133, 147–48, 150–52
indirect discourse, 161–62, 164–66, 168–69, 171, 173
individual, 36, 43–44, 46–47, 49–50, 56, 61–65, 68, 71–72, 76–79, 115, 136–37, 140, 154–55, 162, 168, 191; individuation, 43, 50, 53n3, 72, 78–80, 138, 148, 154–55, 185
intensity, 8, 19–21, 26–29, 50, 56n25, 72, 78–80, 98n40, 122, 148, 153–55, 158n48, 158n55, 185, 195

John of Patmos, 3, 5–6
judgment, 4, 5, 6, 7, 8, 94, 105, 106, 107, 109, 112, 131, 169

Kant, Immanuel, 11–12, 34, 51, 94, 96, 103–9, 112, 116–17, 129, 130–34, 136–37, 139, 140
Kojève, Alexandre, 85, 93, 97n21

language, 12–14, 147, 149, 155, 161–63, 165–73, 177–83, 186–91, 194n24, 195n32, 196n45; *langue*, 178–79, 181, 183, *184*, 186–89, 191; mathematics as, 35–36, 52
Lawrence, David Herbert, 2, 3, 6
Lawrence, Thomas Edward, 2
limit, 36–37, 77, 110–12, 117, 141, 149, 163, 179–80
lines of flight, 172
linguistics, 161–63, 165, 167, 170, 171, 173, 177–79, 181, 182, 184, 185, 191, 193n7, 195n32

literature, 49, 53n2, 147–49, 164–65, 168, 171; experience of writing, 147, 149–50; literary space, 13, 147–49, 155

Marxism, 61–62, 161, 163, 165–67, 173
materialist, 163
mathematics, 35–36, 42–45, 52
metaphysics, 48, 54, 60, 89, 94, 103, 120, 136–37, 155
millennium, 3, 6; millennialist, 4–5
Mnemosyne, 121–22
multiple, 33–34, 43, 52–53, 61, 64–65, 67, 78–79, 88, 105, 110
multiplicity, 43, 57n30, 60, 68, 72, 103, 106, 115, 141n1, 186

nature, 29, 87, 90, 92
negation, 65, 67, 88–89
Nietzsche, Friedrich, 6, 8, 98n40, 110

objectivity, 103, 105, 108, 109, 131, 133, 134, 162, 169
ontology, 52, 55, 85–87, 89, 92–94, 104, 138, 141, 148, 153–54, 180, 191
order-word, 161, 165, 166
orgiastic representation, 88–89
outside, 35, 41, 43–44, 46, 74, 123, 147–49, 151–52, 154–56, 166

passivity, 117, 129–31, 139–41, 150–51, 179, 184
past, 21, 27, 116, 119, 120–24, 153
phenomenology, 115–19, 120–24, 129, 131, 139
physics, 22, 25, 38, 118, 194
Plato, 51, 181–82
positivism, 183, 185, 191
possibility, 63–64, 66, 68, 85, 94, 106, 108, 113, 115–18, 120–21, 124, 130, 135, 139, 148, 150, 186–90
post-Kantians, 57n34, 94–95
pragmatics, 161, 165
pre-reflective experience, 139
present, 27, 116, 119, 120–24, 139, 153, 189

presentism, 125
primitive and derivative, 42, 45–48, 50, 54–55n16
problem, 27, 35–36, 39, 42, 45–46, 48–52, 55n16, 59–61, 64–67, 78, 85–88, 116, 184, 186–87, 191, 195n34. *See also* solution
production, 19, 21, 33, 51–52, 61–62, 64, 93, 103, 112, 151, 166–67, 169–70, 172, 179
productive imagination, 131–32, 135, 141
protention, 123

real, 66, 77, 103, 109, 112, 179–80, 184, 189, 191. *See* actual; virtual
relations, 7, 34–36, 44–49, 52, 61, 63–65, 72, 76–77, 79–80, 87–88, 180, 188–89
representation, 88, 97, 106, 109, 117, 119, 123–24, 130, 139, 149, 151, 156, 161, 166, 184–85, 194
resemblance, 35, 43, 77, 109, 154, 179, 184, 186–88, 191
retention, 119, 120–21, 123–24
return, 6, 29, 90–92, 110–12, 154; eternal, 29, 91–92, 98n40, 110–12, 120, 123, 148, 153
Rilke, Rainer Maria, 149, 151–53, 157n24

self-appearance, 133, 135, 139–40
self-knowledge, 132–33, 139
Selme, Léon, 20, 22, 25–29
sense, 35, 51, 94, 109, 120–21, 137, 163, 166, 171, 191; common, 154; good, 22, 27, 29, 80; internal/inner, 116–18, 130, 133–34
series, 33–37, 43–47, 50, 51–52, 77, 79–80, 88, 93, 112, 138, 181; power series, 37–41, 44–45, 48–49
sign, 35, 79–80, 161–63, 170, 173, 178–79, 183–85, 187–88, 191, 194n24; signal-sign, 79
singular, 42–44, 61, 91, 189–91

singularity, 10, 13, 20, 35, 38–39, 41, 43–45, 49–50, 52, 54n13, 63, 76, 136–38, 154, 181, 186, 188–90
society, 34, 59–61, 64–68, 166, 169
solution, 35–36, 42, 46, 48, 55, 61, 64–67, 78. *See* problem
space, 27, 31n26, 41–43, 52, 76–78, 98n40, 112, 117–18, 189–91
Stalin, Joseph, 167, 170–73
statement-act, 161
structure, 4, 35–36, 44, 47, 49–51, 53n3, 57n30, 60–68, 76, 118, 121, 136–37, 161–62, 180–88; structuralism, 33–35, 51, 62, 177
subjectivity, 116–17, 130, 132, 134–41, 147, 149
superstructure, 169–70, 172
syllogism, 85, 87, 91
synonymy, 103–4
synthesis, 72, 77, 129, 130–39, 140–41
system, 7, 20, 23–25, 27–28, 34, 65, 71, 78–80, 87, 89, 91, 148, 154, 162–63, 173, 187–88

temporality, 61–62, 92, 95, 116, 118–19, 120–21, 123–24, 138
theory of knowledge, 124
thermodynamics, 19–22, 27, 29, 154
thought, 50–53, 86, 89, 91, 94–95, 116–17, 137, 147, 149, 155–56, 178–79, 182–83, *184*, 187, 189–90, 192, 196n45; image of, 95, 105, 115, 117, 137, 139–41, 158n55
time, 7, 21, 27, 52, 61, 64–65, 76–78, 92, 95, 98n40, 104, 112, 115–24, 130–36, 138–40, 142n16, 150, 153, 158n43, 158n55, 189–91; time-consciousness, 135
transcendental: field, 36, 130, 137–42, 147; philosophy, 115, 130, 135–37, 140; subjectivity, 137

unanimous, 106
unity, 52, 57n34, 62, 103, 105–10, 113n12, 118, 120, 130–31, 133, 134–35, 138, 140, 155, 173

universal, 43, 47–48, 54n12, 87, 91, 96n3, 189–91
univocity, 103–5, 107–12

variable (mathematics), 37, 39, 47–48, 56n24; variables of expression, 166
virtual, 36, 42–43, 49–50, 55n16, 61, 66, 72, 77, 80, 87–88, 140, 158n53, 177, 179–82, 184–92, 193n11, 194n26, 195n32. *See* actual; real
voice, 6, 103, 106–11, 161, 164–66, 168–69, 171
Voloshinov, Valentin, 161–73

woof of bodies, 166

Zombies, 1, 8
zygote, 72–73, 75, 80

Contributors

DOROTHEA E. OLKOWSKI is professor and former chair of philosophy at the University of Colorado, Colorado Springs, director of Humanities, director of the Cognitive Studies Program, and former director of Women's Studies. Specializing in contemporary (twentieth-century) continental philosophy, and feminist theory, she has been a fellow at the University of Western Ontario, Rotman Institute of Philosophy and Science, the Australian National University in Canberra, and the University of California, Berkeley. She is the author/editor of twelve books and over one hundred articles, including *Postmodern Philosophy and the Scientific Turn* (2012) and *The Universal (In the Realm of the Sensible)* (2007), and (with Helen Fielding) *Feminist Phenomenology Futures* (2017), Deleuze and Guattari's *Philosophy of Freedom: Freedom's Refrains* (2019), and the forthcoming Deleuze, Bergson, and Merleau-Ponty, *The Logics and Pragmatics of Affect, Perception, and Creation*.

JULIÁN FERREYRA has a PhD in philosophy (Paris X-Nanterre/UBA-Argentina) and is the author of *L'ontologie du capitalisme chez Gilles Deleuze* (2010), "Ideas, from Hegel to Deleuze" (*Comparative and Continental Philosophy Journal*), "La doble vida de la luz: envolvimiento y creación en Fichte y Deleuze" (*Anales Historia de la Filosofía*), "Idea e intensidad en la fase monetaria del capitalismo según Deleuze y Guattari" (*Eidos*), "Esferas y pliegues: la aplicabilidad de la biopolítica de Fichte a Deleuze" (*Estudios de Filosofía*), and "Fichte o Deleuze, ¿quién es el dogmático?" (*Valenciana*), among others. He is independent researcher in the Argentine National Scientific and Technical Research Council and teaches philosophical anthropology in the University of Buenos Aires. He was visitor scholar at Harvard University. He directs the research group *Deleuze, practical ontology* (which has been awarded with many research grants from various scientific research centers), the journal *Ideas, revista de filosofía moderna y contemporánea*, and the book collection *Deleuze y las fuentes de su filosofía* (*Deleuze and the Sources of his Philosophy*).

SEBASTIÁN AMARILLA is finalizing his bachelor's degree in philosophy at the University of Buenos Aires. Currently, his research area is circumscribed to the resonances between biology and embryology in Deleuze's philosophy. He is a member of the collaboration board of the journal *Ideas, revista de filosofía moderna y contemporánea*. He is also a member of the research group *Deleuze, practical ontology*.

SOLANGE HEFFESSE has a bachelor's degree in philosophy from the University of Buenos Aires. She is currently a PhD student at the same university, with an UBACyT scholarship. Her research areas focus on the problem of negativity in Gilles Deleuze's philosophy. She is a member of the research group *Deleuze, practical ontology* since 2012. She has edited, together with Pablo Pachilla and Anabella Schoenle, *Lo que fuerza a pensar. Deleuze, ontología práctica 1* (2019), and has published numerous articles in the volumes of the "*Deleuze y las fuentes de su filosofía*" collection, among other articles. She is also a member of the collaborating board of the journal *Ideas, revista de filosofía moderna y contemporánea*.

VERÓNICA KRETSCHEL has a PhD and a bachelor's degree in philosophy from the University of Buenos Aires. She works at this university's Department of Philosophy, teaching "Contemporary Philosophy." She is a researcher in the Argentine National Scientific and Technical Research Council. Hermain research field is Husserlian and Deleuzian philosophy, focusing on the problem of representing time. She is a member of the research group "Deleuze, practical ontology." She is also a member of the Editorial Board of the journal *Ideas, revista de filosofía moderna y contemporánea* and of RAGIF Editions.

SANTIAGO LO VUOLO has a degree in philosophy from the National University of Litoral (Santa Fe, Argentina). He is currently a PhD student in philosophy at the University of Buenos Aires, directed by Julián Ferreyra. He teaches at the UNLitoral and the Autonomous University of Entre Ríos. His research and philosophical interests are the works of Marx, Althusser, and Deleuze, and their derivations in contemporary thought. He is a member of the research group "Deleuze, practical ontology," as well as other research projects located in the city of Santa Fe.

RAFAEL MC NAMARA has a PhD in philosophy and a bachelor's degree in philosophy from the University of Buenos Aires. His main research fields are Deleuze's ontology of space and practical ontology. He has taught Philosophy and Aesthetics at the National University of Arts (UNA), the National University of La Matanza (UNLaM), and the University of Cinema (FUC), among other institutions. Currently, he is teaching gnoseology and philosophy of culture at the National University of Comahue (UNCo). He is a member of the editorial board of the journal *Ideas, revista de filosofía moderna y contemporánea* and of *RAGIF Editions*. He is also a member of the research group "Deleuze, practical ontology." He is the director of the collection "Deleuze: ontología práctica" (RAGIF Editions).

ANDRÉS M. OSSWALD is a researcher in the Argentine National Scientific and Technical Research Council and assistant professor in the Faculty of Philosophy and Letters at the University of Buenos Aires, where he completed his PhD on Edmund Husserl's Phenomenology of Passivity. His research interest lies mainly in the area of phenomenology but he is also interested in Gilles Deleuze's philosophy and psychoanalytic theory. Currently, he intends to offer a phenomenological response to the question "what is a house?"

PABLO N. PACHILLA holds a double degree PhD in philosophy (Universidad de Buenos Aires—Université Paris 8). He currently teaches ecophilosophy (Universidad de San Martín) and film theory (Universidad del Cine). He has edited, together with Solange Heffesse and Anabella Schoenle, *Lo que fuerza a pensar. Deleuze, ontología práctica 1* (2019), and published several papers in international journals such as *Revue philosophique de la France et de l'étranger*, *Ideas y valores*, and *Areté*. He has been awarded a doctoral and postdoctoral scholarship by CONICET (Consejo Nacional de Investigaciones Científicas y Técnicas) and two short-term grants by DAAD (Deutscher Akademischer Austauschdienst). He is a member of the Buenos Aires–based research group "Deleuze, practical ontology."

GONZALO SANTAYA has a PhD in philosophy (Universidad de Buenos Aires) with a CONICET doctoral scholarship. His area of research is the usage of mathematics throughout Deleuze's philosophy, and on this subject, he has published *El cálculo trascendental* (2017). He has also co-edited *Deleuze y las fuentes de su filosofía V* (2017) with Rafael Mc Namara, and has published articles in all the volumes of that collection. He has published papers in *Revista de Estud(i)os sobre Fichte* y en *Ideas. Revista de filosofía moderna y contemporánea*. He participates in the research group "Deleuze, practical ontology" since 2012, as well as in other research groups related to Sartre's philosophy and German idealism. He is also a high school philosophy teacher.

ANABELLA SCHOENLE is finalizing her bachelor's degree in philosophy at the University of Buenos Aires. She teaches philosophy in various high schools in Buenos Aires. She is a member of the UBACyT project "The Crossroads of Freedom: Spinoza, Deleuze and the First Hegel of Jena" and the PICT-FONCyT 2012–2017 "Deleuze, practical ontology." In the frame of an EVC-CIN scholarship, she has studied the concept of Body Without Organs in relation with the Deleuzian Idea, in a research project untitled: "From the Social Idea to the Body Without Organs: Deleuze and Urondo, around the sense of the paradox." She explores the problems of metaphysics, politics, and the Argentinian and Latin American thought.

MATÍAS SOICH has a PhD in linguistics and a bachelor's degree in philosophy from the University of Buenos Aires. He works at this university's Department of Literature teaching the assignment "Analysis of the Languages of the Mass Media." His main research fields are Deleuzian philosophy and critical discourse analysis, focusing on themes such as gender identity, sexual diversity, and social exclusion. He is a member of the Argentinian team of the Latin American Network for the Analysis of the Discourse of and about Poverty (REDLAD) and of the research group "Deleuze, practical ontology." He is also a member of the editorial board of the journal *Ideas, revista de filosofía moderna y contemporánea* and of RAGIF Editions.

www.ingramcontent.com/pod-product-compliance
Lightning Source LLC
Chambersburg PA
CBHW032044300426
44117CB00009B/1181